Computer Time Sharing
for Managers

Computer Time Sharing
for Managers

John F. Odeneal

Prentice-Hall, Inc.

Englewood Cliffs, N.J.

Prentice-Hall International, Inc., *London*
Prentice-Hall of Australia, Pty. Ltd., *Sydney*
Prentice-Hall of Canada, Ltd., *Toronto*
Prentice-Hall of India Private Ltd., *New Delhi*
Prentice-Hall of Japan, Inc., *Tokyo*

© 1975 by

Prentice-Hall, Inc.
Englewood Cliffs, N.J.

Library of Congress Cataloging in Publication Data
Odeneal, John F
   Computer time sharing for managers.

   1. Time-sharing computer systems. 2. Electronic
data processing--Business. I.   Title.
HF5548.2.O28   658'.05'4404   75-2155
ISBN 0-13-166348-8

Printed in the United States of America

John F. Odeneal is Manager, Management Information Systems, FMC Corporation, New York City, where for ten years he has used time sharing to apply the computer to business problems, models and simulations.

Examples of the broad business background the author brings to time sharing are the implementation of foreign and domestic acquisition programs as well as sales and marketing models.

Mr. Odeneal's main concern has been user-manager involvement and pointing up the efficiencies and cost savings of time sharing. The author has developed the systems that prove the manager can take the helm and do so very profitably.

From this wide experience this book was written. It gives the manager the means to take control of his business environment, enabling him to add full computer capability to his business expertise.

ABOUT THE AUTHOR

What This Book Will Do for You

Have you been frustrated by computer promises that have gone unrealized? Are you hemmed in by computer mystique that builds a barrier between you and the computer? Time sharing lets you surmount these obstacles. Time sharing puts the computer in your hands . . . in the hands of the user.

Time sharing is an immensely powerful new business tool for all levels of management. Chapter 1 describes in precise, step-by-step detail how you can obtain immediate computer power for your everyday business situations; how you can apply the most advanced business techniques without the time-consuming study and mathematical background formerly required to use these techniques.

The unique feature of this book (and of time sharing) is that it puts the user in the driver's seat. Its perspective is user-oriented, and it appreciates and caters to the user unfamiliar *and* uninterested in the technical aspects of computer operations. After all, once you have removed the computer as an in-house responsibility, your only concern should be: "What can it do for me?" not "How does it do it?"

Eighteen Ways to Manage More Profitably with Time Sharing

I. Business Monitoring Techniques

    A. Time sharing's unique contribution to the following is *timeliness*. Other methods function monthly or quarterly; time sharing provides when-you-need-it information.

        1. Output daily or weekly reports on net sales and gross profits.

        2. Maintain current inventory levels with continuous access to inventory status either complete or on an exception report basis whenever required.

        3. Operate a computer-based freight system.

        4. A completely interactive personnel system for personnel skills, payroll and promotion.

        5. Output mark-sense generated orders and billings, thereby reducing intermediate personnel, i.e. order write-up clerks and keypunch operators.

        6. Build interactive accounting systems including balance sheets and aging reports.

        7. Build order control programs to report delinquent shipments.

II. Utilize the most up-to-date business techniques, projection systems and evaluation methods.

    A. Time sharing can immediately apply the most advanced and complicated business formulae without the user needing to understand the mechanics of the procedure.

        8. Four hours of profitability index calculations reduced to four minutes of time-sharing input/output.

        9. Discounted cash flow calculated in minutes rather than hours.

        10. Regression analysis (correlation) applied to business problems without tedious calculating, graphing and charting.

11. Specific business-oriented trade evaluation formulae such as operating efficiency ratings and profit calculations.
12. Performance evaluation and review techniques (PERT) applied to business ventures.
13. Critical Path Method (CPM).
14. Allocation of resources.
15. Minimization of purchase expenses relating to outside suppliers and multiple geographically dispersed plant sites.
16. Maximization of profit by product mix selection.
17. Forecasting.
18. Modeling and simulation.

This book will put immediately within your grasp all the computer capability you will need to cope with even the most complex of your business problems. You can have your own time-sharing terminal operating by the end of chapter 1.

Computer technology and hardware have far exceeded business' capacity to make demands. The challenge now is to make use of this capacity to operate business in a more efficient and profitable fashion. Chapters 5 and 8 delineate several such business systems.

Chapter 9 describes how to handle information. The data base and data bank are explored, and typical examples are provided.

To use the presently available time-sharing and computer capacity, middle and upper management must acquire sufficient basic know-how to seek out computer-susceptible tasks and functions. Elementary and sophisticated time-sharing examples are given in chapters 6 and 7.

Direct interaction with the computer by the user is a new dimension for management. Chapters 2 and 3 show when, where and how to use it. The many people who have found they can interact with it provide opportunities that are expanding as fast as time sharing itself.

Ultimately, time sharing's impact will be felt by every individual in a company. Traffic clerk and president, factory worker and corporate analyst are using time sharing to output meaningful, current, on-line, usable information. Specific examples of on-line company interactive programs are given in chapters 2 and 4.

Although everyone in a company will eventually use time sharing, it will be the responsibility of middle and upper management to apply computer capabilities to the total business environment. This will mean applying new methods and techniques to aid manual operations. This revision of systems and procedures can only be done by those who manage them.

Middle and upper management have traditionally sloughed off computer responsibility on those "computer experts" who are responsible for payroll and billing. Time sharing skips the middleman and delivers computer power direct to management on a day-to-day basis.

Chapter 3 describes such time-sharing management/computer interactions as financial analysis, simulations and modeling. These emphasize more strongly every day the need for the manager to interact directly with the computer. Time sharing satisfies this need companywide, including not only the sales, production, operations, and financial fields, but also complementary and supplementary service to the existing EDP facility.

Thus, this book embraces all segments of a company. The manager who recognizes this interaction with the computer can solve his unique and specific requirements. The EDP facility can use time sharing specifically for program-writing and debugging *and* to provide more interactive operations than those available in-house.

This book takes the reader directly to the heart of time sharing. It strips away the mystique of the computer, and puts the *user* directly in touch with the computer before the first chapter ends.

To use the computer as his own personal problem-solving tool, the manager cannot wait to be led by the hand into some sylvan glade of computer utopia. This book avoids the customary computer gobbledygook and concentrates on acquainting the user only with those things he *needs to know* to get *his* job done. Whether his job is sales, finance, marketing or production, the book explains how to subordinate the computer needs to his requirements. Design and implementation of M.I.S. reports is detailed in chapter 7.

This book recognizes that many people are still computer-shy, but it also emphasizes that computer capabilities are needed at every level. Chapters 10, 11 and 12 describe ways and means of dealing with computer-oriented problems, without getting involved in computerese. Chapter 12, for instance, provides examples of communicating your needs to the programmer.

A unique documentation method is also described in chapter 13. This method allows description and operation of time-sharing programs by one simple technique from first-time user to day-to-day operator. It markedly reduces training and operating time, and again emphasizes user importance over computer complexities. Furthermore, all conventional documentation techniques are covered and flowcharting is described in chapter 12.

Finally, and as briefly as possible, chapters 14 and 15 describe ways of controlling your time-sharing environment. Time-sharing costs and necessary equipment are reviewed and delineated.

John F. Odeneal

CONTENTS

LIST OF ILLUSTRATIONS

1

HOW TO GET TIME SHARING STARTED

We are living in the age of computers; they have become an integral part of everyday life. Technologically, computer development has advanced far beyond our ability to utilize the multitude of capabilities offered. The same computer hardware that is used for moon and space shots is available to anyone through time sharing. In fact, space flights represent the ultimate time-sharing system. Where conventional time sharing serves 40 to 400 customers, time sharing on space flights services only two—ground control and the space capsule.

You have now decided to put this incredible time sharing technology to work for yourself, a wise decision. Time sharing is a one-to-one interaction between man and the computer. Let's waste no time in initiating this relationship.

HOW TIME SHARING OPERATES

A time-sharing computer is no different from any other computer, but it is unique in that it is programmed to give the impression that it is handling only your program. Actually it is handling a multitude of users simultaneously. To do this, it devotes a short span of time to one problem, then another, another, and another. These short spans of time amount to only a millionth of a second each! The trick to the system is that the computer is programmed to work on one problem after another in rapid succession. So rapid, in fact, that to the user the impression is created that the computer is devoted solely to solving his problem alone.

For example, you are at a teletype connected directly to the computer. You type "run program A." The computer activates the teletype and types "program A run." "Answer in file /ONE/." "Do you require another run?" You type "no." The computer replies "Program A filed. Next instruction?" These statements follow one another as fast as you can type replies to the computer's queries. Forever invisible to you are the computer's other activities. While providing the above dialogue with you, it is serving 40 to 400 other users on different telephone lines, with different programs, and with different answers.

Picture the face of a clock with an incoming telephone line at each minute mark. Now speed up the clock until the minute hand is spinning around the face many times a second. Each time the minute hand passes a minute mark, the computer is in contact with the caller on that particular telephone line.

Once data is received, the computer manipulates the information with incredible

15

speed. Subsidiary parts of the computer control input and output to the teletype, in order to slow the action down to more human levels. Other parts store programs to be run, store data for processing, and hold partially completed programs in abeyance while others are being run. In the time-sharing computer all this is going on, not for one customer but for many.

Many individuals have reservations about their ability to understand the complexities of computers. They will be happy to learn that the brief clock analogy is all they will ever need to know about the internal operation of a time-sharing computer. It is like driving in the family car from Boston to New York; you need know only that there is an engine under the hood. What it does and how it does it will not speed the trip by one second.

As you become involved in time sharing, there will be ample opportunity to explore the technological aspects of computer systems. In fact, programmers and technicians usually deluge the user with such information. If it appeals, relax and learn. If it sounds like gibberish, don't hesitate to cut it off. You don't need it.

To paraphrase an old proverb: *"Doing* time sharing is worth a thousand words." In this chapter your objective should be to learn enough to get a time-sharing terminal installed. However, no matter what effort is made to condense this procedure, certain basics must be understood.

The computer field uses a certain technical vocabulary. You must be familiar with a few of these terms in order to communicate effectively. To avoid defining each term as it is used, the Glossary at the end of this book has been compiled. You are probably already familiar with many of these terms. Read through them now, or refer to them as they occur in the text.

A simple time-sharing exercise was used to compile this Glossary. As the book was written, terms were noted and defined as they occurred. Monthly, these terms were typed at the terminal into a data bank and stored by the computer. At the end of the effort, a data bank called GLOSS contained a jumbled list of terms and definitions.

The first five lines read:

```
CRT UNIT    —CATHODE RAY TUBE TERMINAL.
FORTRAN     —A COMPUTER LANGUAGE.
DATA BANK—DATA STORED IN THE COMPUTER.
HEADERS     —CAPTIONS OF OUTPUT DATA.
CPS         —CHARACTERS PER SECOND.
```

Upon completion of the book, the following commands were given to the computer.

```
— SORT/GLOSS 1.12/R240/ALPHA
— PRINT ALPHA
BASIC       —A COMPUTER PROGRAMMING LANGUAGE.
BATCH       —A SINGLE, HOMOGENEOUS ASSEMBLAGE OF DATA.
                        ETC.
```

Sprinkled with a few verbs to enhance human understanding, the first computer command can be easily translated as follows: Prepare to use the SORT program. Find the file named GLOSS. Sort on the first twenty-one characters (1.21). READ each line, which may contain up to 240 characters. Put the sorted result in a file that you should name ALPHA.

The second command simply tells the computer to PRINT out the sorted file ALPHA that it has just created.

```
—LOGOUT
    CPU 9.36
    TERMINAL TIME 0:06:00
```

This command terminates the operator's activity, and confirms the time and cost involved in the job.

Time sharing itself is an ambiguous term and should be clarified before proceeding. Since the word seems almost self-explanatory, it has frequently been used carelessly, arbitrarily, and inaccurately. Time sharing has been casually applied to at least three computer applications other than the specific application described in the preceding paragraphs.

One misapplication of the term refers to sequential batch processing. That is, each job on the computer is scheduled at some time during the day. Literally, appointments are made for the computer to process a particular job. At 10:30 data is put in, processed and output. At 11:00 another job is input, and so on throughout the day. Normally this is called batch processing, but could be misconstrued as time sharing at least often enough to warrant mention, and to caution against confusion.

Another use of the term developed when certain commercial concerns began to solicit work. These firms approached companies too small to buy their own computers. They offered to computerize their orders, billings, accounting, etc. The data delivered by such customers was fed into the computer and processed. In short, forty companies, for instance, shared one computer. Again, however, this was sequential batch processing, i.e. one company after another used the computer; this is not time sharing.

Finally, a third misuse of the term developed as some large companies realized they had developed more computer capacity than they needed. They had invested in computer capacity at the rate of $30,000 per month, yet only used the hardware eight hours a day. To remedy this they set about renting their equipment during their company's off time. Again, several companies were sharing time on the computer.

None of the above satisfies the commercial definition of time sharing. Only the simultaneous use of the computer by a multiplicity of users truly satisfies the definition. This is the field this book will explore. This is the field that gives each individual the impression and the capability of applying computer technology to his everyday business and scientific problems and procedures.

Do not be too concerned about the use to which you will put time sharing. No decisions you make need be irreversible. Your first step can well be a free demonstration. Your longest commitment need only be one month. Your initial outlays and monthly charges can be limited to a few hundred dollars.

CASE IN POINT: Take advantage of a free demonstration. Not only is time sharing a very competitive business today, but time-sharing companies correctly believe that their systems can best sell themselves.

All time-sharing services have free "access numbers." That is, passwords listed exclusively to demonstrate their system at no charge to the client. Usually these are made available to potential users for a few days or a week to demonstrate the system's effectiveness.

One knowledgeable fibers manufacturer in Philadelphia wrote, debugged, and ran a freight minimization program during their free week. Since computer charges are printed out at the terminal after each session, they calculated costs "not charged to them" at nine hundred dollars. The time-sharing company was amply rewarded, however, since acceptance of the program resulted in a contract for their time-sharing services.

Perhaps the only caution that should be given is the potential you will uncover in time sharing. As you explore its possibilities, the temptation to utilize it more and more is very difficult to control.

Consider your initial selection of a time-sharing company as experimental. Naturally avoid any long-term commitment. Expect some pressure from visiting salesmen to sign a long-term contract. Obviously, until you have refined your time-sharing requirements, a month-to-month arrangement is in your own best interests.

Do not hesitate to consider several time-sharing companies simultaneously. Not only can you communicate with all time-sharing companies from one terminal, but access to several systems will help you make prompt performance comparisons. What, how and when to make such comparisons will be the subject of the next few pages.

Initial selection of a time-sharing company should be based on the following criteria:

1. OPERATIONAL PROCEDURES
2. LANGUAGES USED
3. OPERATIONS ASSISTANCE
4. EDITING CAPABILITY
5. UP TIME
6. LIBRARY
7. RESPONSE TIME
8. COST

OPERATIONAL PROCEDURES

Operational procedures are those instructions and commands built into the computer to enable it to react to your questions and requirements. Some time-sharing companies are geared to satisfy scientifically oriented computing. In these cases the time-sharing company pays scant heed to the user, aiming primarily at problem solving. Even under scientific conditions this is not excusable, but once started is hard to change. Avoid this type of service until you are sure of your requirements.

How do you, a novice, judge whether a company meets the requirements of operational simplicity? The answer is obvious. Ask the representative to run through the log in procedure. Ask the representative to explain how he would run one of his library programs.

What criteria do you apply against the answers to the above questions? Again the answer is obvious. If you understand the replies, and feel you can comfortably respond to the procedures described, then the procedures are sound.

Generally speaking, as you become more proficient in time-sharing, individual computer operational procedures will bother you less. Initially, however, they could mean the difference between success and failure, and the acceptance or rejection of time-sharing. The internal complexities of computers are problem enough without allowing them to impinge on the novice user.

Do not be intimidated by the computer in this regard. You are still in an experimental and exploratory stage. You may be asked to compromise simplicity for capacity. It may be claimed that the difficulty of use is offset by the computer's enormous capacity. The realistic response to this ploy is that you will be unlikely, for some time, to tax the capabilities of any time-sharing computer. In almost every field susceptible to time sharing, the computer far outdistances our ability to approach its limitations.

Keep your eye on your objective. If you can understand and respond to the operational procedures, then that time-sharing company is for you. Have confidence in your own judgment regarding the ease or difficulties of the procedures. Remember, ultimately it will be just you and the computer, and these procedures will be your only method of communication.

COMPUTER LANGUAGES

Computer languages will be explored at length in later chapters. Nevertheless some elementary judgment must be made initially so that your utilization of time sharing will not be restricted.

In the time-sharing environment there are usually three types of languages available.

1. Elementary languages.
2. Scientific languages.
3. Batch-processing languages.

There is a constant demand for new unique, and more powerful languages. To the day-to-day time-sharing user, however, this is academic. At this early stage don't sacrifice simplicity or clarity for power. A very powerful computer language might be used to write a time-sharing library program for your use. However, when you run such a program, you are neither aware, nor care, which language was used to write it.

Elementary languages, such as BASIC and scientific languages such as FORTRAN have been most effective with time sharing. Don't be misled by these classifications. Elementary language means easy to learn and use, *not* limited in scope. A scientific language is one structured to be easy to use and structured for the scientific community, not inherently scientific.

To clarify and summarize the language status, perhaps a little history is needed to put the language situation in perspective. Originally computers were not only extremely complex devices, but primarily experimental. In most cases the builders were also the users, and inserting a program or processing sequence was done in machine language, that is, building, programming, and operations were almost one inseparable function.

As computer technology increased, it was only natural that much of the routine operations originally performed by technicians began to be performed by the computer itself. Gradually the computer scientist separated from the computer user. The computer became available to any user, while the computer scientist became a separate entity concerned with making the computer perform better for everyone. Once this stage was reached, it became necessary to develop a separate stage of communication with the computer, one that would enable the user to write his own programs. He no longer needed to be concerned with the internal functioning of the equipment or the means by which his instructions were carried out.

This stage of computer development was reached in the early sixties. The first language designed entirely for the user, called BASIC, was created at Dartmouth College. Since it is continually updated and revised, it continues to be one of the most versatile and effective computer languages available. Variations, ramifications and copies of BASIC are constantly under development. BASIC is unquestionably one of the most viable and powerful computer languages. There is no doubt that with its development time sharing moved from the theoretical into the practical.

Obviously, your first choice for a computer language should be the latest version of BASIC. For the first several months, as you experiment with library programs, BASIC will not concern you. The moment you wish to apply original work or apply your own criteria to data, programming capability will become essential and BASIC will become indispensable.

From the layman's point of view FORTRAN is very similar to BASIC. It is especially valuable as a problem-solving tool, and has gained wide acceptance among time-sharing users. It is generally considered to be more powerful than BASIC. Be wary, however, of such descriptions as "powerful." For all practical purposes, BASIC and FORTRAN are interchangeable from a usage point of view in your initial investigations.

Beyond these two languages lie a host of additional specific and general programming tools. The batch-processing languages, generally used on in-house computer installations have such names as ALGOL and COBOL. Your objectives, however, will best be served by selecting a time-sharing company with BASIC, FORTRAN, or both. Thus they will be available when your skills and requirements dictate their application to your needs.

At the start don't waste your time investigating other languages. A time-sharing company should be able to provide either or both of the latest versions of FORTRAN or BASIC. If it does not, it will not be responsive to your kind of time-sharing requirements.

OPERATIONS ASSISTANCE

Time sharing is a service business. A time-sharing company's only function is to provide its customers with service. Curiously enough, the real value of this service does not revolve around the size of their computer, nor the speed, complexity, flexibility, or uniqueness of their computer.

You'll be able to make empirical judgments on the computer's response time, storage capacity, or library size. Operations assistance is a subjective judgment you must also make. Is the time-sharing company prepared to spend the time, money and personnel to train you in their time-sharing procedures? It is an important question to ask yourself. If you misjudge, you may lose two months waiting for their training expert to appear.

Some companies start you up and then leave you on your own. If you are already familiar with time sharing and only require a specific capability from the time-sharing company, this is fine. As a beginner, however, you need all the help you can get. You need service from your time-sharing company. In its initial stages service means attention—someone to sit down, demonstrate, run, teach, describe, explain; someone to observe as you make mistakes; someone to help you unscramble your errors. This is not too much to ask of a time-sharing company. Not only will you need help initially, but there will be innumerable times when you will require a responsive environment. Determine as soon as possible if such an interactive relationship can be established. You will need it.

The ideal situation is to build a contact with a single individual. If the time-sharing company assigns one, ask him or her to visit you. Often the salesman only initiates the relationship. If you build your assumptions about the company on his competence, you may be disappointed in not finding him available later.

In short, as in most situations (and here, even with computers), people are important. Make sure you know who will be responsible for your account. Base your time-sharing company selection partially on your judgment of this individual.

EDITING CAPABILITY

This capability varies widely among computers. Usually many time-sharing companies, with the same computers, have similar editing facilities. From the user's point of view, editing can be a critical characteristic. It is the capability that enables the user to edit, that is, to correct, change, adjust, or reorganize a program or data base.

Editing is the commands you give the computer to tell it how to manipulate its files and its programs. Here again a demonstration by the representative is essential. Here again your subjective reaction to the procedures should be the criteria.

For example, while this chapter was being written two members of my staff were updating the same data base on two different time-sharing systems (each system had capabilities the other lacked). However, one had a much stronger *editor* than the other.

It became necessary to correct a customer name buried within a 2,000-line data bank. Staff member A had to refer to his original input dating back several months, locate the correct line number and then request (operator's commands are underlined):

```
* FIND LINE 657
= 892
* TYPE 892
657 TUDOR,852.79,I,B,AREORROW,8297,CWT,657.25
```

He then retyped the complete line with the corrected wording.

```
CORRECT LINE 657
657 TUDOR,852.79,I,B,AROW,8297,CWT,657.25
SAVE
```

The job is done.

Staff member B proceeded as follows:

```
* S (SUBSTITUTE)
"AROW" for "AREORROW"
1 SUBSTITION MADE
* SAVE
```

The job is done.

In the latter case the same command could have corrected twenty "AREORROW" entries. In the former, twenty lines would have had to be rewritten.

There are many different types of program editors and procedures. Naturally, each has been designed to be efficient and easy to use. Whether they are easy to use depends on the user. Some people prefer one procedure, some another.

At this early stage in your familiarization with time sharing, this may be a hard decision to make. If you elect to use two time-sharing companies side by side, you will find that the editing capability may be the deciding factor between the two. This is a good reason to consider side-by-side comparisons.

If this is not feasible, demonstrations should be requested. A word of caution: Once you become familiar with an editing technique you will be reluctant to change. Make every effort to select that technique best suited to your needs. Here switching horses in midstream can be an unnecessary hardship.

For some applications the editing facility is not essential. However, it will become more critical as your expertise develops. The situation will solve itself if you elect to use two time-sharing companies; if not, select your editing capability with as much range as possible.

UP TIME

Perhaps this book should have started with the one fact of life every time-sharing user lives with—*crashes!* This is the word used when the computer malfunctions. In other words, when the computer is right in the middle of printing out your answers, and . . . *stops!* The only solution, when a real crash occurs, is to go back to the beginning and start again.

Needless to say, crashes are the bane of a time-sharing user's existence. They not only terminate the normal processing of a program, but it can also be anywhere from ten minutes to twenty-four hours before the computer is operational or "up" again. "Is the computer up?" or "Is the computer down again?" are the two queries familiar to most time-sharing milieus. The only protection against losing valuable up time is astute questioning of the representative. Acceptable up time should be over 95%.

Most time-sharing companies are up 16 to 18 hours a day, i.e. 7:00 a.m. to 12:00 p.m. Early morning and late evening hours are the most economical times to use the computer. Furthermore, companies routinely run on Saturdays and Sundays. Although these times may seem inconvenient, this type of up time will be provided by most time-sharing companies.

Percentage of up time and operating hours should be taken into consideration when evaluating prospects.

LIBRARY

Library programs are those computer programs already written and available to the time-sharing user. Naturally they are generalized to cover as wide a range of potential applications and customers as possible. There is rarely an extra charge for using these programs other than that normally incurred to run them.

Broadly speaking, there are two types of library programs, structured and unstructured. A structured program requires only that the user input specific data, that is, to project a trend; the user types the numbers 2,4,6,8 and is provided the projection 10,12,14.

CASE IN POINT: Never assume your problem is unique. A large New York bank decided to take on time sharing. They already had an extensive EDP staff, but decided that the interactive environment of time sharing would provide computer services to their banking and loan staff.

Programmers and systems analysts were freed from EDP duties, and programs and procedures were designed and written for their unique requirements. The whole package worked out fine.

It worked out so well that they proudly demonstrated it to the time-sharing company. The time-sharing company commended them on their skill and industry. Then, as politely as possible, made a suggestion. Before undertaking another such effort, they might like to look at the library of programs available to them when they signed up for the service.

When this library was investigated, the bank discovered it had reinvented the wheel. Most of the capabilities designed were already available: a profitability index, regression analysis, an interest rate program and a sort program.

With considerable chagrin, it was estimated that ten thousand dollars of program writing and debugging costs had been expended. All these programs were already written and available in the library.

The unstructured program requires that the user provide more than just the raw data. These kinds of programs require that the user provide such details as headers, formula, processing and sequences.

Both types of programs have value. Structured programs can be used immediately. They are written to be almost self-explanatory and little or no training is required to initiate and run them. These characteristics are also their drawbacks. Obviously they are generalized, and obviously they don't apply directly to anyone's specific requirements. In spite of this, many time-sharing companies offer a wide range of programs, frequently numbering in the hundreds. Almost inevitably something of interest can be found that can serve your needs.

Unstructured programs require much more attention. They provide great computer flexibility without the need for specific programming knowledge. More and more unstructured program capability is being offered. It fills a much-needed void between user and programmer.

For the first time in the user's evaluation of time-sharing companies he must ask, "What specific activities do I wish to computerize?" A list of requirements should be made, for instance:

1. Projections
2. Statistical analysis
3. Profitability index
4. Sort systems
5. Balance sheet
6. Accounts payable package

A list should be presented to each time-sharing company you contact. They will do the rest. Their response to your requirements and their demonstrations of their capability will easily separate the men from the boys.

> CASE IN POINT: A medium-sized export-import concern in New York with an enlightened management decided that time sharing could provide it with "all the computer services it would ever need." The president supervised installation of the equipment and signed up the time-sharing service. Everything was installed and made ready to run.
>
> Two months and five hundred dollars later (equipment charges and minimum time-sharing charges), nothing had been done. To the uninitiated, the console was a mystery. To the few brave souls who tried it, the question "What?" when they struck the wrong key was incriminating.
>
> The time-sharing company was called in. They, too, were concerned over the lack of use. A meeting with management defined their objectives. Personnel were selected for training, and procedures were established for operation. Management was right. There were many opportunities for time sharing.
>
> In short, time sharing is still new and unfamiliar to many. Training and familiarity must be developed before value can be received.

Don't be caught short. For each type of requirement have company data, or a reasonable facsimile thereof available. The representative will be anxious to demonstrate his capability. Don't make the mistake of asking for something and not have the means to take full advantage of a demonstration.

If you are going to explore a company's ability to handle your requirements, you must have your data available. Take the time to prepare your data your way. Have it ready when evaluation time comes. Your judgment of their performance should be made on two factors. Your data should be fed into the computer with little or no revision. The preparation to process your information should be simple and brief.

Computer library programs are designed and supposed to be fast and efficient. If the computer library appears well stocked with programs you can use, consider it. If the procedures seem clumsy, the programs complex or the operations long and involved, be wary.

Your first month will probably be spent on library programs. Make certain they suit your requirements.

RESPONSE TIME

Response time is the time lag between your instruction to the computer and its reply. Remember that time sharing relies on sequential-user processing of the users currently "on line." As the number of users increases, the time spent on each decreases. The time between your request to the computer and your answer from the computer increases as it services more users.

As computers improve and software is revised, response time is reduced to a minimum. Nevertheless, there is a noticeable difference in response time when the computer is servicing one account and when it is servicing forty. Sometimes a very successful time-sharing company will oversell its services. When this occurs, too many customers are being serviced and response time deteriorates (grows longer).

The user is entitled to a prompt response. If a noticeable delay occurs between responses, care should be exercised before serious commitments to such a company are made.

COSTS

Competitive pressures have kept time-sharing charges down. There are two general ways of billing customers: on a single monthly charge, or on a time-used basis.

A single monthly billing charge is usually negotiated between the time-sharing company and a user after several years of use has given both a pattern of needs. For the new computer user such time-sharing contracts are a bit far down the road to be explored extensively at this time.

The more conventional method of charging is based on a minimum monthly rate, C.P.U., on time and storage.

Minimum Monthly Charge

Some companies charge a flat minimum fee. Usually this runs no more than $100.00 per month. It is usually refunded out of the first hundred spent on the computer. Its primary purpose is to discourage a signed-up user who doesn't use the system. As with any other computer charge, it is inconsequential in relationship to the overall potential of the computer.

Central Processing Unit Charge

Think of this as the actual cost of computer time. After each session on the computer you will be given the Central Processing Unit (C.P.U.) time as the computer signs off. The C.P.U. time is given in seconds and you are charged 5 C.P.U., 25 C.P.U. etc. as the occasion demands.

Seconds of C.P.U. time range in cost from three to five cents. Multiplying the cost per second times the C.P.U. will provide the C.P.U. cost of each computer run. Initially, with library programs, these charges will run rarely over a few dollars per session.

On-line Charges

These refer to the time from when you log in to the computer until you log out. Prices range from five dollars per hour to fifteen dollars per hour depending on the type of service you require. This is a flat fee and covers what is referred to as your "connect time." Again, competitive pressures keep this cost within reasonable bounds.

Storage Charges

These charges are levied against those stored programs, files, and data that you may wish to maintain exclusively for your use. These charges are based on the quantity of the stored data. Prices range from fifty cents to two dollars per thousand words, but competitive activity again keeps these prices down.

The minimum charge plus the above three charges will be your monthly time-sharing bill, i.e. the amount of information you have stored in the computer; the amount of time you have spent connected to the computer; and the number of central processing units (C.P.U.) you have used to run your programs.

For example, the cost of running the SORT program used for the Glossary was provided after the log out command. They read:

```
–LOGOUT
   CPU 9.36
   TERMINAL TIME 0:06:00
```

The user can now calculate the job costs very simply. C.P.U. costs are $.05 per second and terminal time is $10.00 per hour. Thus, 9.36 X $.05 = $.47. Six minutes is a tenth of an hour equaling $1.00. Total cost for the job is $1.47.

As a matter of course, ask each time-sharing company to provide you with their:

1. Minimum monthly charge, if any
2. Storage charges ($/1,000 words)
3. C.P.U. charges ($/second)
4. On-line charge ($/hour)

Comparisons between companies will be easy, but will tend to even out. This factor need not be emphasized unless the price discrepancies are particularly evident.

In summary, initial selection of a time-sharing company should be based on eight criteria:

1. Operational procedures—How comfortable are you when using the system?
2. Languages—BASIC and FORTRAN are essential.
3. Operations assistance—How much help will the company give you?
4. Editing capability—Does the computer have an easy-to-use text and file-editing program?
5. Up time—Is the computer always ready to run when you are?
6. Library—Are there enough available stock programs to help you process your information?
7. Response time—Does the computer accept and process your work promptly?
8. Costs—Are operating costs within the current competitive framework?

Now that you have the criteria, start contacting time-sharing companies. For an in-house demonstration you need only one thing—a telephone.

Any time-sharing company should be able to supply you with a portable terminal and a data set. Once these have been brought to your office, you can communicate with the computer.

There are innumerable ways to get in touch with time-sharing companies. If you have not already contacted a time-sharing company or have one in mind, try these sources for recommendations:

1. Large hardware manufacturers, i.e. I.B.M., Honeywell, Burroughs, etc.
2. Computer trade publications, i.e. *Data-Mation, Computer Age,* etc.
3. In-house computer personnel.
4. Even the yellow pages under "Data Processing Service."

Do not hesitate to contact several companies, and schedule their visits over several days. Certainly one or two will make themselves available immediately.

Don't waste time trying to define your requirements too precisely. Simply inform the company of your situation, for instance:

1. You have not previously used time sharing.
2. You have no terminal or data set.
3. You want an in-house demonstration by their salesman on a portable terminal.
4. You intend to use their library programs so come prepared to demonstrate.

The above will insure that the salesman comes prepared. To insure that you will be prepared, rough out several areas you feel are susceptible to time sharing, and have data available when the opportunity to demonstrate is offered.

If the session goes well, ask the salesman to leave the equipment for a few days. Nothing will prove the value of time sharing faster than the ready availability of such equipment.

Your task now is to evaluate the presentations of the time-sharing companies. Evaluate their services based on the eight points made earlier. Keep your eye firmly on your own specific objectives and requirements.

Don't be high pressured or impressed with sales gimmicks. Remember, almost any time-sharing company can cope with your immediate needs. The critical factor should be whether you function comfortably within the operational procedures. If the company makes you feel confident about using their system, that's the system for you.

And now, before sending you out into the marketplace, consider this analogy: You are going to buy a car to drive from New York to Boston. You have your map, you know the speed limits, and you wish to take the scenic route. You are looking forward to a comfortable, pleasant drive.

Two salesmen give you their story: Salesman "A" says he has a nice family car with power steering, power brakes, and air conditioning. Salesman "B" says his car has four-barrel carburetion, an overhead cam engine, five hundred horsepower, and overdrive.

Advice: Buy your car from salesman "A."

2

PINPOINTING INITIAL JOBS
TO PUT ON TIME SHARING

Interest in time sharing, i.e. reading this book, usually occurs for one of the following reasons.

1. Outside advisors recommended time sharing.
2. You feel computers should do more than write the payroll.
3. No in-house services meet your needs.
4. You suspect you are overlooking a valuable business or scientific tool.
5. Others are using time sharing, why not you?

In the broadest terms, almost any problem can be computerized. Present-day time-sharing capability can undertake, formalize, and program most business and scientific requirements. Failure usually occurs, not at the hardware level, but at the conception level. As usual, it is the people not the computer that fail.

For example, you wish to project the sale of a product. To do this, you use a time-sharing library projection program. Activate the program and insert sales for the past three years. These figures are 20,000, 40,000, and 80,000. The computer projects 160,000, 320,000, and 640,000 for the next three years. Upon inspection these numbers are ridiculous since you know, but failed to inform the computer, that your maximum production capacity is 100,000 units. In short, the computer can do infinite calculations for you, but it cannot do your thinking.

You will find that this book does much the same. Descriptions and examples will abound, but you will rarely find a specific solution to your specific situation. Modify, adjust, twist and turn the examples to your own purposes. View them not as examples but near misses for your requirements. What library programs should you use? How should you use them? When should you use them? These questions depend entirely on your specific needs.

Two broad categories of time-sharing users exist: first, electronic data processing (EDP) specialists who realize that in-house computers can't be all things to all people; second, business managers, and educational and scientific personnel who care nothing about computers, but simply want to get a job done.

Time sharing's value to the first group has yet to be fully realized. It can be used to provide a more interactive computer environment than most in-house EDP facilities are capable of supplying. Programming and debugging are more powerful and flexible on time sharing. Compare these two situations. A programmer works a week writing a program. When completed he requests time on the computer. This is usually scheduled two or three days in advance. When the proper time arrives, his program is fed into the computer. Once the computer has digested (compiled) the program, it outputs a list of errors, logic inconsistencies, and format and syntax discrepancies.

In a normal, busy in-house computer situation, it is customary to turn error output over to the programmer for correction. Once corrections are made, a new appointment is made for computer time and a new list of errors produced. Such programming, compiling, error output, appointment making, and rewriting can go on for weeks. Using time sharing, a program can be input, compiled, debugged, and rewritten during a single session at the console. For more difficult situations the programmer can return to debugging at *his* convenience. Furthermore many time-sharing companies have program writing assistance programs that make programming and debugging much more interactive and immediate.

Another advantage of time sharing to the EDP manager is its flexibility. One-shot requests for access to the in-house computer are constantly being evaluated and refused on the basis of "too costly" or "too time-consuming." At one time or another everyone has asked "Can't this be done on the computer?" The EDP manager wants to provide all the service he can. Unfortunately equipment designed for payroll and order and billing processing is not very flexible. Reluctantly the computer facility must turn down those requests that call for two weeks' programming and one-shot ten seconds of output.

With assistance from a good time-sharing service, the EDP manager can provide company personnel with an additional variety of computer services. Computer time and a wide range of programs is then made available at a minimum of expense and effort.

The second category of user is obvious. It is everyone, other than EDP personnel, who has a job to do and needs a computer to do it. Time sharing has the flexibility, capability, and capacity to service any number and variety of business or scientific requests. Its flexibility ranges from the simplest mathematical calculations to the most involved projections and transformations. Time sharing is geared so the user can progress very quickly from novice to expert.

Time sharing offers three levels of sophistication:

1. Library programs.
2. Specifically written programs.
3. Report-generating programs.

Library programs are those programs already written by the time-sharing company and stored in the computer. They are immediately available to users upon command. Library programs are generalized and cover such areas as sorting information, projecting trends, drawing graphs, processing data through specific formulae, and manipulating common scientific and business equations. These programs may further be broken down into those requiring minimum input and those utilizing massive data bases.

This distinction is important in the early stages of your exploration of time sharing. If you wish to take your first step into time sharing, you require a minimum input program. This means that you insert from one to thirty numbers, and the computer supplies the answer. Perhaps the simplest example of this is a regression

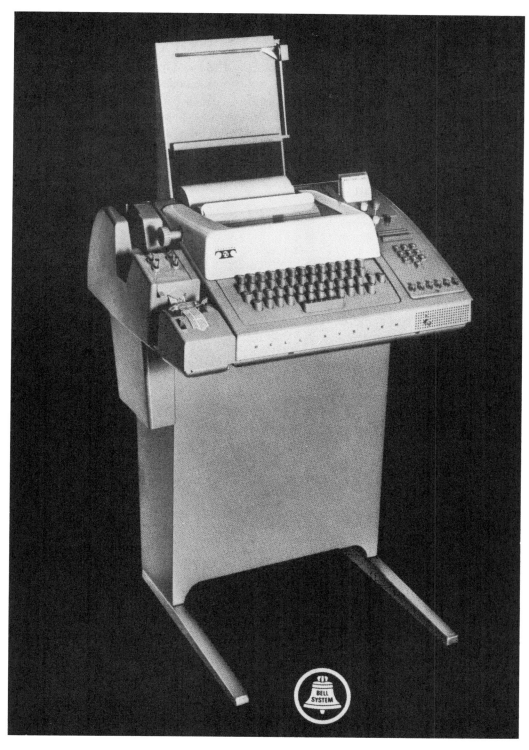

FIGURE 1   COMPUTER TERMINAL

analysis. A stream of numbers is inserted. For example 3,6,9,12 and the computer outputs the continuation 15, 18, 21 and 24.

A sorting program would exemplify the massive data type. Here you would insert 1,000 lines of consistent but unsorted data, and the computer would sequence it as requested. Obviously for your initial efforts you do not wish to start by inserting 1,000 lines of data. Your initial efforts, therefore, should be directed to investigation of minimum input programs.

What job to put on time sharing, therefore, is dictated by the skill, knowledge, and sophistication of the user. These qualities grow with time-sharing experience, and the progression of events is:

1. Minimum input library programs.
2. Massive input library programs.
3. Specifically written programs.
4. Report-generating programs.

Once time sharing is available, applications will suggest themselves. Initially, however, thought must be given to specific applications. These will serve to introduce and familiarize personnel with time-sharing techniques and procedures.

Every time-sharing company has a series of procedures for initiating action with the computer. These are simple procedures for telephoning the computer, identifying yourself, and calling library programs. These procedures are called "logging in."

For the first time, let's stick a toe in the cold water of computerese. Your terminal has been delivered, probably much like the one shown in Figure 1. The time-sharing company has assigned you identification, i.e. a series of letters, such as "HAP103." You are ready to log in.

The format we will use to describe time-sharing operations lists computer output on the left third of the page. Comments are provided in the center column, and operator responses are given on the right-hand third of the page:

COMPUTER (left third)	COMMENT (center column)	OPERATOR (right third)
	Let's assume the time-sharing service has delivered the two devices you require to utilize their service.	
	1. A portable terminal (much like a typewriter).	
	2. A data set. This is a rectangular box 8″ x 18″ with a top slot for inserting a telephone.	
	Your first move is to turn	

COMPUTER	COMMENT	OPERATOR
	on the terminal and to activate the data set. Details for turning on both the terminal and the data set vary from equipment to equipment. However, a maximum of two minutes should suffice to acquaint you with the specific procedures required.	
	Once the equipment is ready, be prepared to dial the time-sharing service. Dial the number provided by the time-sharing service. Dial 123-4567.	
AAA TIME-SHARING SERVICE PLEASE LOG IN:		
	You type your code number, and strike the carriage return (CR):	HAP103 (CR)
	Usually the computer then responds with	
READY		
—	The dash indicates the computer is ready to accept commands.	

Thus, with a simple procedure you have established your identity and made computer services available to you.

Minimum input computer programs should be your first concern. To provide examples of these a consistent format will be used.

1. The problem.
2. Input/output (question/answer).
3. Comment.

Keep in mind that these examples are used to describe time sharing. No attempt will be made to explain or describe uses for these programs except where it bears on a description of the technique. The basic assumption must be made that an individual's interest in time sharing is based on his desire to put manual work he is familiar with on the computer.

CASE IN POINT: A planning department manager for one division of a large conglomerate devoted much time to product projections. One individual in his department spent most of his time "fitting" lines and graphing product growth. These patterns were then "fitted" to national statistics. Since the product mix was large and varied, it was estimated that half a man-year was devoted to this activity. The other half was used to collect and extract data.

During a visit to another division, the manager observed a time-sharing facility already installed. Regression analysis, line fit, and a variety of other statistical results were being run routinely. He immediately recognized the value of this work to his own efforts. In fact, the applications were so pertinent that he started using time sharing by telephoning data to the other division before his own equipment could be installed.

In this instance, ten thousand dollars a year was saved merely by using the time-sharing company's free library programs. No new programs were required.

Regression analysis is a perfect example of minimum input programming.

Problem: You have been marketing a product for the last ten years. Sales have been fluctuating, but now they cannot be increased without building a new plant. Question: How big a plant is needed to accommodate sales ten years in the future?

Input/Output: Each library program has a specific name. Determine what program you wish to run and assemble the necessary input data. This should be completed before you log in.

Each time-sharing service has a directory that describes the programs and procedures. Assume you have selected from the program directory the regression analysis program REGAN. Now assemble your ten years of sales figures. These might be:

Year	Sales	Year	Sales
1	$ 1,420,000	6	$1,750,000
2	1,440,000	7	1,640,000
3	1,600,000	8	1,700,000
4	1,500,000	9	1,870,000
5	1,540,000	10	1,840,000

With your data assembled and the program selected, activate the computer.

COMPUTER	COMMENT	OPERATOR
	Dial 123-4567	
AAA TIME-SHARING SERVICE		
PLEASE LOG IN	Type your identification number (ID)	HAP103
READY		
—	You can now call the program previously selected. You type:	CALL REGAN

COMPUTER	COMMENT	OPERATOR
REGAN READY		

Reference to the time-sharing directory has informed you that X is for years, and Y is for projective data.

You now type in the data as described in the program description, i.e. first the year, next the sales amount.

1,1420,2,1440,3,1600,4,1500,5,1540,6,1750,7,1640, 8,1700,9,1870,10,1840

NOTE: To reduce input effort 1, 2, 3 serves for consecutive years, and trailing zeros may be omitted.

You instruct the computer to process the data by typing "RUN 10" indicating a ten-year projection. Without hesitation the computer will output its results.

RUN 10 (CR)

The program REGAN has applied your data to six types of curves.

As per your last input, "RUN 10," it has projected this data ten years out. Furthermore, the program has tested each curve for fit and reliability.

The computer now prints its results and requests instructions as to which set of projections you wish to see.

COMPUTER	COMMENT		OPERATOR
	INDEX OF		
CURVE TYPE	DETERMINATION	A	B
1. Y=A+(B*X)	0.83662	1366	48
2. Y=A*EXP(B*X)	0.841174	1380.34	2.94526E-2
3. Y=A*(X^B)	0.759136	1363.1	0.115566
4. Y=A+(B/X)	0.526384	1751.77	-415.757
5. Y=A/(A+B*X)	0.843219	7.18634E-4	-1.81636E-5
6. Y=X/(A+B*X)	0.578909	1.64342E-4	5.70599E-4

FOR WHICH CURVE ARE DETAILS DESIRED (NUMBER)?

You study this output and select that curve showing the highest degree of fit, in this instance curve 5 (0.843219).

5 (CR)

As soon as 5 and a carriage return are struck, specific data on that curve is output. The output describes the curve, confirms the input data (actual) and lists the calculated results from year one to year ten and the projection from year eleven to year twenty.

5. Y=A/(A+B*X)

The computer indicates the equation from which the following output was generated.

X—ACTUAL	Y—ACTUAL	Y—CALC
1	1420	1427.61
2	1440	1465.62
3	1600	1505.7
4	1500	1548.04
5	1540	1592.82
6	1750	1640.28
7	1640	1690.65
8	1700	1744.21
9	1870	1801.28
10	1840	1862.2

X—ACTUAL	Y—ACTUAL	Y—CALC
11		1927.4
13		2027.51
14		2072.51
15		2241.25
16		2336.36
18		2439.9
19		2553.04
20		2814.03

As in many programs, REGAN now cycles and gives the user an opportunity to reuse the data by selecting another curve.

FOR WHICH CURVE ARE DETAILS REQUIRED?   2   (CR)

Under most conditions only the "best fit" data is required. However, if curve 2 is also wanted, the above instruction, i.e. 2, will immediately produce the additional information.

2. Y=A*EXP(B*X)   Equation used.

X—ACTUAL	Y—ACTUAL	Y—CALC
1	1420	1421.6
2	1440	1464.6
3	1600	1507.85
4	1500	1552.93
5	1540	1599.34
6	1750	1647.15
7	1640	1606.38
8	1700	1747.09
9	1870	1799.31
10	1840	1853.09
11		1908.48
12		1965.53
13		2024.28
14		2084.79
15		2147.1
16		2211.28

X—ACTUAL	Y—ACTUAL	Y—CALC
17		2277.38
18		2345.45
19		2415.56
20		2487.76

Stop here for a moment, and consider what has been accomplished by the insertion of these twenty numbers (ten years, ten sales totals). A complete review, analysis, and projection has been made. Six choices have been presented, and an evaluation of the data reliability has been produced.

If such an operation were attempted manually, it would not only require an hour of mathematical calculation, but another hour of graphing. The five minutes on the computer represents several hours of manual effort, not to mention the background knowledge and skill many executives lack for this type of analysis.

Thus, the single command, "CALL REGAN," has condensed several hours of manual calculations, projections and graphing to no more than minutes. Beyond this, however, is the ability to change one or two numbers in the input and take another and different look at the results.

The real value of time sharing only now becomes apparent. A single run-through of this data provides a single perspective. If you had spent three hours calculating these results manually, you would hesitate before undertaking another such project. Human inertia, laziness or rationalization could prevent you from taking a second look at this problem. Even an in-house computer setup might discourage a second look because of the scheduling, computer tie-up, or other roadblocks.

Let's take advantage of this time-sharing "second look" capability. Study the sales data given previously and consult your records. Note that years three, six and nine are unusual. Nonrepeatable government contracts, competitors' supply position, and new product introduction biased these years upward.

Return to the raw data, adjust your sales to reflect these trends, and change your input data accordingly.

COMPUTER	COMMENT	OPERATOR
—		CALL REGAN
REGAN READY		CHANGE
	The "change" command instructs the program that you wish to insert new data.	
NEW DATA?		3,1470,6,1590,9,1770 (CR)
REGAN READY		RUN 10 (CR)
	This command again initiates the program, and indicates a ten-year projection.	

COMPUTER	COMMENT	OPERATOR
	The computer now outputs the new curve fits based on the new data.	

CURVE TYPE	INDEX OF DETERMINATION	A	B
1. Y=A+(B*X)	0.969033	1334	46.7273
2. Y=A*EXP(B*X)	0.979616	1350.76	2.91079E-2
3. Y=A/(A+B^X)	0.811128	1343.82	0.1094
4. Y=A+(B/X)	0.503745	1698.75	-367.889
5. Y=1/(A+B*X)	0.987922	7.33179E-4	-1.82083E-5
6. Y=X/(A+B*X)	0.555865	1.49143E-4	5.8935E-4

Note the vastly improved index of determination with the new data.

With this more reliable data a new projection can now be requested.

Curve 5 is still the best fit, but with much greater reliability.

FOR WHICH CURVE ARE DETAILS REQUIRED? 5 (CR)

5. Y=A/(A+B*X)

X—ACTUAL	Y—ACTUAL	Y CALC
1	1420	1398.66
2	1440	1435.21
3	1470	1473.72
4	1500	1514.36
5	1540	1557.3
6	1590	1602.75
7	1640	1650.93
8	1700	1702.09
9	1770	1756.53
10	1840	1814.57
11		1876.57
12		1942.96
13		2014.22
14		2090.9
15		2173.66
16		2263.23

X—ACTUAL	Y—ACTUAL	Y CALC
17		2360.51
18		2466.52
19		2582.5
20		2709.93

LOG OUT (CR)

AAA TIME-SHARING SERVICE ENDED 15:12

No more than five minutes was consumed by this rerun. If attempted manually a completely new set of values would have had to be calculated, and a new chart constructed.

Comment: Note that the revised data confirms the original, and increases its reliability factor thereby increasing the confidence with which one can work with this information. This "looping" capability provides confidence and insight that would have been lacking in a single manual extrapolation. One, incidentally, that would have consumed several additional valuable hours.

For years the complexity of such operations has prevented the pragmatic businessman from applying these techniques. Time sharing sweeps away the incomprehensible details and provides only the specific numbers required.

CASE IN POINT: A large industrial company has for years utilized a standard procedure for proposing, approving, and finding major projects. For this practice they have devised their own standard practice manual. This has been formalized into a sixty-page booklet referred to as the A.F.E. (Authorization For Expenditure).

One part of this study is the Profitability Index (P.I.). It calls for three pages of tedious calculations. Because each option required this type of investigation, rarely were more than two presented to management. These evaluations required several hours of work per option. The work was prone to error, the calculations and recalculations frustrating and time consuming.

Time sharing solved this problem completely. It not only saved an estimated five hundred dollars per analysis, but also allowed, because of the time and aggravation saved, more options to be explored.

On time sharing, the same answers are now being generated at $5.00 per run.

A second brief example should serve to pin down the effort- and time-saving elements of time sharing.

Problem: The profitability index is a new business concept. It is not too frequently used because of the complexity of its calculations. It provides businessmen with a new tool to evaluate business ventures and vastly improves on the concept of payout. Here are two examples with the same five-year payouts, but vastly different profitability indexes.

Input/Output: Profitability index studies are initiated by the development of an income stream. This is built by a detailed study of the venture. Once satisfactory data is generated, it is written on an input sheet for ready insertion in the program. Such an input sheet might look like that shown in Figure 2.

PROFITABILITY INDEX

A. TO CALL PROGRAM:

At dial tone, dial 123-4567

COMPUTER PRINTS:	YOU REPLY:
AAA TIME-SHARING SERVICE	
PLEASE LOG IN	HAP 103
READY	
—	CALL PIRUN
PIRUN READY	

Data should be separated by a comma only. After the CR wait for the ? to appear before inserting the information.

ENTER RUN IDENTIFICA-
TION? RUN A

Insert four numbers: *disbursements* made at *start* of one to three calendar years before initiation of project (if none, use zeros), and initial investment. (First year after project startup).

?	10000	10000	10000	10000000
	3 years prior	2 years prior	1 year prior	initial investment

Insert *disbursements* made *during* each year of life of project consisting of three years prior to initiation and ten years after start of project. (Total: 13 years). Use zeros where necessary.

?	10000	10000	10000	5000000	10000
	10000	10000	10000	10000	10000
	10000	10000	2130000		

Insert *receipts* in years one to thirty. Use zeros if no receipts are expected. (Total: 30 years).

?	10000000	5000000	2000000	200000	70000
	100000	100000	100000	10000	100000
	100000	100000	100000	10000	100000
	100000	100000	100000	10000	100000
	100000	100000	100000	10000	100000
	100000	100000	100000	10000	330000

FIGURE 2   PROFITABILITY INDEX INPUT SHEET

Note that each input sheet carries full instructions for running the program. Since this type of program is not run every day, input sheets should be designed to be self-explanatory.

Following the input sheet exactly, we generate a PI within minutes.

COMPUTER	COMMENT	OPERATOR
	Dial 123-4567	
AAA TIME-SHARING SERVICE		
PLEASE LOG IN		HAP103
READY		
—		CALL PIRUN
PIRUN READY		
?	Insert run ID name, using a CR after each line.	RUN A
	Note: While the program runs, a question mark is used to request the next line of data.	
?		10000,10000,10000,10000000
?		10000,10000,10000,5000000,10000
?		10000,10000,10000,10000,10000
?		10000,10000,2130000
?		100000000,5000000,2000000,200000,70000
?		10000,10000,10000,10000,10000
?		10000,10000,10000,10000,10000
?		10000,10000,10000,10000,10000
?		10000,10000,10000,10000,10000
?		10000,10000,10000,10000,330000
	As soon as all data is in, the results are calculated and output.	
PAYOUT PERIOD 5 YEARS		
PROFITABILITY INDEX 17.5%		
PIRUN READY		
?	The program has now cycled and is ready for additional input. A second PI may now be inserted.	RUN B

COMPUTER	COMMENT	OPERATOR
?		10000000,1000000,1000000,1000000
?		1000000,1000000,1000000,1000000,100000
?		100000,100000,10000,10000,10000
?		10000,10000,10000
?		10000,10000,10000,240000,17000000
?		100000,100000,100000,100000,100000
?		100000,100000,100000,100000,100000
?		100000,100000,100000,100000,100000
?		100000,100000,100000,100000,100000
?		100000,100000,100000,100000,330000

PAYOUT PERIOD 5 YEARS
PROFITABILITY INDEX 1.5%

PIRUN READY	Hit escape ESC	ESC
STOP	key	
—		LOGOUT
TIME 0:0:.5,0:15:23		

Turn off data set to end transmission.

Comment: A more effective tool than payout is available to evaluate business ventures, namely the profitability index (PI). The complexity of its calculations (see Figures 3, 4 and 5) often discourages users. However, by putting these calculations on the computer, the full advantages of the profitability index is realized.

That the profitability index is an effective tool there is no doubt. In the example given, a payout of five years for both ventures is a poor measure of their desirability. Further refinement via the profitability index is essential to clarify the risks inherent in the two opportunities. Not only can two such evaluations be made, but five, ten or twenty refinements can be inspected in the time it would take to do one manual analysis.

Time sharing has provided a viable, thinking tool for the evaluation of business ventures. Few businessmen have the time, experience, or training to apply these mathematical techniques themselves. Furthermore, most businessmen will not entrust such calculations to individuals who do not understand the full implications and ramifications of such evaluations. Result: Until time sharing became available, few profitability index studies were made.

Innumerable minimum input programs can be developed or utilized via time-sharing libraries. They take the tedious error-ridden manual effort out of evaluation efforts and leave the user free to apply his thinking to the problem rather than become entangled in the mechanics of it.

There is enormous scope and application to the minimum input library programs

CALCULATION OF PROFITABILITY INDEX

RUN A

TIMING (CAL. YEAR / PERIOD)	TRIAL #1 0% INTEREST RATE — ACTUAL AMOUNT OF DISBURSEMENTS	TRIAL #2 10% — FACTOR	TRIAL #2 — PRESENT WORTH	TRIAL #3 15% — FACTOR	TRIAL #3 — PRESENT WORTH	TRIAL #4 25% — FACTOR	TRIAL #4 — PRESENT WORTH	TRIAL #5 40% — FACTOR	TRIAL #5 — PRESENT WORTH
BEFORE ZERO POINT									
3RD YR. AT ST.	10,000	1.350	13,500	1.568	15,680	2.117	21,170	3.320	
3RD YR. DURING	10,000	1.285	12,850	1.456	14,560	1.873	18,730	2.736	
2ND YR. AT ST.	10,000	1.221	12,210	1.350	13,500	1.649	16,490	2.225	
2ND YR. DURING	10,000	1.162	11,620	1.253	12,530	1.459	14,590	1.834	
1ST YR. AT ST.	10,000	1.105	11,050	1.162	11,620	1.284	12,840	1.492	
1ST YR. DURING	10,000	1.052	10,520	1.079	10,790	1.136	11,360	1.230	
AFTER ZERO POINT									
1ST YR. AT ST.	10,000,000	1.000	10,000,000	1.000	10,000,000	1.000	10,000,000	1.000	
1ST YR. DURING	5,000,000	.952	4,760,000	.929	4,645,000	.885	4,425,000	.824	
2ND YEAR DURING	10,000	.861	8,610	.799	7,990	.689	6,890	.553	
3RD	10,000	.779	7,790	.688	6,880	.537	5,370	.370	
4TH	10,000	.705	7,050	.592	5,920	.418	4,180	.248	
5TH	10,000	.638	6,380	.510	5,100	.326	3,260	.166	
6TH	10,000	.577	5,770	.439	4,390	.254	2,540	.112	
7TH	10,000	.522	5,220	.378	3,780	.197	1,970	.075	
8TH	10,000	.473	4,730	.325	3,250	.154	1,540	.050	
9TH	10,000	.428	4,280	.280	2,800	.120	1,200	.034	
10TH	2,130,000	.387	3,870	.241	2,410	.093	930	.023	
TOTALS (A)	17,270,000		14,885,450		14,766,200		14,548,060		

TIMING (CAL. YEAR / PERIOD)	ACTUAL AMOUNT OF RECEIPTS	FACTOR	PRESENT WORTH	FACTOR	PRESENT WORTH	FACTOR	PRESENT WORTH	FACTOR	PRESENT WORTH
1ST YEAR DURING	10,000,000	.952	9,520,000	.929	9,290,000	.885	8,850,000	.824	
2ND	5,000,000	.861	4,305,000	.799	3,995,000	.689	3,445,000	.553	
3RD	2,000,000	.779	1,558,000	.688	1,376,000	.537	1,074,000	.370	
4TH	200,000	.705	141,000	.592	118,400	.418	83,600	.248	
5TH	70,000	.638	44,660	.510	35,700	.326	22,820	.166	
6TH	100,000	.577	57,700	.439	43,900	.254	25,400	.112	
7TH	100,000	.522	52,200	.378	37,800	.197	19,700	.075	
8TH	100,000	.473	47,300	.325	32,500	.154	15,400	.050	
9TH	100,000	.428	42,800	.280	28,000	.119	11,900	.034	
10TH	100,000	.387	38,700	.241	24,100	.093	9,300	.023	
11TH	100,000	.350	35,000	.207	20,700	.073	7,300	.015	
12TH	100,000	.317	31,700	.178	17,800	.057	5,700	.010	
13TH	100,000	.287	28,700	.154	15,400	.044	4,400	.007	
14TH	100,000	.259	25,900	.132	13,200	.034	3,400	.005	
15TH	100,000	.235	23,500	.114	11,400	.027	2,700	.003	
16TH	100,000	.212	21,200	.098	9,800	.021	2,100	.002	
17TH	100,000	.192	19,200	.084	8,400	.016	1,600	.001	
18TH	100,000	.174	17,400	.073	7,300	.013	1,300	.001	
19TH	100,000	.157	15,700	.062	6,200	.010	1,000	.001	
20TH	100,000	.142	14,200	.054	5,400	.008	800		
21ST	100,000	.129	12,900	.046	4,500	.006	600		
22ND	100,000	.117	11,700	.040	4,000	.005	500		
23RD	100,000	.105	10,500	.034	3,400	.004	400		
24TH	100,000	.095	9,500	.029	2,900	.003	300		
25TH	100,000	.086	8,600	.025	2,500	.002	200		
26TH	100,000	.078	7,800	.022	2,200	.002	200		
27TH	100,000	.071	7,100	.019	1,900	.001	100		
28TH	100,000	.064	6,400	.016	1,600	.001	100		
29TH	100,000	.058	5,800	.014	1,400	.001	100		
30TH	330,000	.052	17,160	.012	3,960	.001	100		
TOTALS (B)	20,000,000		16,137,320		15,125,360		13,590,020		
RATIO A/B	.864		.922		.976		1.07		

FIGURE 3　　CALCULATION OF PROFITABILITY INDEX

CALCULATION OF PROFITABILITY INDEX

RUN B

CAL. YEAR	PERIOD		TRIAL #1 0% INTEREST RATE — ACTUAL AMOUNT OF DISBURSEMENTS	TRIAL #2 10% — FACTOR	PRESENT WORTH	TRIAL #3 15% — FACTOR	PRESENT WORTH	TRIAL #4 25% — FACTOR	PRESENT WORTH	TRIAL #5 40% — FACTOR	PRESENT WORTH
3RD YR.	AT ST.		10,000,000	1.350	13,500,000	1.568	15,568,000	2.117		3.320	
	DURING		1,000,000	1.285	1,285,000	1.456	1,456,000	1.873		2.736	
2ND YR.	AT ST.		1,000,000	1.221	1,221,000	1.350	1,350,000	1.649		2.225	
	DURING		1,000,000	1.162	1,162,000	1.253	1,253,000	1.459		1.834	
1ST YR.	AT ST.		1,000,000	1.105	1,105,000	1.162	1,162,000	1.284		1.492	
	DURING		1,000,000	1.052	1,052,000	1.079	1,079,000	1.136		1.230	
1ST YR.	AT ST.		1,000,000	1.000	1,000,000	1.000	1,000,000	1.000		1.000	
	DURING		1,000,000	.952	952,000	.929	929,000	.885		.824	
2ND YEAR DURING			100,000	.861	86,100	.799	79,900	.689		.553	
3RD " "			100,000	.779	77,900	.688	68,800	.537		.370	
4TH " "			10,000	.705	7,050	.592	5,920	.418		.248	
5TH " "			10,000	.638	6,380	.510	5,100	.326		.166	
6TH " "			10,000	.577	5,770	.439	4,390	.254		.112	
7TH " "			10,000	.522	5,220	.378	3,780	.197		.075	
8TH " "			10,000	.473	4,730	.325	3,250	.154		.050	
9TH " "			10,000	.428	4,280	.280	2,800	.120		.034	
10TH " "			10,000	.387	3,870	.241	2,410	.093		.023	
TOTALS (A)			17,270,000		21,478,300		23,973,350				

CAL. YEAR	PERIOD		ACTUAL AMOUNT OF RECEIPTS	FACTOR	PRESENT WORTH	FACTOR	PRESENT WORTH	FACTOR	PRESENT WORTH	FACTOR	PRESENT WORTH
1ST YEAR DURING			10,000	.952	9,520	.929	9,290	.885		.824	
2ND " "			10,000	.861	8,610	.799	7,990	.689		.553	
3RD " "			10,000	.779	7,790	.688	5,880	.537		.370	
4TH " "			240,000	.705	169,200	.592	142,080	.418		.248	
5TH " "			17,000,000	.638	10,846,000	.510	8,670,000	.326		.166	
6TH " "			100,000	.577	57,700	.439	43,900	.254		.112	
7TH " "			100,000	.522	52,200	.378	37,800	.197		.075	
8TH " "			100,000	.473	47,300	.325	32,500	.154		.050	
9TH " "			100,000	.428	42,800	.280	28,000	.119		.034	
10TH " "			100,000	.387	38,700	.241	24,100	.093		.023	
11TH " "			100,000	.350	35,000	.207	20,700	.073		.015	
12TH " "			100,000	.317	31,700	.178	17,800	.057		.010	
13TH " "			100,000	.287	28,700	.154	15,400	.044		.007	
14TH " "			100,000	.259	25,900	.132	13,200	.034		.005	
15TH " "			100,000	.235	23,500	.114	11,400	.027		.003	
16TH " "			100,000	.212	21,200	.098	9,800	.021		.002	
17TH " "			100,000	.192	19,200	.084	8,400	.016		.001	
18TH " "			100,000	.174	17,400	.073	7,300	.013		.001	
19TH " "			100,000	.157	15,700	.062	6,200	.010		.001	
20TH " "			100,000	.142	14,200	.054	5,400	.008			
21ST " "			100,000	.129	12,900	.046	4,600	.006			
22ND " "			100,000	.117	11,700	.040	4,000	.005			
23RD " "			100,000	.105	10,500	.034	3,400	.004			
24TH " "			100,000	.095	9,500	.029	2,900	.003			
25TH " "			100,000	.086	8,600	.025	2,500	.002			
26TH " "			100,000	.078	7,800	.022	2,200	.002			
27TH " "			100,000	.071	7,100	.019	1,900	.001			
28TH " "			100,000	.064	6,400	.016	1,600	.001			
29TH " "			100,000	.058	5,800	.014	1,400	.001			
30TH " "			330,000	.052	17,160	.012	3,960	.001			
TOTALS (B)			20,000,000		11,609,780		9,150,540				
RATIO A/B			.864		1.85		2.62				

FIGURE 4   CALCULATION OF PROFITABILITY INDEX

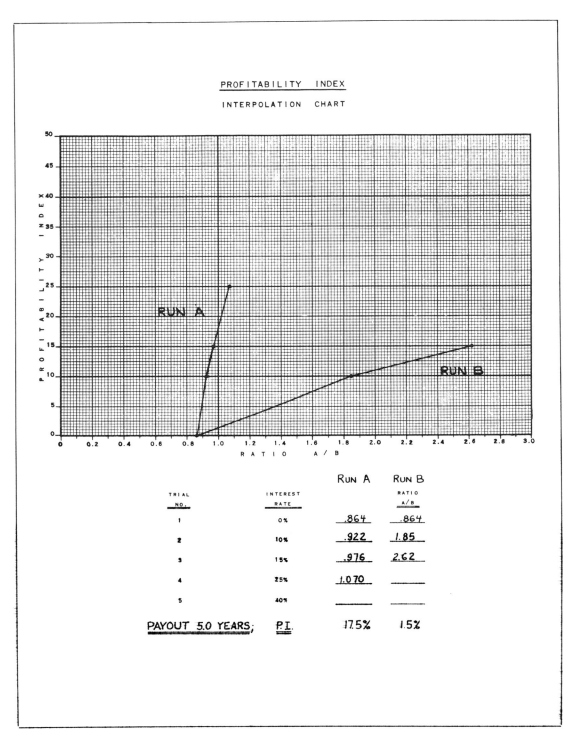

FIGURE 5   P.I. INTERPOLATION CHART

available from time-sharing services. These cover a range from frivolous (tic, tac, toe) to sophisticated projection evaluation and analysis operations. Minimum input programs provide fast, efficient, accurate results for many hard-to-do scientific and business procedures.

As expertise develops and additional projects are undertaken, the scope and range of minimum input programs begins to restrict the user. It is then that he becomes anxious to explore additional alternatives such as:

1. Massive input programs.
2. Specifically written programs.
3. Report-generating programs.

3

EXPANDING THE SCOPE
OF TIME-SHARING JOBS

Massive input programs are more difficult to initiate than minimum input programs. However, they are not difficult to operate once the data has been input. Assemblage, organization, and preparation of the output format of the data is time-consuming. The value of massive data-base programs is the continuing ability to manipulate the data once it is available.

Volumes of data can be inserted in a variety of ways. Direct input from the console is a tedious, but workable method. Keypunching the data on tab cards is a commonly used technique. The preferred technique would be the extraction of specific data from a data base. This would be an in-computer operation requiring no manual effort. In any case, the objective is to have available several thousand lines of information and then manipulate the data to produce meaningful output.

Perhaps the most common of these manipulative programs is the "sort" program. This program sorts alphabetically whatever lines of data are in the file (data bank). Thus, several thousand customers may be sorted by name, city, street address or whatever may be required. The simplest of these programs operates on one line of data, sorts on any segment of it, and prints a file containing the results of the sort. Furthermore, it need not affect the original file, which is retained for future processing.

One example might use a simple, specifically written program to combine and sum invoices, and a library program to sort the results. This combination of library and proprietary programs is typical of the multifaceted aspects of time sharing.

The combination of massive input and a specifically written program neatly exemplifies points two and three, namely:

2. Massive input programs.
3. Specifically written programs.

CASE IN POINT: A tedious manual sorting chore was put on time sharing. This task had been done for years manually. Each month a copy of all invoices was put aside. Quarterly the task of determining gross sales by country was undertaken by the accounting department.

Each invoice was inspected. To make sorting easier, the country of destination was circled. A clerk was then assigned to sorting the invoices by country. This usually amounted to fifty or sixty invoice piles.

Then each pile was summed on an adding machine, and the total recorded. These piles were then checked to determine that all invoices were accounted for. The fifty or sixty country totals were then added and reconciled with the gross sales total.

The next step was to sort the country bundles by sales value. This sort was then typed in a list arranged alphabetically by country.

The final step was to re-sort the bundles alphabetically by country. This was then typed as the second listing.

Arranging for the extra invoice, filing and saving the invoice copies quarterly, and highlighting dollar value and country was a continuous, costly chore. The final sorting and reconciliation took the better part of two days.

The company estimated that at least $1,000.00 was spent quarterly with this record keeping.

Problem: A large international organization sells products around the world. For tax, personnel, sales allocations and D.I.S.C. (Domestic International Sales Corporation) purposes, it is important to know the gross dollar amount sold to each country. Fortunately, each invoice is summarized and captured in a data base. The problem is to summarize this miscellaneous collection of invoice data and list it by country and dollar amount.

Input/Output: A data base is available from the processing of hundreds of monthly billings. This data base contains nineteen essential details on each billing. Such a data base might look like this:

Billing #1	45906,1,1,CHAIN ARC 1475,STO,64.20,27.90,16.5,CANAD
	6533.80,45906,TAINTO, 1,A,02SEP72, 09OCT72, FOB N 30, NY
Billing #2	47806,2,1,TRIG NEG 274,MTO,32.1,26.5,5.12,ARGEN
	1116.33,47806,GLANE ,B,F,09SEP72,31NOV72, CIF LC,BA

This gibberish can go on forever, literally thousands of lines long. It contains, however, the nineteen essential elements on an invoice, and from this it is possible to extract just those elements necessary to satisfy our requirements.

Our problem concerns only two of these nineteen fields, specifically the country field (field ten) underlined in the above example as CANAD and ARGEN, and the "Gross Receivables Amount" (field eleven) as 6533.80 and 1116.33, also underlined.

A simple program is written to read each pair of lines and construct a new data base consisting of only these two data elements, country and gross receivables. This will in no way affect the original data base. It is retained for whatever additional purposes may be appropriate.

The extracted new data base, however, will contain only information pertinent to the present investigation. It will look like this.

CANAD	6533.
ARGEN	1116.
ETC.	

And continues for 2,108 entries containing a scrambled list of countries and gross receivables.

The sort program described previously is now run and the countries are sorted. This creates a new data base with all country sales together. The new data base looks like this:

ARGEN	5876.
ARGEN	206.
ARGEN	53062.
ARUBA	240.
ARUBA	250.
AUSTR	25.
AUSTR	8406.
BELGI	502.
BELGI	5402.
ETC.	

A second run now totals each set of countries i.e., all Argentina sales, all Aruba sales, and so on. A new data base is written containing each country name and its summed sales. This data base now looks as follows:

ARGEN	59,144.
ARUBA	491.
AUSTR	8,431.
BELGI	3,926,407.
ETC.	

The sort program is run again with the same simple command used in chapter 1.

—SORT/COUNTRY/ 10.20/ R72/ DOLLARS/

A new data base is now written ranking the countries by their dollar sales. If we consider only the above four countries (rather than the 2,108 sales and 56 countries actually used), the final result would be:

BELGI	3,926,407.
ARGEN	59,144.
AUSTR	8,431.
ARUBA	491.
ETC.	

Written descriptions tend to complicate the simplicity of the actual operation. In practice, the above takes five minutes and consists of:

STEP 1. Extract two fields from a data base.
STEP 2. Sort the result by country.
STEP 3. Sum the country totals.
STEP 4. Sort the result by gross receivables.

Stop to consider for a moment what an enormous manual effort such a job would entail.

As briefly as possible and by the number, this would consist of:

1. Collect the 2,108 invoices for the month.
2. Separate the 2,108 invoices by country of destination.
3. Sum each bundle of country invoices.
4. Sort country totals from high to low.

Estimated time: 8 hours.

Let's see how this looks conducted directly from the terminal. To operate, one source file, one proprietary program, and one library program are required:

Source File   : "INVOICES," contains 2,108 entries.

Proprietary Program: "BILLSUM," has two options:
          1. To extract country and gross receivables from data lines in source file "INVOICES."
          2. To summarize dollar amounts by country.

Library Program   : "SORT," to sort data as directed.

COMPUTER	COMMENT	OPERATOR
	Dial 123-4567	
AAA TIME-SHARING SERVICE		
PLEASE LOG IN		HAP103
READY		
	STEP 1—*Extract two fields from a data base.* First extract the two pertinent pieces of data from the file "INVOICES." Use the proprietary program "BILLSUM." The computer command is:	CALL BILLSUM
	The computer asks which option is required.	
EXTRACT DATA (1), SUM DATA (2)?		1
	You select the first option.	
THE FILE "EXTRAC" HAS BEEN WRITTEN		
	"EXTRAC" contains the two extracted pieces of data you require.	
	The file "EXTRAC," just written, looks like this:	
	SOAFR 35642.10	

COMPUTER   COMMENT   OPERATOR

MEXIC	5906.21
CANAD	72503.67
MEXIC	21404.89
BRAZI	2486.21
GERMA	75062.80
CANAD	3304.60
CANAD	97104.20
SWEDE	106245.21
GERMA	4573.20
FRANC	43217.01
ARGEN	24145.07
ARGEN	81805.12

STEP 2— *Sort the results by country.*

"EXTRAC" is now sorted with the library SORT program. You command

—   SORT/EXTRAC/1.8/R72/COUNTRY/

THE FILE "COUNTRY" HAS BEEN WRITTEN

The file "COUNTRY," just sorted, looks like this:

ARGEN	24145.07
ARGEN	81805.12
ARGEN	125236.01
ARGEN	60250.12
AUSTR	93276.21
AUSTR	4682.76
AUSTR	36458.93
ETC.	

Option two of the program "BILLSUM" is now run to develop a total sales per country figure. The second option is used.

STEP 3—*Sum the country totals.*

                                                         CALL BILLSUM

EXTRACT DATA (1), SUM DATA (2)

You respond   2

THE FILE "SUMTRY" HAS BEEN WRITTEN

COMPUTER	COMMENT	OPERATOR
—	The file "SUMTRY" contains the summed gross receivables for each country. The file "SUMTRY" looks like this:	

ARGEN	59,144.
AUSTR	520,604.
AUSTR	982,521.
BAHAM	184,376.
BELGI	3,926,407.
ETC.	

STEP 4—*Sort the result by gross receivables.*

The library SORT program is again used.

—		SORT/SUMTRY/10.20/R72/DOLLAR/

THE FILE "DOLLAR" HAS BEEN WRITTEN

The data base "DOLLAR" contains a list of countries with sales ranked from high to low.

The "DOLLAR" file looks like this:

UKGB	5706240
JAPAN	5152046
GERMA	4872156
CANAD	4215605
BELGI	3926407
ETC.	

—		LOGOUT

Comment: Time sharing has condensed a day's work into five minutes—what more can be said?

REPORT-GENERATING PROGRAMS (RGPs)

RGPs are unquestionably the future of time sharing. They provide great individual latitude in manipulating data without requiring programming knowledge or training. Essentially, RGPs are designed for the busy executive who knows precisely what he wants. This know-how is useless, however, if he must first learn programming in order to use the computer. Report-generating programs allow the executive to manipulate output data in a variety of formats, to process the data through a complexity of mathematical equations, and to output only the results he requires.

The program provides for insertion from the keyboard of all the elements necessary to build a program. These elements include:

1. Column and row titles (called headers).
2. Variables—input.
3. Variables—output.
4. Equations.

Given these options, any type of data manipulation can be built right at the console. Reports can be generated without recourse to a programmer. RGPs provide the user with a computer tool, rather than forcing the user to dilute his efforts by program building. In return for this flexibility, however, the computer demands study and concentration. The user cannot simply turn on the AAA Time-Sharing Company's RGP program and go. Care, time, effort, and study all must be expended before real results can be achieved.

Assuming that all the preliminaries of technique and method have been overcome, let's undertake the construction of an RGP program concerned with the financial analysis of two companies. The objective of this study is to determine whether one company (the parent) should acquire another (the candidate). Furthermore, the program should be built so that any candidate can be compared with the parent company whenever acquisition interest develops.

Problem: To build a corporate acquisition program. The program should input pertinent candidate company financial data, compare it to the parent company, and output data permitting judgments as to acquisition desirability.

Input/Output: Report-generating programs require extremely careful analysis before approaching the computer. The power and flexibility of RGPs allow analysis in depth, but can also result in hours of wasted effort if the objectives are not clearly defined.

After a thorough evaluation of company objectives, management requirements, and executive capabilities, a framework for the acquisition analysis should be constructed. Nothing can be hazy or ill-defined in a computer program. Frequently the discipline imposed by the computer forces refinement and clarity to an evaluation that casual inspection would never reveal.

Before approaching the computer or attempting to activate the report-generating program, each detail of input and output must be precisely laid out:

1. Headers.
2. Input variable (I).
3. Output variable (O).
4. Equations.

Such an exercise might look like this:

Page 1, headers (titles):

PARENT-CANDIDATE
FINANCIAL ANALYSIS
ACQUISITION PROGRAM

DATE	PARENT	CANDIDATE	CONSOLIDATION

Sales.
Before-tax earnings.
Net earnings.
Margin on sales.
Common shares.
Earnings/share.
Cash flow.
Cash flow/share.
Stockholder equity.
etc.

Page 2, headers

COMMON STOCK
NONDILUTION PREMIUM PERCENTAGES
EARN/SH=   CF/SH=   EQTY/SH=

| PARENT STOCK FOR CANDIDATE AT PCNT PREMIUM OF | MM PAR. SHARES REQUIRED FOR ACQUISITION | PERFORMANCE/NEW PAR. SHARES | | | PAR. DIV. PER. ACQ. |
| | | EARNINGS/ SHARE | C-FLOW SHARE | EQUITY/ SHARE | SHARE |

TIMES EARNINGS   ACQUISITION $ COST NO. OF PAR. SHARES REQ.

| CONSOLIDATION WITH IM CANDIDATE AT PCT PREMIUM OF | PAR. SHARES AFTER TRADE | CONSOLIDATION PERFORMANCE ACT. | | | VAL/SH OF ACQ. PCT PREM. |
| | | EARNINGS/ SHARE | C-FLOW SHARE | EQUITY/ SHARE | |

Each header in the report and each row of output must be formatted in advance. The most effective way to organize such a report is to prepare it in its entirety with dummy numbers. This can then be converted to input for the RGP program.

Format and layout are only the first step. Following this, variables for each financial element must be devised, and equations for each calculation must be constructed.

Let's explore an example of this using the earnings per share portion of the report.

VARIABLES	SUBJECT
IPE	= Parent's net earnings
IPS	= Parent's number of shares
ICE	= Candidate's earnings
ICS	= Candidate's number of shares
IPMV	= Parent's and market value/share
ICMV	= Candidate's and market value/share
IPES and ICES	= Earning per share, parent and candidate
OESA	= Earnings per share after acquisition

Thus, the equations for earnings per share would look like this:

$$OPES = IPE/IPS$$
$$OCES = ICE/ICS$$

The formula for earnings per share for the two corporations after acquisition without premium payments would be:

$$OESA = (IPE+ICE)/(ICS/(IPMV/ICMV))+IPS)$$

The above merely serves to indicate not only the flexibility but also the complexity that can be built into such programs.

Report-generating programs are available from most time-sharing companies. They may be simple or elaborate, but one thing you can be certain of—each will be different. Some companies build generalized RGPs for any purpose. Some slant the program toward financial matters, some scientific, some transportation.

Do not be discouraged by a certain superficial complexity. Remember, the alternative is to write a program. In order to write a program you must still lay out the problem in equal detail. A programmable, detailed description of an acquisition analysis will require the same effort as needed to construct your own RGP.

To summarize, a report-generating program requires five things:

1. Careful analysis of the problem.
2. Specific definition and assignment of input variables.
3. Specific definition and assignment of output variables.
4. Precise delineation of equations.
5. Headers and formatting.

Assuming all preliminary work has been accomplished, let's proceed to the console for an example of data input and RGP operation.

COMPUTER	COMMENT	OPERATOR
	Dial 123-4567	

AAA TIME-SHARING SERVICE

COMPUTER	COMMENT	OPERATOR
READY		RUN RGP
HEADERS:	At this point you type the headers you have determined are suitable for the report. These are coded by you, and typed and positioned exactly as they will appear on the page of the final report.	
	You type:	HEADER 1
PARENT	PARENT-CANDIDATE FINANCIAL ANALYSIS ACQUISITION PROGRAM CANDIDATE	CONSOLIDATION
DATE		
SALES		
BEFORE-TAX EARNINGS		
NET EARNINGS		
MARGIN ON SALES		
	This continues until all page-one headers are in. You then type:	HEADER 2
	And so forth, until all the report's headers have been written. When finished you type:	DONE HEADERS
	The program then asks	
INPUT VARIABLES?		
	You now type the variable name of the input variable and its actual value.	
		IPCN = USCORP
		IPCD = 10/10
		IPNS = 17.41
		IPBT = 4.346
		IPNE = 2.49
		IPS = 1.415
		IPD = .804
		IPE = 10.766
		IPD = .85
		IPMP = 30.00

COMPUTER	COMMENT	OPERATOR

OPERATOR: IPMP = 30.00

COMMENT: Now the candidate company data is inserted.

OPERATOR:
ICCN = CANDID
ICCD = 10/19
ICNS = 10.948
etc.

COMMENT: Following this the formulae are input.

Note: The output variable initiates with an "O" while the above input variables initiated with an "I."

OPES = IPE/IPS
OCES = ICE/ICS
OESA = (IPE+ICE)/(ICS/(IPMV/ICMV))+IPS

COMMENT: After all the equations are inserted, an output listing is written to conform to the headers.

Type: OUTPUT FORMAT

Page 1

COMPUTER: DATE

OPNS	OCNS	OPNS+ICNS
OPBT	OCBT	OPBT+OCBT
OPE	OCE	OPE+OCE
OPMS	OCMS	OPCMS
OPS	OPS	IPS+OPS

COMMENT: This outlines the format for page 1. Pages 2, 3 and 4 are constructed in a similar fashion.

Naturally only a part of the RGP can be described here. For instance, the simple transformation of an input number (IPBT) to an output number (OPBT) by the equation OPBT= IPBT explains the first five

COMPUTER	COMMENT	OPERATOR
	outputs that require no further manipulation.	

Obviously the construction and input of data to the RGPs can cover any degree of complexity. It is impossible to detail every step in building a report-generating program. The previous explanation is provided only to give a feel for the thinking, planning, and operation involved.

> CASE IN POINT: This acquisition study was originally done manually and used by a multinational company. It was investigating overseas acquisitions.
>
> At one time thirty-five studies were backed up waiting for review. The original data used were the financial statements and annual reports of foreign businesses. This type of data extraction, manipulation and evaluation could not be left to clerks. As a result, various management staff people were assigned the work.
>
> The financial reports were in foreign currency. The first task was converting this to dollars. Then the pertinent numbers were extracted. Finally, the individual entered the extracted data on a standard form. This then led through various calculations, and the final manipulation was the acquisition analysis.
>
> It was estimated that a man, attending to his other duties as well, could complete one analysis in about two weeks. The cost estimated was between three and five hundred dollars.
>
> When the RGP program was implemented, a particularly ingenious device was used. The foreign financial report was inserted in the system in its own currency. Then one data input required only the current foreign exchange rate. When the program ran, the computer automatically converted the appropriate numbers into U.S. dollars. Actually it was quite spectacular; data input in Japanese yen, information output in U.S. currency.
>
> During the time of changing exchange rates, it was invaluable. Normally, each time currency was revaluated it would be necessary to redo the whole exercise by converting the base data to its new dollar value. On time sharing, only the exchange rate values needed changing. With this single adjustment, a whole new report could be immediately output.
>
> Evaluations taking weeks were reduced to fifteen minutes, and costs to five dollars per run.

Is such an effort worth it? Naturally each case must be judged on its merits. In the case of the acquisition program described above, it required the off-and-on attention of a middle manager for several weeks to complete manually the financial portion of such an acquisition study.

Once the acquisition RGP was established, the parent company data was held constant (except for the current market price), and only the candidate company's data needed to be input. Furthermore, this input data was collected on an input sheet and could be input in a couple of minutes. Four pages of acquisition analysis ensued, printed out at thirty characters per second. All in all a single analysis required no more than fifteen minutes. Two weeks versus fifteen minutes? Well worth the week's work that might be entailed when establishing the initial RGP.

Obviously acquisition analysis is not a one-time job. The objective of this RGP was to provide a capability that would test candidate after candidate as a prospective acquisition. Once the program was functioning, its value was the speed and low cost with which it could process candidate companies. Eleven pieces of data are inserted.

ACQUISITION ANALYSIS. CANDIDATE COMPANY:		
DESCRIPTION	INPUT DATA	
	VARIABLE	DATA
COMPANY NAME	ICCN =	CANDID
CURRENT DATA	ICCD =	10/20
NET SALES	ICNS =	10.948
BEFORE-TAX EARNINGS	ICBT =	.668
NET EARNINGS	ICNE =	.420
SHARES OUTSTANDING	ICS =	4.500
DEPRECIATION	ICD =	.947
EQUITY	ICE =	6.668
DIVIDEND PER SHARE (COMMON)	ICD =	.048
MARKET PRICE	ICMP =	1.918
PARENT COMPANY MARKET PRICE	IPMP =	30.000

Once this input is organized on the input sheet, operation can further be simplified as follows:

COMPUTER	COMMENT	OPERATOR
	Dial 123-4567.	
AAA TIME-SHARING SERVICE READY		
—		RUN RGP ACQUIS
INPUT DATA		CANDID,10/20,10.948,.668,.42,4.50
INPUT DATA		.947,6.668,.048,1.917,30
—	The program counts the input and is expecting eleven pieces of data. Any more or less will result in an error message.	

COMPUTER	COMMENT	OPERATOR
	With all in order, the report-generating program outputs in the next ten minutes four pages of detailed financial acquisition analysis.	
	[See Figures 6, 7, 8, 9, and 10.]	

Comment: Admittedly, RGPs are sophisticated computer tools. The time saved over manual efforts in complicated analyses amply justifies the initial output in time and cost.

Naturally the reports to be generated must be selected with care and understanding. Undoubtedly, this type of program represents time sharing at its best. The success of RGPs will obviously be dependent on the skill and ingenuity of the user. There are no common business problems and few scientific exercises that could not be improved with this type of application.

PARENT AND CANDIDATE
FINANCIAL ANALYSIS
ACQUISITION PROGRAM

DATE 22SEP		PARENT	CANDIDATE	CONSOLIDATION
SALES	$MM	17.410	10.948	28.358
BEFORE-TAX EARNINGS	$MM	4.346	.668	5.014
NET EARNINGS	MM	2.490	.420	2.910
MARGIN ON SALES	PCT	14.300	3.834	10.261
COMMON SHARES	MM	1.415	4.500	1.703
EARNINGS/COMMON SH	$	1.76	.093	1.709
CASH FLOW	$MM	3.294	1.367	4.661
CASH FLOW/COMMON SH	$	2.33	.304	2.737
STOCKHOLDER EQUITY	$MM	10.766	6.668	17.434
MARGIN ON EQUITY	PCT	23.13	6.296	16.690
EQUITY/COMMON SH	$	7.61	1.482	10.239
CONVERTIBLE PREF SH	MM	00.000	.000	.000
DIVIDEND/PREF SH	$	0.000	.000	.000
DIVIDEND/COMMON SH	$	.85	.048	
MARKET PRICE	$	30.000	1.918	
PR/EARNINGS RATIO		17.045	20.565	
PRE/CASH FLOW RATIO		12.876	6.316	

FIGURE 6   ACQUISITION OUTPUT PAGE 1

COMMON STOCK
NONDILUTION PREMIUM PERCENTAGES
EARN/SH = -17.10 CF/SH = 104.05 EQTY/SH = 204.54

PAR. STOCK FOR CANDIDATE AT PCNT PREMIUM OF	MM PAR. SHARES REQUIRED FOR ACQUISITION	PERFORMANCE/NEW PAR. SHARES			PAR DIV. PER ACQ. SHARE
		EARNINGS/ SHARE	C-FLOW/ SHARE	EQUITY/ SHARE	
.00	.288	1.459	4.750	23.171	.054
10.00	.317	1.326	4.318	21.065	.060
20.00	.345	1.216	3.958	19.309	.065
30.00	.374	1.122	3.654	17.824	.071
40.00	.403	1.042	3.393	16.551	.076
50.00	.432	.973	3.167	15.447	.082
60.00	.460	.912	2.969	14.482	.087
70.00	.489	.858	2.794	13.630	.092
80.00	.518	.810	2.639	12.873	.098
90.00	.547	.768	2.500	12.195	.103
100.00	.576	.729	2.375	11.586	.109
-17.10	.239	1.760	5.730	27.951	.045

TIMES EARNINGS	ACQUISITION $ COST	NO. OF PAR. SHARES REQ.
5X	2098992.81	69966.43
10X	4197985.61	139932.85
15X	6296978.42	209899.28
20X	8395971.22	279865.71

CONSOLIDATION WITH CANDIDATE AT PCT PREMIUM OF	IM PAR. SHARES AFTER TRADE	CONSOLIDATION PERFORMANCE ACT.			VAL/SH OF ACQ. PCT PREM.
		EARNINGS/ SHARE	C-FLOW/ SHARE	EQUITY/ SHARE	
.00	1.703	1.709	2.737	10.239	1.918
10.00	1.732	1.680	2.692	10.068	2.110
20.00	1.760	1.653	2.648	9.904	2.302
30.00	1.789	1.626	2.605	9.745	2.494
40.00	1.818	1.601	2.564	9.590	2.686
50.00	1.847	1.576	2.524	9.441	2.878
60.00	1.875	1.552	2.485	9.296	3.070
70.00	1.904	1.528	2.448	9.155	3.261
80.00	1.933	1.505	2.411	9.019	3.453
90.00	1.962	1.483	2.376	8.887	3.645
100.00	1.991	1.462	2.342	8.758	3.837
-17.10	1.654	1.760	2.819	10.543	1.590

FIGURE 7   ACQUISITION OUTPUT PAGE 2

CONSOLIDATED ERNGS/SHARE AT VARIOUS MKT PRICES FOR PAR. + CAND.

PAR. PRICE= 22.00 24.00 26.00 28.00 30.00 32.00 34.00 36.00 38.00

CANDIDATE

1.10	1.77	1.79	1.81	1.83	1.84	1.85	1.86	1.87	1.88
1.20	1.75	1.77	1.79	1.81	1.82	1.84	1.85	1.86	1.87
1.30	1.73	1.75	1.77	1.79	1.81	1.82	1.83	1.84	1.85
1.40	1.71	1.73	1.76	1.77	1.79	1.81	1.82	1.83	1.84
1.50	1.69	1.72	1.74	1.76	1.77	1.79	1.80	1.82	1.83
1.60	1.67	1.70	1.72	1.74	1.76	1.77	1.79	1.80	1.81
1.70	1.65	1.68	1.70	1.72	1.74	1.76	1.77	1.79	1.80
1.80	1.63	1.66	1.69	1.71	1.73	1.74	1.76	1.77	1.79
1.90	1.61	1.64	1.67	1.69	1.71	1.73	1.75	1.76	1.77
2.00	1.60	1.63	1.65	1.68	1.70	1.72	1.73	1.75	1.76
2.10	1.58	1.61	1.64	1.66	1.68	1.70	1.72	1.73	1.75
2.20	1.56	1.59	1.62	1.65	1.67	1.69	1.71	1.72	1.74
2.30	1.54	1.58	1.60	1.63	1.65	1.67	1.69	1.71	1.72
2.40	1.53	1.56	1.59	1.62	1.64	1.66	1.68	1.70	1.71
2.50	1.51	1.54	1.57	1.60	1.63	1.65	1.67	1.68	1.70
2.60	1.49	1.53	1.56	1.59	1.61	1.63	1.65	1.67	1.69
2.70	1.48	1.51	1.55	1.57	1.60	1.62	1.64	1.66	1.68
2.80	1.46	1.50	1.53	1.56	1.59	1.61	1.63	1.65	1.67
2.90	1.45	1.49	1.52	1.55	1.57	1.60	1.62	1.64	1.65
3.00	1.43	1.47	1.50	1.53	1.56	1.58	1.61	1.63	1.64
3.10	1.42	1.46	1.49	1.52	1.55	1.57	1.59	1.61	1.63

FIGURE 8   ACQUISITION OUTPUT PAGE 3

PCNT NONDILUTION PREMIUM AT VARIOUS MKT PRICES FOR PAR. + CAND.
    BASED ON EARNINGS PER SHARE.

PAR. PRICE= 26.00 27.00 28.00 29.00 30.00 31.00 32.00 33.00 34.00

CANDIDATE

	26.00	27.00	28.00	29.00	30.00	31.00	32.00	33.00	34.00
1.10	25.30	34.94	39.76	44.58	49.40	54.22	30.12	59.04	63.86
1.20	14.86	23.70	28.12	32.53	36.95	41.37	19.28	45.79	50.20
1.30	6.03	14.18	18.26	22.34	26.42	30.49	10.10	34.57	38.65
1.40	-1.55	6.03	9.81	13.60	17.39	21.17	2.24	24.96	28.75
1.50	-8.11	-1.04	2.49	6.03	9.56	13.10	-4.58	16.63	20.16
1.60	-13.85	-7.23	-3.91	-.60	2.71	6.03	-10.54	9.34	12.65
1.70	-18.92	-12.68	-9.57	-6.45	-3.33	-.21	-15.80	2.91	6.03
1.80	-23.43	-17.53	-14.59	-11.64	-8.70	-5.75	-20.48	-2.81	.14
1.90	-27.46	-21.88	-19.08	-16.29	-13.50	-10.71	-24.67	-7.92	-5.13
2.00	-31.08	-25.78	-23.13	-20.48	-17.83	-15.18	-28.43	-12.53	-9.88
2.10	-34.36	-29.32	-26.79	-24.27	-21.74	-19.22	-31.84	-16.69	-14.17
2.20	-37.35	-32.53	-30.12	-27.71	-25.30	-22.89	-34.94	-20.48	-18.07
2.30	-40.07	-35.46	-33.16	-30.85	-28.55	-26.24	-37.77	-23.94	-21.63
2.40	-42.57	-38.15	-35.94	-33.73	-31.52	-29.32	-40.36	-27.11	-24.90
2.50	-44.87	-40.63	-38.50	-36.38	-34.26	-32.14	-42.75	-30.02	-27.90
2.60	-46.99	-42.91	-40.87	-38.83	-36.79	-34.75	-44.95	-32.71	-30.67
2.70	-48.95	-45.02	-43.06	-41.10	-39.13	-37.17	-46.99	-35.21	-33.24
2.80	-50.77	-46.99	-45.09	-43.20	-41.31	-39.41	-48.88	-37.52	-35.63
2.90	-52.47	-48.81	-46.99	-45.16	-43.33	-41.50	-50.64	-39.67	-37.85
3.00	-54.06	-50.52	-48.75	-46.99	-45.22	-43.45	-52.29	-41.69	-39.92
3.10	-55.54	-52.12	-50.41	-48.70	-46.99	-45.28	-53.83	-43.57	-41.86

FIGURE 9   ACQUISITION OUTPUT PAGE 4

CONVERTIBLE PREFERRED STOCK

| PAR. STOCK FOR CANDIDATE AT PCNT PREMIUM OF | MM PAR. SHARES REQUIRED FOR ACQUISITION | PERFORMANCE/NEW PAR. SHARES | | | PAR. DIV |
		EARNINGS/ SHARE	C-FLOW/ SHARE	EQUITY/ SHARE	PER ACQ. SHARE
.00	.230	1.824	5.938	28.964	.000
10.00	.253	1.658	5.398	26.331	.000
20.00	.276	1.520	4.948	24.137	.000
30.00	.299	1.403	4.567	22.280	.000
40.00	.322	1.303	4.241	20.689	.000
50.00	.345	1.216	3.958	19.309	.000
60.00	.368	1.140	3.711	18.102	.000
70.00	.391	1.073	3.493	17.038	.000
80.00	.414	1.013	3.299	16.091	.000
90.00	.437	.960	3.125	15.244	.000
100.00	.460	.912	2.969	14.482	.000

STOP

+

FIGURE 10   ACQUISITION OUTPUT PAGE 5

4

FREE COMPUTER PROGRAMS
VIA TIME SHARING

You know your car can take you from New York to Chicago. Would you consider climbing in the back seat of your empty vehicle and announcing, "Take me to Chicago"? If you did, you would soon realize that you were sitting in nothing but an assemblage of upholstered steel, aluminum and rubber. Attractive and sparkly perhaps, but not even a rival for your living room sofa.

If you want to avoid the analogous situation of sitting in front of a computer exclaiming, "Compute for me," you must carefully review your jobs for computer-susceptible tasks. The computer is not going to solve problems you can't solve yourself. It won't predict trends with insufficient data. It won't solve problems you don't understand yourself. In short, it won't take you to Chicago unless you study the maps and do the steering.

During the twenties, thirties, and forties, scientists developed many complex theories and equations. Some were so involved that their authors took delight in explaining that it would take a hundred men a hundred years to perform the calculations. In a way they had drawn the road map, but the trip was simply too long for a man to take. Since the forties, the computer, like the jet plane, has begun to make our world smaller. The analogy is quite apt. Both jet and computer in the course of the twentieth century have reduced man's travel time, both physically and mentally, to a remarkable degree.

What time sharing offers us is the muscle to do those things we know we should do, but have been too busy, preoccupied, or understaffed to take time to do. Consider the following example.

Problem: The Wexler company employs fifty salesmen around the country to sell heavy, bulk commodities in a very competitive environment. The freight, packing, and delivery costs vary widely from customer to customer. Result, the fifty salesmen are forced to quote "on the spot." Result: Too many low-profit orders and no "feel for the market" except the month-end profit and loss statement.

Solution: A data base generated when the order is computer output. The computer then outputs a listing each week of all orders and the calculated gross profit. This list is then distributed to management and all salesmen. It is used like an exception report (see Figure 11.)

The salesmen merely glance down the Est. G/P% column. The corporation has set

		ALL SHIPMENTS				
ORDER NO. (6)	CUSTOMER NAME (2) (5)	PRODUCT NAME (4)	QUANTITY IN LBS (3)	PLANT NET (7)	DOLLARS /UNIT	EST GP% (1)
722205	STANFHARO	DUST	200000.	9.40	CWT	5.3
722464	KLAASSENS	KALI	100000.	11.73	CWT	5.0
722578	MARSHALPRE	FARA	40000.	8.43	CWT	11.6
722527	CONSOGLOTT	ISOL ASH	194660.	21.94	ST	27.8
722371	GILLIN	LEODINAC	800.	15.97	CWT	27.2
722461	OTOKI	KALLOS	3220.	46.43	CWT	36.7
722438	QUIMPITIKI	LOKO BULK	40700.	8.50	CWT	8.2
722487	ALLISRAEL	CAN LOR CHOS	7700.	2.20	CWT	25.0
722498	OTOKI	KALLOS	6900.	47.09	CWT	37.6
722564	KLAASSENS	FARA	40000.	7.93	CWT	5.0
722579	KLAASSENS	KLAS DICA	24200.	16.39	CWT	32.6
722619	COTROMAL	SANDED TECH	1500.	1.45	LB	58.6
722736	CHLINMECH	BIOKALIKAN	40800.	49.67	CWT	2.2
722737	VARILONET	BIOKALIKAN	4500.	55.86	CWT	39.7
721782	TONGUATIMO	SODCARFD	10000.	4.12	CWT	17.7
722662	TORRIA	BIOKALIKAN	11100.	47.15	CWT	28.6
722663	SOLARSKIES	CYANOLUM	250.	56.45	CWT	56.1
722668	ILKO	BIOKOLIKON	3300.	59.00	CWT	37.1
		BIOKALIKAN	1500.	59.00	CWT	2.9

TOTAL PLANT NET   325362.65
TOTAL TRANSFER COST   245961.22

TOTAL GROSS PROFIT   79401.43   AVE. G/P PERCENTAGE   24.4

FIGURE 11   GROSS PROFIT REPORT

certain gross profit percentage parameters. Anything under 5%, (1) for instance, is undesirable. Wherever 5% or less is shown, the salesman looks to the left to see if the customer is one of his accounts (2). If not he goes on. If it is his account, he checks the other details provided by the computer to the left of the G/P percentage. He may then ask himself: Does the quantity indicate a sample shipment (3)? Is the product a consistently high- or low-profit item (4)? Is this customer under contract (5)? Should he request further file information on that order number (6)? Is the selling price within a competitive range (7)?

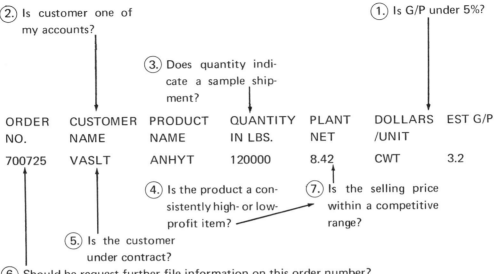

CASE IN POINT: How much money is saved by preventing errors? This is difficult to assess. If you know errors are occurring, you correct them. How can you total up the number of errors made that you don't know about?

A New York industrial concern gained a momentary glimpse of the answer. They utilized the gross profit program just described. The first report output showed ten of fifty gross profits outside the established parameters. Six months later, one in a hundred was more the rule.

Perhaps it is a meaningless exercise, but for purposes of comparison, a review was made. Comparison of the first report with the one six months later revealed a gross profit variance of thirty-one thousand dollars.

To an experienced salesman this sort of a report can be reviewed in seconds. In fact, profit discrepancies will practically leap off the page with their demand for attention. From a scan of only a few moments, forty of the fifty salesmen will confirm that their activities are going well. The remaining ten will have the necessary information to begin checking on their low-profit sales.

Simultaneously management is reviewing these reports. They also scan for the profit exceptions. Furthermore, they can promptly explore or request explanations for poor profit performance. At the end of each report an actual total dollar percentage provides a true reading of the market and of sales trends for management from week to week.

Only with the computer can collection, calculation and computation of these thousands of weekly sales be undertaken. If attempted manually, at best it would be a week late, at worst, its accuracy would always be in question.

The speed and accuracy of the computer has added a new dimension to the business operation. It has assembled and organized information fast enough and accurately enough so that a continuing control of company profits may be maintained.

Many people consider their jobs too complicated for the computer. Perhaps this may be true for the overall operation, the direction and initiative, but frequently the individual segments, the "nuts and bolts," can be easily organized for computer manipulation.

Not only can the computer process various elements of a job faster and more efficiently, but it also can provide more information. It can do so simply because it can intake, calculate, process, and output faster than would be economically feasible by manual means.

Take, for example, a financial evaluation of a business enterprise. Individual conclusions drawn from the evaluation of a balance sheet and a profit and loss statement vary enormously. Overall "feel," existing trends, comparison with similar businesses and/or current ratios all may serve as a businessman's criteria. Innumerable methods and techniques have been proposed. Not infrequently several men in the same company will base decisions on the same matter using completely different criteria. These different perspectives, of course, are not a disadvantage, but the amount of manual effort involved both by the decision maker and his subordinates is enormous. Furthermore, in the rush of the moment details can be erroneously calculated, overlooked or ignored.

Financial evaluation is subject to computer analysis. To solve the question of multiple perspective, the computer simply processes and manipulates all points of view. The final report shows all sides of the picture. The evaluator and decision maker simply chooses that information he can use and ignores the other data.

> Problem: Financial analysis of Company A.
> Input: [See Figure 12.]
> Output: [See Figure 13.]
> Comment: There is something here for any business or financial point of view. This is a
>   perfect example of where the computer does the work and the people do
>   the evaluation.

This type of output serves an additional purpose. Each evaluator is expected to have his preferred ratios. Others are unfamiliar or unknown to him. By including brief explanations with each ratio, users are encouraged to expand their evaluation tools.

Time sharing offers a host of applications to line and staff management. Whole structures of interacting computer programs can be built on time sharing. On the other hand, limitless individual evaluations, previously done manually, are instantly available via time sharing.

> CASE IN POINT: A large chemical company routinely compared its yearly financial performance with that reported by its ten major competitors. This evaluation was prepared by the controller's department. Not only was it a tedious chore, but yearly changes were made in the format that required a constant up-date of the previous years' reports. Extracting, calculating, reformatting and retyping was a month-long chore. The estimated yearly cost was five thousand dollars.

COMPANY NAME: XXX INC.   DATE:

1. Fiscal Year	1
2. Net Sales	1009702886
3. Gross Profit	141365987
4. Net Profit (NPAT)	62921187
5. Number of Shares	30361000
6. Depreciation	37078834
7. Equity (Net Worth)	382459000
8. Dividends/Share	0.71
11. FMC Market Price	38

PROGRAM 2—FINANCIAL ANALYSIS
    ASSETS

12. Cash and Market Securities	20523665
13. Receivables	161156574
14. Inventory	19954980
15. Other	12285378
16. Other	55235815
17. Fixed Assets	234787494
18. Prepaid Expenses	0
19. Other	2646211
20. Other	8069369

    LIABILITIES

21. Payables	87006779
22. Accruals	37979936
23. Taxes	25739953
24. Other	10643507
25. Other	0
26. Long-term Debt	131208164
27. Deferred Investment	7249111
28. Other	3894525
29. Other	0
30. Cost of Sales	780732342
31. Selling, Adm., R&D, Exp.	97922149
32. Taxes	46800000

FIGURE 12   FINANCIAL ANALYSIS INPUT SHEET

XXX INC.
FINANCIAL RATIOS

EQUITY/TOTAL ASSETS, higher, more conservative financing.   55.0%
NPAT/EQUITY, return on investment.   16.5%
NPAT/TOTAL ASSETS, managerial efficiency.   9.0%
NPAT/EMPLOYED CAP, similar to return on investment.   11.0%
NPAT/NET SALES, profit on each merchandizing dollar.   6.2%

EARNINGS/SHARE $ 2.07
PRICE-EARNING RATIO
EQUITY/SHARE $12.58
PRICE EQUITY RATIO
CASH FLOW/SHARE $ 3.29
PRICE CASH FLOW RATIO

CURRENT RATIO, adequacy of working capital test.   2.4
ACID TEST, stricter adequacy of working capital test.   1.2
CST SAL/NET SALES, efficiency of management planning.   77.0%
SLG EXP/NET SALES, selling efficiency.   9.7%
DEPC/CASH FLOW, proportion of earnings.   37.0%

CASH/CRRNT DEBT, liquidity ratio.   .13
FIXED ASSETS/EQUITY, amount of capital depreciating.   62.0%
NET SALES/INV'N'TY, merchandizing efficiency, turnover.   5.1 times
NET SALES/EQUITY, trading ratio, invested capital turnover.   2.6 times
MISC. ASSETS/EQUITY, noncompany objectives for equity.   17.0%

COLLECTION PERIOD, average time to collect debts.   57 days
CURRENT DEBT/EQUITY, degree of freedom from day-to-day debt.   42.0%
TOT'L DEBT/EQUITY, degree of limitation on future financing.   79.0%
INV./WRKG CAPITAL, cash tied up in inventory.   86.0%
REC'V'B WRKG CAP, cash tied up in receivables.   69.0%

LG TM DEBT/WRK CAP, measure of borrowing power.   56.0%
SALES/FXD ASSETS, efficiency of plant and equipment.   4.3 times
SALES/WRKG CAP, gauges efficient use of working capital.   4.4 times

FIGURE 13   FINANCIAL ANALYSIS OUTPUT SHEET

The controller's department put this project on time sharing. One set of data was now extracted from each annual report. Prior years' data was saved on tape from year to year.

When the report was run, a final, complete version was typed out at the rate of five minutes per company. Format changes made in the program and all reports of prior and present years were consistent.

The estimated yearly saving was four thousand dollars. This included whatever reprogramming was required from year to year.

There is no room between the manager and the computer for intermediary personnel. It takes longer to explain it to a third party than to do it yourself. Time sharing is ideal for the type of program that solves problems from limited data, for the type of program that encourages looping.

"Looping" is a term used to describe observing the results of a program, changing the input data, and rerunning the program for a new result. This result is reviewed, input data again adjusted, and new results output. Here is the epitome of man-computer interaction. The enormous calculating capacity of the computer is tied into a loop involving the judgment capacity of man.

Direct, at-the-terminal problem solving by the user is time sharing's greatest asset. Nothing will duplicate this activity but the experience itself. Some feeling for this can be generated by examples, especially if they are carefully studied. The format for presenting time-sharing examples has been carefully worked out to simulate computer activity. Pursue the following examples as if you were actually seated before a console manipulating the keyboard.

Plotting graphs is a tedious and time-consuming problem. Fortunately, computers are ideally suited for this type of activity. An almost infinite variety of plotting programs are available from time-sharing services. Plotting programs for business, science, education, or mathematical purposes are available in profusion.

POINT TO PONDER: Some people work comfortably with numbers. Some react more favorably to graphs. Unfortunately, providing graphs is a time-consuming exercise. Management works with many tools. The more comfortable they are with them, the more effective are their decisions.

To attempt to provide management with a constant, timely and graphic picture would require a resident graphic artist. In the business environment, this has always been considered too costly a luxury. Spot year-end presentations are common, but timely and current graphic presentations are rare.

Time sharing is ideal for this purpose. Library programs are available to convert any numerical output to charts or graphs. The numeric results of any proprietary program can be converted to graphic output within the time-sharing environment and output on paper or displayed on a C.R.T. console.

What would cost hundreds of dollars to undertake manually is reduced literally to pennies via time sharing.

Mathematics

Problem: To plot simultaneously two functions of a single variable.

Input/Output: Reference is made to the directory of time-sharing programs and a suitable program found. Usually it is accompanied by a description similar to the following, which provides an example of how the program functions. Assume the program required is named "PLOT."

COMPUTER	COMMENT	OPERATOR
	Dial 123-4567	
AAA TIME-SHARING SERVICE		
PLEASE LOG IN		HAP103
READY		CALL PLOT
FIRST FUNCTION OF X?		1-EXP(-X)

With this reply the computer will establish the equation Y=1-EXP(-X)

THE SECOND FUNCTION OF X AND/OR Y?   X$\uparrow$2

An up arrow ($\uparrow$) indicates squaring.

The computer sets up another equation
$$Z=X\uparrow 2$$

WHAT RANGE FOR VERTICAL AXIS?   0.1
WHAT INCREMENT FOR THE X-AXIS?   .05

With all questions answered, the computer now outputs the plot.

(NOTE: Y IS PLOTTED "X," Z IS "." AND "O" IS COMMON POINT)

FOR X:	TOP = 0	BOTTOM = 1	INCREMENT = .05
FOR PCTS:	LEFT = 0	RIGHT = 1	INCREMENT = 1.66667 E-2

Business

Problem: To project future sales based on prior years' sales.

Input/Output: Unlike the scientifically oriented regression analysis, this simply satisfies the businessman's desire to investigate the company's growth rate.

COMPUTER	COMMENT	OPERATOR
READY	Note: Trailing zeros may be omitted. The last number with no comma indicates the end of the series.	RUN GROWTH
INPUT EQUISPACED SALES		3139,3165,4664,4679, 5051,6032,6600,7273, 7617
	This input may be in days, months, years or any other increment as long as it is over equal periods.	
PROJECT FORWARD (NO. OF PERIODS)?		3
	The program now has all the necessary information, i.e.:	
	Nine years of sales figures, and instructions to project three years into the future. With the final command to project three years, the computer outputs its results.	

AVERAGE PERIOD RATE (PCT) = 12.3564
CONTINUOUS RATE (PCT) = 11.6506
THE DOUBLE LIFE (PERIODS) = 5.94947

	PERIOD	ESTIMATE	ACTUAL
	-8	3212.37	3139
	-7	3609.31	3165
	-6	4055.29	4664
	-5	4556.38	4679
HISTORY	-4	5119.38	5051
	-3	5751.95	6032
	-2	6462.69	6600

PERIOD	ESTIMATE	ACTUAL
-1	7261.24	7273
0	8158.47	7617
PROJECTION 1	9166.56	
2	10299.2	
3	11571.8	

Program recycles

MORE EQUISPACED SALES?   5051,6032,6600,7273,7617
PROJECT FORWARD (NO. OF PERIODS)?   10

AVERAGE PERIOD RATE (PCT) = 10.6131
CONTINUOUS RATE (PCT) = 10.0868
THE DOUBLE LIFE (PERIODS) = 6.87181

PERIOD	ESTIMATE	ACTUAL
-4	5269.42	5051
-3	5828.67	6032
-2	6447.27	6600
-1	7131.53	7273
0	7888.4	7617
1	8725.61	
2	9651.66	
3	10676.	
4	11809.1	
5	13062.4	
6	14448.7	
7	15982.1	
8	17678.3	
9	19554.6	
10	21629.9	

Time-sharing programs, when written properly, should recognize two things:

1. Programs are run erratically, that is, they may be used for a day or two, then not returned to for several months.
2. When a time-sharing program is used it may be used intensively for several hours, for instance, two dozen projections might be cranked through in half a day.

For these reasons the structuring of time sharing programs is important. It is desirable to have the computer explain the inputs as it requests them. For instance, "What is the cash flow for the first year?" "What is the cash flow for the second year?" "What is the cash flow for the third year?" However, such clumsy requests would infuriate anyone waiting to insert a ten-year stream of cash flows.

Organizing and designing computer-assisted input is an art in itself. You should insist on clear, concise library programs or go elsewhere. Furthermore, when designing your own programs great care should be devoted to this human-computer interaction. The following example shows how such an input activity may be streamlined.

Financial

A simple banking problem might involve calculation of the annual interest rate charged on an installment plan. Such a program might also be used by retailers to review the terms they are offering customers.

Problem: Calculation of the true annual interest rate charged on an installment loan.

Input/Output: Naturally the actual numbers to be used should be assembled on an input sheet before starting. Ten or twenty sets of data might be assembled before approaching the computer.

COMPUTER	COMMENT	OPERATOR
READY		RUN INT
1. AMOUNT OF LOAN IN DOLLARS?		600
2. AMOUNT OF EACH PAYMENT?		31.99
3. HOW MANY PAYMENTS DUE?		21
4. YEARLY PAYMENTS?		12
THE INTEREST RATE IS 12.61%		
	Note that for each wordy computer question the operator merely has to supply a single number. This, however, has its value if the operator has not run the program before, or has reactivated it after a month's absence. However, the well-structured program will now cycle and ask:	
SECOND RUN?	To this you reply "YES" or "NO."	YES
INPUT 1,2,3,&4	Note: The original questions were numbered. This request asks you to insert your new data in the same sequence as the original, but omits retyping the full question.	

COMPUTER	COMMENT	OPERATOR
		1400,54.9,30,12
THE INTEREST RATE IS 12.98%		
THIRD RUN?	A "NO" reply ends the program.	NO
		LOGOUT

Every variety of chart, graph, calculation, or mathematical exercise is available via time sharing. Histograms are a frequently used evaluation device and there are a variety of these programs from any time-sharing company.

Here again, care should be exercised in finding the simplest, easiest and clearest method for your specific purposes and applications.

COMPUTER	COMMENT	OPERATOR
READY		RUN HIST
ENTER VARIABLE DATA		109,90,97,89,103,106,116,
		110,95,85,98,108,121,94,
		107,104,98,107,88,99,100,
		101
PRINT SYMBOL?		+
NUMBER OF INTERVALS		6

The computer then prints out a page-wide chart.

[COMPUTER PRINTOUT]

FREQUENCY	4	2	6	6	2	2
6			+	+		
5			+	+		
4	+		+	+		
3	+		+	+		
2	+	+	+	+	+	+
1	+	+	+	+	+	+
INTERVAL	85-90	91-96	97-102	103-108	109-114	115-121

MINIMUM 85.0   SPACING 6.0   MAXIMUM 121.0

Time-sharing programs come in any degree of complexity. Many companies are still struggling with manual solutions to problems that are now available from every time-sharing service. There are several reasons for this:

1. Most people consider their problems too difficult and unique for computer solution.
2. A company has built-up in-house know-how and is too lazy or indifferent to rethink its requirements with the computer in mind.
3. To initiate computer applications requires that someone study and learn something new!

All these very human foibles tend to discourage applying time sharing to a company's problems. Unless time sharing has top management support, its application to everyday business problems will be difficult.

In the fields of science and education the attitude is the same. An individual who is accustomed to sweating for hours over a regression analysis is initially distrustful of the computer. Somehow, the twenty-second output loses the flavor of the problem as far as he is concerned.

Concentrate first on problems involving simple input and output. "Seeing it happen" is time sharing's greatest convincer. There are, of course, programs of much greater sophistication. Naturally, the more sophisticated, the more specific the problem.

CASE IN POINT: There are 13,000,000,000,000,000,000,000,000,000 freight rate combinations and permutations in the U.S. alone. Even the computer would have a hard time struggling through this complexity. Fortunately, a company transportation system does not ship from "everywhere to everywhere" as the above number implies. Fifteen plants shipping to 1,500 customers is still a reasonable problem.

A large national chemical manufacturer started an effort to computerize this problem. The previous effort (normal for the trade) hired a lot of clerks to look up the rates and see what looked best.

A small segment of this problem was tackled on time sharing. Selected were the major products. After one year of operation, a review of the program reported a $300,000 savings on gross freight charges had been realized.

The last line of the year's summary, reporting on the undertaking, reads as follows:

Last year the savings due almost entirely to this program and the information it generated was $300,000 arrived at in the following manner:

Last year freight $1,045,848   for 199,821 tons
This year freight $1,021,370   for 219,894 tons

Freight rate increases amounting to 15%

The freight rate increases should have raised the total freight charges by $157,000. The ten percent increase in shipments should have further raised it by $120,000. Instead, freight costs decreased by $24,500, an indicated savings of over $300,000.

Until now the examples have been as general as possible. The objective has been to present programs using techniques familiar to anyone. However, an example of a slightly more sophisticated program may be appropriate as a last example.

Transportation

Problem: To determine the minimum total shipping costs within a network of plants and warehouses. Specifically, a manufacturer has three plants in Chicago, Hartford and Trenton, and five warehouses in New York, Dearborn, St. Louis, Houston and Richmond, all handling the same product.

Input/Output: A table is constructed encompassing all the necessary details.

PLANTS	SHIPPING COSTS/UNIT WAREHOUSES					PLANT CAPACITY
	NEW YORK	DEARBORN	ST. LOUIS	HOUSTON	RICHMOND	
CHICAGO	$4^{(3)}$	6	7	4	6	$1000^{(1)}$
HARTFORD	7	5	8	5	8	800
TRENTON	6	4	6	7	5	600
WAREHOUSE REQUIREMENT	$400^{(2)}$	700	300	500	500	2400

For a given time period plant supply capacities (1), individual warehouse requirements (2), and shipping costs per unit of product from plant to warehouse (3) are given.

When this data is assembled, you are ready to run the program. Let's assume the computer is logged in.

COMPUTER	COMMENT	OPERATOR
READY		RUN TRANSPORT
PLANT CAPACITY?	(1)	100,800,600
WAREHOUSE CAPACITY?	(2)	400,700,300,500,500
	Regardless of plant or warehouse number, the program will check by comparing plant capacity to warehouse requirements. If they are inconsistent, the program will output an error message.	
INPUT SHIPPING COSTS PER UNIT?		4,6,7,4,6
		7,5,8,5,8
	(3)	6,4,6,7,5

COMPUTER	COMMENT	OPERATOR
	Insert the exact numbers as they appear in the transportation grid you constructed earlier.	
	Once the computer has all the necessary data it runs and outputs the results.	
	In this instance a simple transportation grid was used. The complexity of some transportation problems create grids 10x50 or 18x100.	
	In any case, like this simple 3x5, the answer is output promptly by the computer as:	

MINIMUM SHIPPING COST = $11700.00

And further a full summary is output:

PLANTS	QUANTITIES TO BE SHIPPED TO WAREHOUSES WAREHOUSES					TOTAL PLANT REQUIREMENT
	NEW YORK,	DEARBORN,	ST. LOUIS,	HOUSTON,	RICHMOND	
NEW YORK	400	0	0	400	200	1000
BOSTON	0	700	0	100	0	800
BALTIMORE	0	0	300	0	300	600
WAREHOUSE REQUIREMENT	400	700	300	500	500	2400

LOGOUT

SUMMARY

Present time-sharing companies offer an almost infinite variety and complexity of programs. Taking advantage of these free programs is entirely dependent on the ingenuity, perseverance, and skill of the time-sharing customer.

Time sharing can be used to replace present tedious manual operations. Time sharing offers the businessman, scientist, and educator techniques previously too complicated, too time-consuming or too expensive to apply.

5

INTEGRATING TIME SHARING INTO THE TOTAL MANAGEMENT INFORMATION SYSTEM

Peter Drucker, in his book *Technology, Management and Society,* summarizes best what the computer sciences do today. In the same paragraph he suggests what they should be doing tomorrow.

> So these are the instructions I give to my computer people. I say: "By now children, you have learned how to do the payroll; you may even have learned how to do credits; you may even have learned how to follow an order through the plant so that one can coordinate plant scheduling with shipping and customer promises (although that is something everybody says he has done, I have yet to see anybody who really has). Fine, you have learned how to do large-scale clerical work. *Now I want you to start working on information.* "[1]

In another essay in the same work, Mr. Drucker foresees the decline of in-house computer facilities. He predicts the rise of the "computer utility." Like electric utility companies, he envisions central computer facilities providing a whole area of a city with computer services. Specifically, he puts it this way:

> Already the time-sharing principle has begun to take hold. I don't think it takes too much imagination to see that a typical large company is about as likely to have its own computer twenty years hence as it is to have its own steam-generating plant today. It is reasonably predictable that computers will become a common carrier, a public utility, and that only organizations with quite extraordinary needs will have their own. Steel mills today have their own generators because they need such an enormous amount of power. Twenty years hence, an institution that's the equivalent of a steel mill in terms of mental work—MIT, for example—might well have its own computer. But I think most other universities, for most purposes, will simply plug into time-sharing systems.[2]

Anyone with even the most cursory knowledge of the computer field can anticipate its direction. Its hardware growth is toward bigger and faster machines. As these objectives are achieved, the fourth, fifth, or sixth generation computers will become extremely powerful. Within the very near future they will be capable of

---

[1] Drucker, Peter F. *Technology, Management and Society* (New York: Harper and Row) 1970.
[2] Ibid.

handling dozens of businesses. Only the very largest of institutions will be able to cost-justify proprietary (in-house) computers.

Time sharing is unquestionably the first evidence of Mr. Drucker's prediction. Its greatest assets are an ability to provide user-computer interaction and to be immediately responsive to user needs.

Anyone exploring time sharing's potential becomes aware of one thing: Although the majority of the computer establishment does not share Mr. Drucker's insight, it definitely views time sharing as a threat to its in-house existence. As long as time sharing restricts its operations to individual problem solving, to incremental input and output, the users will find little in-house objection. If, however, an integrated, continuous operation is attempted, the cries of, "It's cheaper in-house" will be heard along the institution's corridors.

In the present "state of the art" there is no generalized answer to this complaint. Essentially time sharing supplies much greater flexibility to the user. It is up to you, the time-sharing user, to pick projects, and build programs that are cost-justifiable. Programs that satisfy the users and provide the information, flexibility, and immediacy that can't be provided in-house constitute such programs.

In these early stages of time sharing, the proprietary computer establishment has, in many instances, strong grounds for complaint. Frequently the fascinating experience of computer power at instant beck and call has led to considerable misuse.

Time sharing's first attraction is to problem-solvers in a company or in the scientific community. These people frequently ignore cost, concentrate on experimentation, and fail to evaluate the dollar return on their effort. The reader of this book is quite likely to fall into this category. This explanation is put forth as a caution to emphasize that the computer establishment has a point: Time-sharing can be wasteful. It is the responsibility of the user to justify his applications of time sharing.

Obviously, until the computer utility is a reality, time sharing must find a place alongside the in-house computer. It must be realized that both have functions they can serve. Since, by the very nature of the beast, the in-house operation is already established, "leave to Caesar that which is Caesar's."

We have now made our admonishments about, and genuflections to, the in-house computer. In previous chapters, we have described a half dozen problem-solving time-sharing programs. In this and the following two chapters we will describe a more advanced and sophisticated time-sharing package.

Many packages of time-sharing programs have been constructed. "Packages" consist of groups of programs, each processing data and outputting this processed data so it becomes input information for a succeeding program. Packages serve the purpose of manipulating data and information through a series of transformations. The purpose of this is to provide the user with information.

The package we will describe is designed to provide the business executive, at all levels, with a continual monitoring of the daily status of the organization's business. To produce such a package, specific objectives, procedural outlines, and operational theory must be established.

The package to be described is a Management Information System. In the last few years a great deal of attention has been devoted to this management tool. To build an M.I.S. package, a clear concept must be proposed, and then computer programs designed to achieve its objectives.

M.I.S. is still under intensive debate, exploration, and construction. For our purposes, and to provide us with a structure, we will advance an M.I.S. definition. On this basis we will then describe a computer package designed to meet these objectives, in this instance, the sales, financial, and management objectives. Production and operational functions will be omitted as extraneous and repetitious to our objective, that is, of demonstrating the daily interaction and functioning of time sharing.

The theory and structure for a management information system must be established first. The M.I.S. concept is relatively new. It is not yet completely defined. All the ifs and buts about M.I.S. make it the most interesting and intriguing concept to enter the business community in many a year. In a nutshell, it challenges the old seat-of-the-pants operator, and attempts to formalize and organize the data used to make business decisions.

Business enterprises come in an infinite variety of forms. For this reason, an equally infinite variety of M.I.S. structures is possible, although several characteristics must be common to every M.I.S. Here we tread on delicate ground. A myriad of M.I.S. definitions have been proposed; a variety of descriptions have been advanced. We will not try to advance the ultimate M.I.S. definition, but merely to build an M.I.S. framework—a definition off which we may bounce questions. Such questions might be:

1. "Is this data really necessary?"
2. "Is this output really necessary?"
3. "Does this operation contribute to our objectives?"

Let's boil our definition down to five points:

A. SYMBIOTIC
B. VIABLE
C. DYNAMIC
D. CURRENT
E. TO PROVIDE A PEEK INTO THE FUTURE

A. Symbiotic, because an M.I.S. must use the information already available. The whole operation of a company cannot be stopped to collect extraneous data for special reports to management.
B. Viable, because no business remains in business if it is not always striving to increase its effectiveness and improve its operations. An M.I.S. must grow to meet management's demands, and to encompass whatever new management techniques, methods, or systems may be needed.
C. Dynamic, because an M.I.S. must operate continuously, accepting a daily stream of data, manipulating it, and outputting a variety of scheduled and unscheduled reports whenever called upon.
   1. This is where time sharing enters the picture, for this technique provides:
      a. Immediacy

    b. Real-time response to adjustments and errors

    c. Minute-to-minute update of data

    d. Direct-user access to the computer

    e. Minute-to-minute output of information

D. Current, because to manage you must first know where you are before you can navigate a course toward your objective. This requirement was best pictured by J. W. Forrester in his book *Industrial Dynamics* when he described an executive as "an individual driving a car blindfolded while a colleague tells him how to steer by looking through the rear window." Reports, summaries and statistics are all necessary, but they are usually "looking through the rear window."

E. And finally, a new concept: To provide management with a "peek into the future."

Although an M.I.S. can do many things, whenever it takes this "peek into the future" it is turning "data" into "information." If you will stop to consider, all present management techniques support this peek-into-the-future hypothesis. Profitability index, present value (of future income), budgeting, rate of return, payback period, modelling, risk analysis, and simulations are all management's efforts to anticipate future events.

The concept of an M.I.S. as symbiotic, viable, dynamic, current, and providing a peek into the future make time sharing and M.I.S. a most challenging marriage. It offers businessmen a package of great power and effectiveness. It requires a current, daily, on-line activity accepting a continuous daily stream of data. Manipulating this and outputting a variety of scheduled and unscheduled reports is its objective.

Finally, M.I.S. means precisely that. As the recording companies like to say, "music to love by" or "music to relax by," M.I.S. should say "information to manage by." "What information to manage by?" and "What is managing?" then become critical questions in developing an M.I.S. Some definition, some foundation, some target, if you will, must be set up before any sort of M.I.S. can be attempted.

First, why is a definition necessary? Primarily so we may ask ourselves what specific data and equipment is required to meet our objectives. Second, to allow definition of output so we may pattern the output to satisfy our requirements.

Without a specific target, building an M.I.S. becomes a haphazard collection of data. Nothing is omitted because it is feared something will always be needed that may be overlooked. Until one single set of clearly defined M.I.S. objectives is established, vacillation and indecision will be rampant.

M.I.S. has been difficult to define because it encompasses a wide variety of disciplines. Not only are the computer and mathematical sciences involved, but also the financial and management arts. Who then is to come forward with the definition? The computer specialist who has never managed a business or the businessman whose art of managing has never been clearly defined?

Alchemy, a medieval chemical science and speculative philosophy, remained an art for several hundred years before it became the science of chemistry. The term "management science" has been extant for only twenty years, and many managers were managing ten or twenty years before the concept was proposed.

It is not surprising that such a disparate group as mathematicians, businessmen, programmers, accountants, and systems analysts would find it difficult to concur on a single definition for M.I.S. The approach favored by the computer people would be to survey the field and determine what objectives and requirements must be met.

Perversely enough, the field to be surveyed is the business manager's, who admittedly is still practicing an art rather than conducting scientific investigations. To ask most managers what they are doing and what information they require to do it is a futile exercise. For anyone who has attempted this survey, the vagueness and generalities encountered are frustrating. Such questions and answers as the following are common:

Question : Precisely what shipping details do you require?
Answer   : All details.
Question : How many customers do you want listed?
Answer   : All customers.
Question : How often do you want summaries?
Answer   : Daily.

In short, the art of management and the science of computers make a difficult mix. Given time, management will most certainly develop individuals who employ the scientific method. At present, truly scientific methods are not applicable nor employed on a day-to-day basis.

To ask a manager to enumerate precisely which specific elements he needs to manage is like asking a sculptor precisely what he needs to sculpt. After a superficial description of the basic materials, both sculptor and manager play it by ear.

It is no wonder then that both managers and scientists have found M.I.S. difficult to define. M.I.S. bridges the gap between a discipline and an art and attempts to apply scientific measurements and criteria to the art of management.

M.I.S. was initially a computer concept. The task of defining it fell to the systems analyst. The computer's ability to handle, store, and process vast quantities of data almost demanded a summation of the total information. It became then the computer expert's job to define this total information summation. Unfortunately, the programmers, technicians, analysts, mathematicians, and scientists involved in the development of the computer were not schooled in business management. They proceeded to employ standard scientific methods but unfortunately found few management "artists" sufficiently articulate to describe their activities.

Our final conclusion regarding M.I.S. might be rather like Columbus and the egg. Once he demonstrated that one merely needed to crack the bottom of the egg to make it stand on end, anyone could do it.

M.I.S. should be designed to do only two things:

1. To tell management its current position.
2. To provide management with a "peek into the future."

Present position is important simply as the record-keeping and orientation phase of management. A manager must know where he is before he can plan to go elsewhere.

The real insight into M.I.S. is the realization that its sole function is to assist management to foresee the future. Perhaps the art part of management is not so unrealistic from this point of view. Clairvoyance is still classified as an art rather than a science.

Based on this concept, information may be stored and rejected, processed or ignored, analyzed or voided depending on its value, quality, and ability to provide management with a "peek into the future." Once this concept is grasped, it becomes possible to sort the wheat from the chaff, and concentrate on that data and those techniques that will serve to fulfill this peek-into-the-future objective.

Now let's take a look at a business structure and determine where, in such a picture, M.I.S. fits. Sometimes in the overenthusiasm of the pursuit of an M.I.S., the definition seems to include the total corporation. Try to apply such a definition of M.I.S., and M.I.S. has gobbled up your whole company This rapacious approach has scared off more businessmen than any other single factor. M.I.S. is not trying to take over the company. It should try to provide management with information to manage by, to provide management with its "peek into the future."

Figure 14 is an illustration of the M.I.S. concept. Spooky-looking it may be. The eye at the top does not represent management's eternal vigilance, it symbolizes "the peek into the future" M.I.S. should be designed to provide.

Think of this pyramid as the total business. It is drawn open merely so we may see all four sides. The total pyramid is, in effect, the total business system: the company, the corporation, the business utility itself. Call this total the B.I.S. if you like, the business information system. At the bottom is the data base. All systems draw information from here. Years ago this data base was made up of file cabinets and the contents of men's minds. Gradually the computer memory is holding much of this information today. It's more permanent, more available and less temperamental.

The four sides of the pyramid provide the structure for the four major business information systems of a business:

1. The sales information system.
2. The financial information system.
3. The operations information system.
   a) personnel, traffic, etc.
4. The production/manufacturing information system.

It is obvious that not all the information needed or used in the sales information system is needed all the way up the management ladder. The processing of payrolls and acquisition of supplies utilizes systems, but does not generate information used by top management. In short, many systems are functioning simultaneously in a B.I.S., but only those that have special characteristics and qualities are used by management. Essentially an M.I.S. seeks out those specific types of information that tell management where they are now, and those that give management a "peek into the future."

Thus, each of these four portions of the B.I.S. contain a vast variety of systems and data. However, each provides only a small portion of the "information to manage by." Management data must be drawn from each portion of the structure. When properly selected, it should provide management with the information and guidance to make effective management decisions.

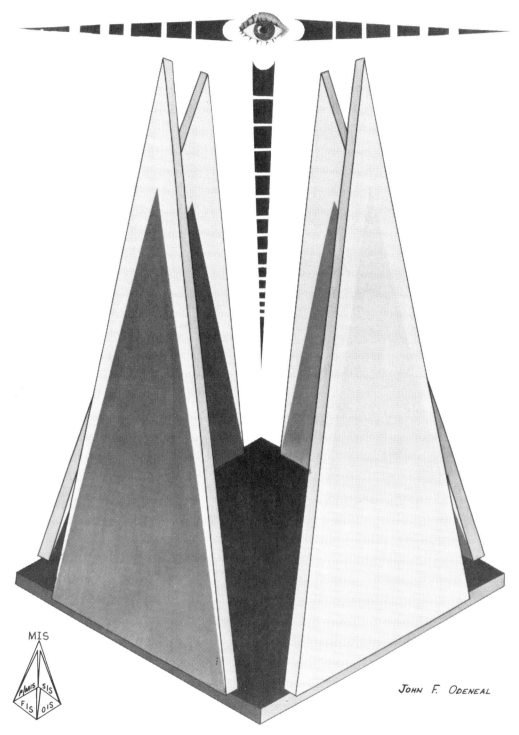

FIGURE 14   M.I.S. STRUCTURE

Why have the last few pages been devoted to the definition of an M.I.S. structure? To emphasize the fact that time-sharing packages are a complex and unique undertaking. Don't discount the requirement for careful and meticulous planning. Don't undertake package building without first setting out precisely and clearly defined goals.

Simple, conventional packages such as accounting, payroll, and library search and retrieval are built on already accepted premises. These generally can be modified to meet most conventional requirements.

A solid foundation of theory, data selection, and information input/output is essential whenever you construct packages uniquely tailored to your own requirements. In time sharing, you, the user, are the important element. Your objectives must be clearly defined before you undertake a package. Of the many horror stories of computer failures, at least 90 percent can be attributed to the designer having no clear idea of his ultimate objective.

If you come away from this book with only one point in mind, let it be: *Don't undertake any computer package before you have meticulously recorded its theory, details, objectives, and output in writing.*

The user of time sharing accepts much greater responsibility than was ever accorded the programmer, systems analyst, or computer technician. In the past each could claim his phase of operation worked, and pass the buck down the line. The programmer claimed the computer wasn't powerful enough. The systems analyst indicated the input was inadequate or inaccurate. The computer technician claimed the programmer was at fault. These excuses have frustrated a generation of potential computer users. Now time sharing enters the arena. For the first time you, the user, can interact with the computer. Like every blessing, this one is mixed!

You can now be in control of your own computer activities. You can accomplish wonders, but if you fail, you will only have yourself to blame.

The next ten pages describe, as a series of slides, the typical output of a package of programs used to generate an M.I.S.

The term "M.I.S." used throughout this book describes information generated via a computer data base. Recently a number of other terms have been used to define this technique. Thus the management information system (M.I.S.) described can just as well be called a Computer Based Information System (C.B.I.S.), Data Base Management (D.B.M.), or an Integrated Management Information System (I.M.I.S.).

In the next chapter the theories, mechanics and operating details of such information systems are more fully delineated and elaborated.

THE INTERNATIONAL
MANAGEMENT INFORMATION SYSTEM.

THE PRIMARY VALUE OF THE
INTERNATIONAL M.I.S. IS

TIMELY INFORMATION

..... CONSIDER THE FOLLOWING

FMCI, 1969

1. DAILY NET SALES ESTIMATED MANUALLY — VARIANCE ±30%

2. WEEKLY GROSS PROFIT ESTIMATED MANUALLY — VARIANCE ±50%

3. NO ORGANIZED OPEN ORDER CONTROL.

4. MARKET REPORT RECEIVED 25 DAYS AFTER MONTH END, AND INACCURATE.

AN EXECUTIVE IS LIKE A MAN DRIVING A CAR BLINDFOLDED, BEING TOLD HOW TO STEER BY A COLLEAGUE LOOKING THROUGH THE REAR WINDOW.

.... J. W. FORRESTER
INDUSTRIAL DYNAMICS

SO WE DID SOMETHING ...

FIRST, ESTABLISHED OBJECTIVES

A. <u>TO TRACK</u> ALL ORDERS AND BILLINGS FROM CUSTOMER ORDER ENTRY TO CUSTOMER BILLING.

B. <u>TO COMPARE</u> PERFORMANCE TO BUDGET AND PRIOR YEAR.

C. <u>TO INFORM</u> THREE LEVELS OF MANAGEMENT, AND TO PROVIDE BACKUP DETAILS FOR ALL ECHELONS.

A. TO TRACK

TO KEEP TRACK OF THE FLOW OF BUSINESS ACTIVITY A **UNIQUE** **METHOD** WAS USED.

1. ORDER AND BILLING WRITE–UP DIRECTLY ON IBM CARDS.

2. INPUT VIA AN OPTICAL MARK–SENSE READER.

3. COMPUTER PRINTING OF ORDERS AND BILLINGS.

4. DATA BASES CREATED AS INFORMATION SOURCES FOR MANAGEMENT ORGANIZING, PLANNING AND CONTROL.

B. TO COMPARE
C. TO INFORM

DAILY, WEEKLY AND MONTHLY M.I.S. REPORTS ARE OUTPUT FROM THESE DATA BASES.

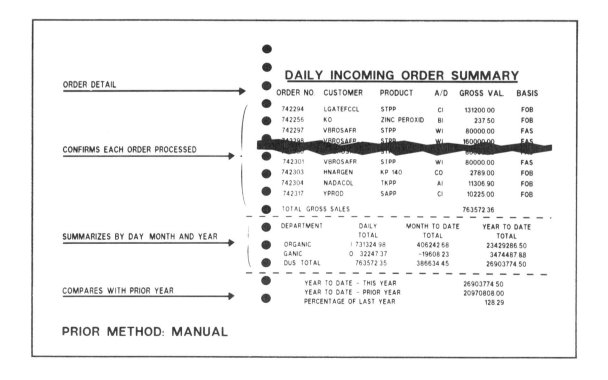

ORDER DETAIL

CONFIRMS EACH ORDER PROCESSED

SUMMARIZES BY DAY MONTH AND YEAR

COMPARES WITH PRIOR YEAR

DAILY INCOMING ORDER SUMMARY

ORDER NO.	CUSTOMER	PRODUCT	A/D	GROSS VAL.	BASIS
742294	LGATEFCCL	STPP	CI	131200.00	FOB
742256	KO	ZINC PEROXID	BI	237.50	FOB
742297	VBROSAFR	STPP	WI	80000.00	FAS
742298	VBROSAFR	STPP	WI	160000.00	FAS
		STP		80	
742301	VBROSAFR	STPP	WI	80000.00	FAS
742303	HNARGEN	KP 140	CO	2789.00	FOB
742304	NADACOL	TKPP	AI	11306.90	FOB
742317	YPROD	SAPP	CI	10225.00	FOB
TOTAL GROSS SALES				763572.36	

DEPARTMENT	DAILY TOTAL	MONTH TO DATE TOTAL	YEAR TO DATE TOTAL
ORGANIC	1 731324.98	4062426 8	234292 86.50
GANIC	O 3224737	-1960823	3474487.88
DUS TOTAL	763572.35	386634 45	26903774.50

YEAR TO DATE - THIS YEAR		2690377450
YEAR TO DATE - PRIOR YEAR		20970808.00
PERCENTAGE OF LAST YEAR		128.29

PRIOR METHOD: MANUAL

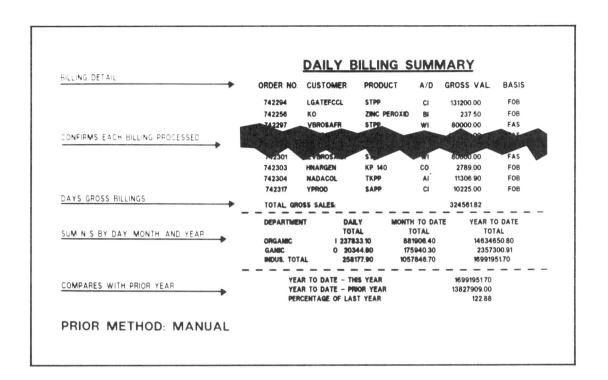

DAILY BILLING SUMMARY

BILLING DETAIL →

ORDER NO.	CUSTOMER	PRODUCT	A/D	GROSS VAL.	BASIS
742294	LGATEFCCL	STPP	CI	131200.00	FOB
742256	KO	ZINC PEROXID	BI	237.50	FOB
742297	VBROSAFR	STPP	WI	80000.00	FAS

CONFIRMS EACH BILLING PROCESSED →

742301	VBROSA..	S..	WI	80000.00	FAS
742303	HNARGEN	KP 140	CO	2789.00	FOB
742304	NADACOL	TKPP	AI	11306.90	FOB
742317	YPROD	SAPP	CI	10225.00	FOB

DAYS GROSS BILLINGS →

TOTAL GROSS SALES: 324561.82

SUM N S BY DAY MONTH AND YEAR →

DEPARTMENT	DAILY TOTAL	MONTH TO DATE TOTAL	YEAR TO DATE TOTAL
ORGANIC	I 237833.10	881906.40	14634650.80
GANIC	O 20344.80	175940.30	2357300.91
INDUS. TOTAL	258177.90	1057846.70	16991951.70

COMPARES WITH PRIOR YEAR →

YEAR TO DATE – THIS YEAR	16991951.70
YEAR TO DATE – PRIOR YEAR	13827909.00
PERCENTAGE OF LAST YEAR	122.88

PRIOR METHOD: MANUAL

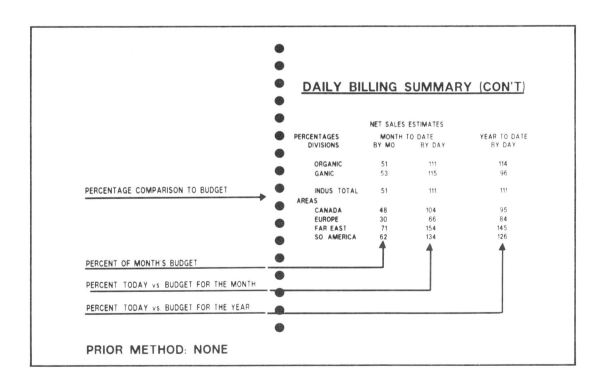

DAILY BILLING SUMMARY (CON'T)

NET SALES ESTIMATES

PERCENTAGES DIVISIONS	MONTH TO DATE BY MO	BY DAY	YEAR TO DATE BY DAY
ORGANIC	51	111	114
GANIC	53	115	96
INDUS TOTAL	51	111	111
AREAS			
CANADA	48	104	95
EUROPE	30	66	84
FAR EAST	71	154	145
SO AMERICA	62	134	126

PERCENTAGE COMPARISON TO BUDGET →

PERCENT OF MONTH'S BUDGET →

PERCENT TODAY vs BUDGET FOR THE MONTH →

PERCENT TODAY vs BUDGET FOR THE YEAR →

PRIOR METHOD: NONE

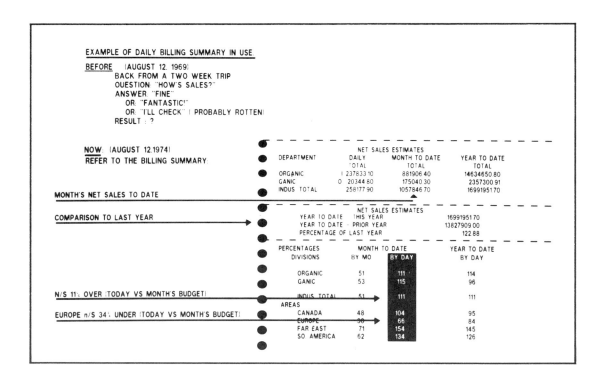

EXAMPLE OF DAILY BILLING SUMMARY IN USE.

BEFORE   (AUGUST 12. 1969)
        BACK FROM A TWO WEEK TRIP
        QUESTION: "HOW'S SALES?"
        ANSWER: "FINE"
          OR: "FANTASTIC!"
          OR: "I'LL CHECK" (PROBABLY ROTTEN)
        RESULT : ?

NOW: (AUGUST 12.1974)
REFER TO THE BILLING SUMMARY:

DEPARTMENT	NET SALES ESTIMATES		
	DAILY TOTAL	MONTH TO DATE TOTAL	YEAR TO DATE TOTAL
ORGANIC	1 237833 10	881906 40	14634650 80
GANIC	0 20344 80	175040 30	2357300 91
INDUS TOTAL	258177 90	1057846 70	1699195170

MONTH'S NET SALES TO DATE

COMPARISON TO LAST YEAR

NET SALES ESTIMATES	
YEAR TO DATE THIS YEAR	1699195170
YEAR TO DATE - PRIOR YEAR	1382790900
PERCENTAGE OF LAST YEAR	122 88

PERCENTAGES DIVISIONS	MONTH TO DATE BY MO	BY DAY	YEAR TO DATE BY DAY
ORGANIC	51	111	114
GANIC	53	115	96
INDUS TOTAL	51	111	111

N/S 11% OVER (TODAY VS MONTH'S BUDGET)

EUROPE n/s 34% UNDER (TODAY VS MONTH'S BUDGET)

AREAS			
CANADA	48	104	95
EUROPE	50	66	84
FAR EAST	71	154	145
SO AMERICA	62	134	126

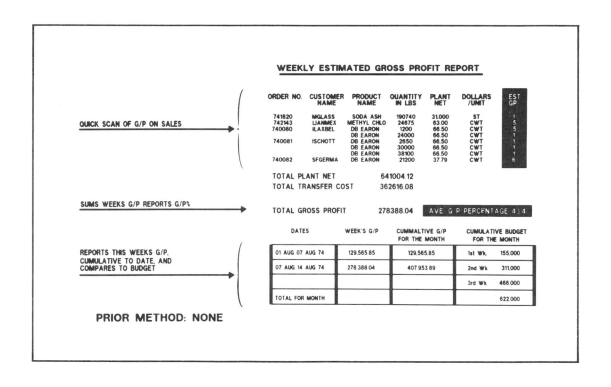

WEEKLY ESTIMATED GROSS PROFIT REPORT

QUICK SCAN OF G/P ON SALES

ORDER NO.	CUSTOMER NAME	PRODUCT NAME	QUANTITY IN LBS	PLANT NET	DOLLARS /UNIT	EST GP
741820	MGLASS	SODA ASH	190740	31.000	ST	1
742143	LIAMMEX	METHYL CHLO	24675	63.00	CWT	5
740080	ILAXBEL	DB EARON	1200	66.50	CWT	5
		DB EARON	24000	66.50	CWT	1
740081	ISCHOTT	DB EARON	2650	66.50	CWT	1
		DB EARON	30000	66.50	CWT	1
		DB EARON	38100	66.50	CWT	1
740082	SFGERMA	DB EARON	21200	37.79	CWT	6

TOTAL PLANT NET   641004.12
TOTAL TRANSFER COST   362616.08

SUMS WEEKS G/P REPORTS G/P%

TOTAL GROSS PROFIT   278388.04   AVE. G P PERCENTAGE 43.4

REPORTS THIS WEEKS G/P,
CUMULATIVE TO DATE, AND
COMPARES TO BUDGET

DATES	WEEK'S G/P	CUMMALTIVE G/P FOR THE MONTH	CUMULATIVE BUDGET FOR THE MONTH	
01 AUG 07 AUG 74	129.565.85	129.565.85	1st Wk.	155.000
07 AUG 14 AUG 74	278.388.04	407.953.89	2nd Wk	311.000
			3rd Wk	466.000
TOTAL FOR MONTH				622.000

PRIOR METHOD: NONE

EXAMPLE OF G/P REPORT IN USE
BEFORE: (AUGUST 12, 1969)
    QUESTION: WHAT'S OUR G/P?
    ANSWER: 30% OF NET SALES—USUALLY
    QUESTION: PRODUCT MIX
    ANSWER: I DON'T KNOW, IF SALES ARE IN LOW PROFIT ITEMS
    FIGURE 20% OF GROSS SALES.
      IF HIGH, FIGURE 40% OF GROSS SALES.
    RESULT: ?

NOW: (AUGUST 12,1974)
REFER TO THE G/P REPORT.

THIS WEEKS GROSS PROFIT, CUMULATIVE AND BUDGET.

DATES	WEEKS G/P	CUMULATIVE G/P FOR THE MONTH	CUMULATIVE BUDGET FOR THE MONTH
07 AUG 14 AUG 74	362.431.32	491,997.17	2nd. Wk. 311,000

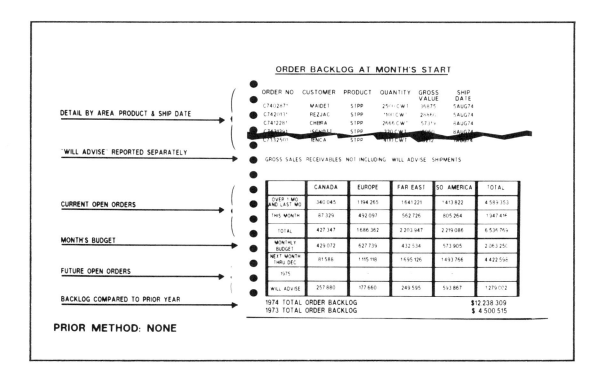

ORDER BACKLOG AT MONTH'S START

DETAIL BY AREA PRODUCT & SHIP DATE

ORDER NO	CUSTOMER	PRODUCT	QUANTITY	GROSS VALUE	SHIP DATE
C7402H7	MAIDET	STPP	250 CWT	36875	5AUG74
C742013	REZJAC	STPP	1100 CWT	26860	5AUG74
C741228	CHBRA	STPP	2666 CWT	57314	8AUG74
C7413131	JSCNOLL	STPP	220 CWT		8AUG74
C7332501	IENCA	STPP	400 CWT		8AUG74

"WILL ADVISE" REPORTED SEPARATELY

GROSS SALES RECEIVABLES NOT INCLUDING WILL ADVISE SHIPMENTS

	CANADA	EUROPE	FAR EAST	SO AMERICA	TOTAL
OVER 1 MO AND LAST MO	340.045	1 194 265	1 641 221	1 413 822	4 589 353
THIS MONTH	87.329	492.097	562 726	805 264	1 947 416
TOTAL	427.347	1 686 362	2 203 947	2 219 086	6 536 769
MONTHLY BUDGET	429.072	627 739	432 534	573 905	2 063 250
NEXT MONTH THRU DEC	81 586	1 115 118	1 695 126	1 493 766	4 422 596
1975		·	·		
WILL ADVISE	257.880	177.660	249 595	593 867	1 279 002

CURRENT OPEN ORDERS

MONTH'S BUDGET

FUTURE OPEN ORDERS

BACKLOG COMPARED TO PRIOR YEAR

1974 TOTAL ORDER BACKLOG $12 238 309
1973 TOTAL ORDER BACKLOG $ 4 500 515

PRIOR METHOD: NONE

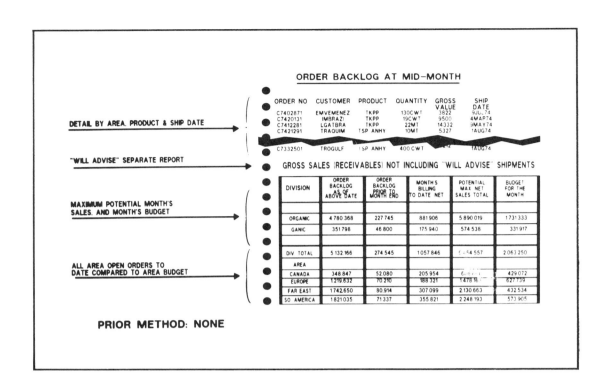

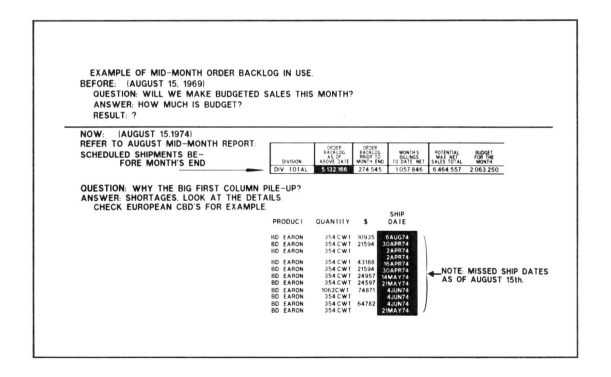

SUMMARY OF MONTHS ACTIVITY BY AREA BY N S G P →

SUMMARY OF MONTHS ACTIVITY BY DIVISION COMPARED TO BUDGET →

PRIOR METHOD NONE

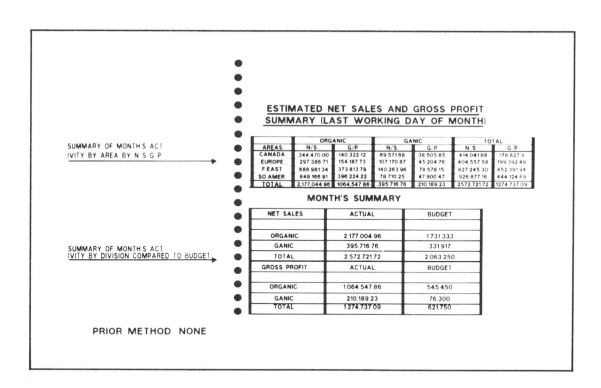

ESTIMATED NET SALES AND GROSS PROFIT SUMMARY (LAST WORKING DAY OF MONTH)

AREAS	ORGANIC		GANIC		TOTAL	
	N/S	G/P	N/S	G/P	N S	G P
CANADA	344 470.00	140 322.12	69 571.68	38 505.85	414 041.68	178 827.9
EUROPE	297 386.71	154 187.73	107 170.87	45 204.76	404 557.58	199 392.49
F EAST	686 981.34	373 813.79	140 263.96	78 578.15	827 245.30	452 391.94
SO AMER	848 166.91	396 224.22	78 710.25	47 900.47	926 877.16	444 124.69
TOTAL	2,177,044.96	1064,547.86	395 716.76	210 189.23	2572 721.72	1274 737.09

MONTH'S SUMMARY

NET SALES	ACTUAL	BUDGET
ORGANIC	2.177.004.96	1.731.333
GANIC	395.716.76	331.917
TOTAL	2.572.721.72	2.063.250
GROSS PROFIT	ACTUAL	BUDGET
ORGANIC	1.064.547.86	545.450
GANIC	210.189.23	76.300
TOTAL	1.274.737.09	621.750

EXAMPLE OF ESTIMATE N/S & G/P REPORT IN USE.
BEFORE: (AUGUST 31, 1969)
QUESTION: HOW WERE OUR NET SALES THIS MONTH?
ANSWER: I'LL LET YOU KNOW A WEEK FROM TOMORROW.
QUESTION: GROSS PROFITS?
ANSWER: SEE ME IN TWO WEEKS.
RESULT: ?

NOW: (AUGUST 31,1974)
REFER TO THE EST. N/S AND G/P REPORT.

VARIES LESS THAN 1.0% FROM ACTUAL →

NET SALES	ACTUAL	BUDGET
TOTAL:	2.572.721.72	2.063.250
GROSS PROFIT	ACTUAL	BUDGET
TOTAL:	1.274.737.09	621.750

SUMMARY: WHAT THIS SYSTEM DOES FOR MANAGEMENT:

1. CONFIRMS, CAPTURES, AND TRACKS ALL MONTH'S TRANSACTIONS.
2. SUMMARIZES SALES ACTIVITIES BY DAY, MONTH AND YEAR.
3. REPORTS WEEKLY GROSS PROFIT.
4. REPORTS OPEN ORDER POTENTIAL AT MONTH'S START.
5. FORECASTS MONTH-END SALES AT MID-MONTH.
6. SUMMARIZES N/S AND G/P ON THE LAST DAY OF THE MONTH (+ 1.0%)

AND OUTPUTS FOR OTHER ECHELONS AND DEPARTMENTS:

A. SALES AND MARKETING
1. THE MARKET REPORT.
2. MAJOR PRODUCT BILLING SUMMARY.
3. SPECIAL OPEN ORDER REPORT BY $.
4. MAJOR OPEN ORDER PRODUCT REPORT.
5. BILLINGS BY AREA.
6. OPEN ORDER DETAILS AT MONTH-START.
7. OPEN ORDER DETAILS AT MID-MONTH.
8. SELECTED OPEN ORDER PRODUCT REPORT.
9. SELECTED PRODUCT BILLING COMPARISON.

B. ACCOUNTING.
1. SALES REGISTER SUMMARY
2. SALES REGISTER
3. D.I.S.C.
4. COUNTRY NET SALES REPORT (QUARTERLY)

C. TRAFFIC
1. ORDER DOCUMENTS
2. BILLING DOCUMENTS
3. CREDITS & DEBITS
4. INSURANCE REPORTS.

D. CREDIT.
1. AGEING REPORT

NOTE:
MONTH'S COMPUTER ACTIVITIES AND REPORT DISTRIBUTION ARE COMPLETED THREE DAYS AFTER MONTH-END. PRIOR METHOD: TWENTY-FIVE DAYS AFTER MONTH-END.

6

REACHING FIVE KEY OBJECTIVES OF AN INTEGRATED, TIME-SHARING M.I.S. SYSTEM

One day M.I.S. will be all things to all men. Today, some consider it a m.i.s.take. I disagree. In the preceding chapter we have established a working theory for a time-sharing M.I.S. package. The need for a detailed theory has been emphasized. To recapitulate, an M.I.S. should be:

1. Symbiotic
2. Viable
3. Dynamic
4. Current
5. Provide a "peek into the future"

This chapter will be devoted to a detailed description of such a structure with emphasis on its achievement of each of the above objectives.

Symbiosis is the opposite of parasitism. It is the intimate living together of two dissimilar organisms in a mutually *beneficial* relationship.

In order to produce payroll, credit, and accounting tasks, special extra steps have always been necessary to accommodate the computer. Attempts to establish an M.I.S. in this environment exaggerated this data demand even further.

Grist for the computer had to be manually assembled and then keypunched into the system. This type of operation involved two levels of personnel not used before:

1. Someone to collect and organize the data from records, billings, orders or other documents.
2. Keypunch operators to input the data to the computer.

This personnel was added for the computer's benefit, or converted from their other jobs when computers replaced them. Essentially, these people were parasitic. They stood between the user and the computer. They did not originate information. They processed it. A typical and common example of this is the order clerk at a distant sales location. He receives the customer's order, extracts those details useful to his company, and teletypes or mails a properly filled-in input form to the head office.

At the head office this form is handed to a keypunch operator who keypunches the data into the computer. Neither clerk nor keypunch operator ever see the order again. An order expeditor later has the responsibility of directing the order to the customer.

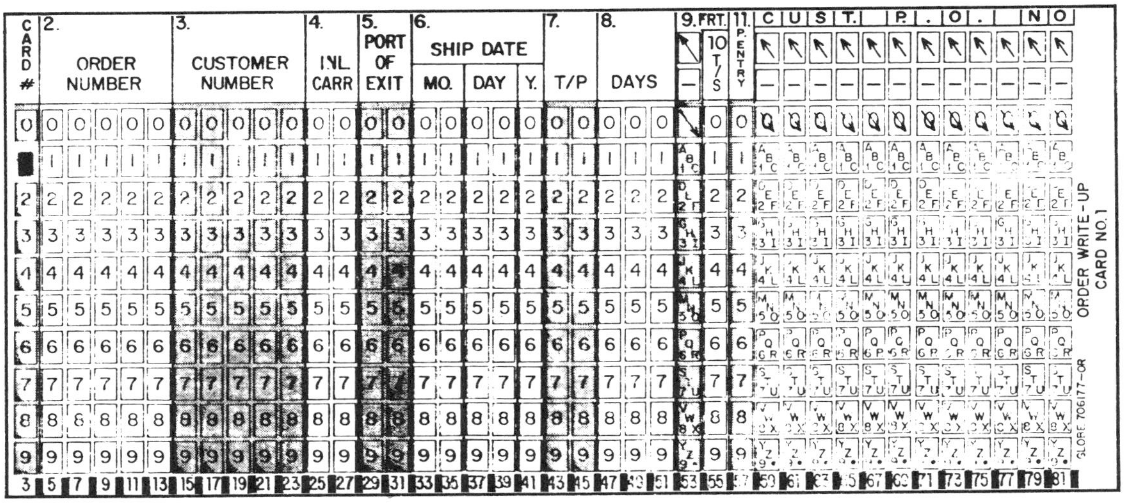

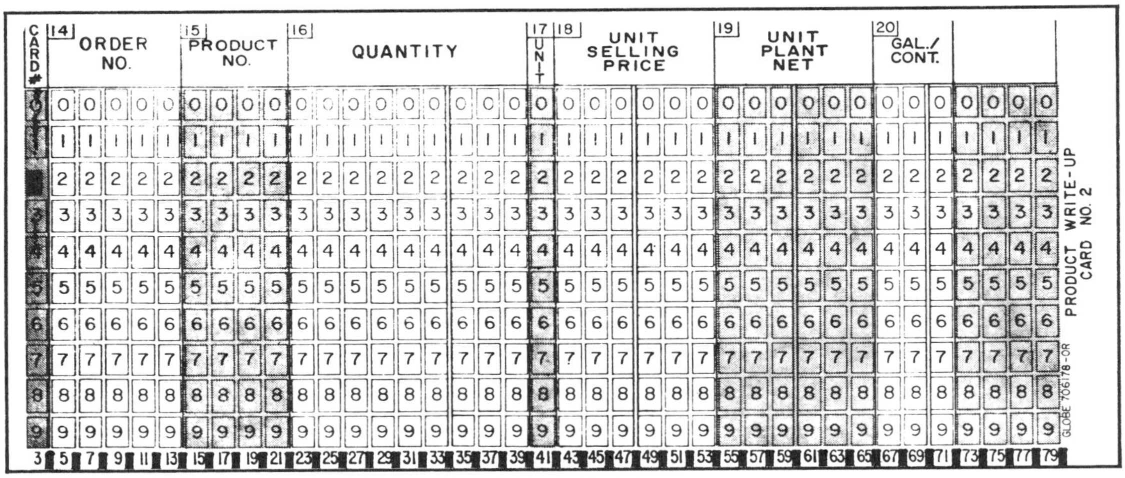

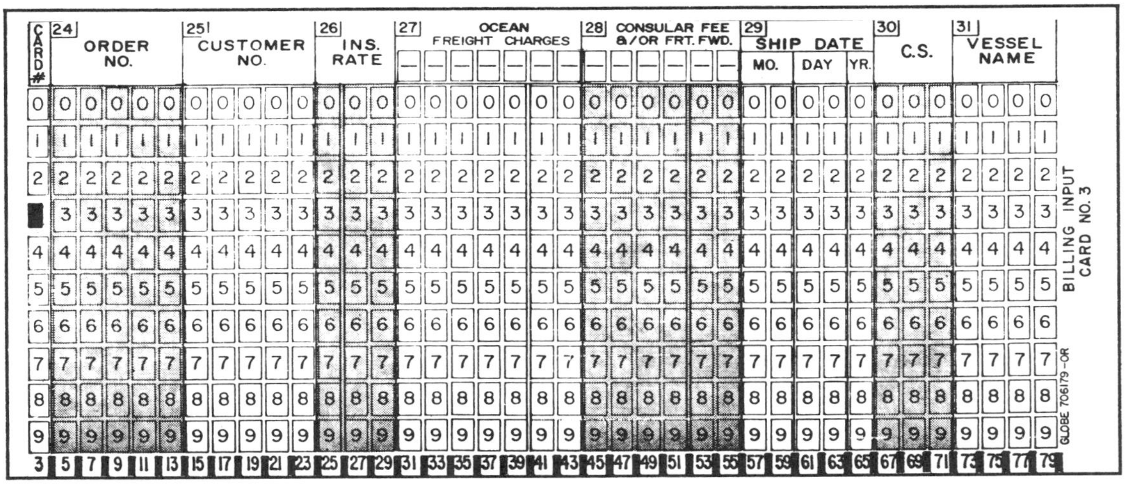

FIGURE 15 OPTICAL MARK-SENSE CARDS

CASE IN POINT: There are thousands, perhaps hundreds of thousands, of manual order entry systems functioning in the U.S. today. These consist of order clerks and typists "doing their thing" to the daily influx of customer orders.

Major companies with massive order entry requirements have moved to computers to do this job. They may have replaced the clerk-typist for order write-up, but they have substituted the write-up clerk, keypunch operator, and a whole EDP staff.

One medium-sized company developed a time-sharing alternative. Their traffic expeditors fill out a mark-sense card. This is fed directly into the time-sharing computer, and orders and billings are output. This not only eliminates the manual clerk-typist, but also the keypunch operator in conventional computer configurations.

This system will be outlined in the following pages. Its implementation, however, reduced an order-entry staff of eight to a time-sharing staff of three. Result: Forty thousand dollars a year was saved.

The following describes a symbiotic M.I.S. environment in which optical mark-sense cards are used (see Figure 15). The order expeditor, the person responsible for the order itself, marks the cards by pencil. These cards then are read directly into the computer via a mark-sense reader (Figure 16) and no further human intermediary is required. Not only does this input enable the computer to write the order and/or billing required, but more importantly the computer can now construct a data base from which all management reports are generated.

Thus the keypunching and manual data extraction superimposed on the business system (parasitic) has been eliminated. The natural process of order and billing output has been utilized to generate a data base, symbiotically, as the starting point for a management information system.

Establishing your data base on the individual order and billing output keeps it current as of the last written order or billing. Such timeliness demands immediate access to correct errors, and to review and revise the data base.

Viable and dynamic are the watchwords of time sharing. With a continuous daily influx of information a similar flexibility must be available. Only time sharing can provide this capability. It is here that time sharing for packaged programs justifies itself.

The ability to enter the data base, review, revise, and adjust this data base is essential in a dynamic system. The flexibility to add new reports, change the emphasis on regular reports, and to modify existing reports to meet your changing requirements is also essential. Of all the features of M.I.S. and time sharing, the dynamics and viability of such systems are best achieved via this constant interaction.

Pause here a moment and consider exactly what time sharing permits in such dynamic systems. In the current "state of the art," electronic data processing massages volumes of data, modified only by rigid routines built into the computer. This is why there is a proliferation of funny computer stories. This is why one person is charged a million dollars for a toothbrush by his friendly department store computer.

Time sharing ties an operator into the system. It emphasizes user/computer interaction. The input and the output circulate, not only through the computer, but also through a human mind. The computer processing and the mind evaluating create a

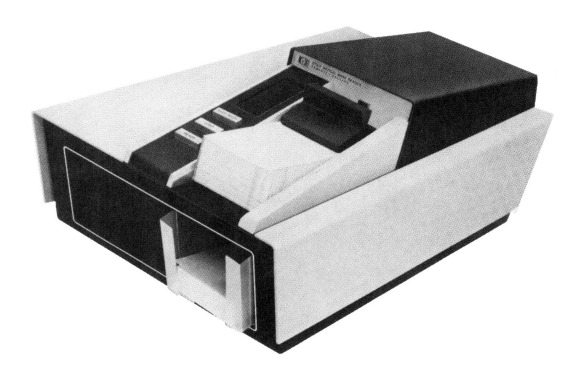

FIGURE 16   OPTICAL MARK-SENSE READER

truly viable and dynamic data base, a data base responsive to day-to-day requirements, to data manipulation, to input correction and to output review.

The input of mark-sense cards, and the output of orders and billings represent the only clerical activity. Management information starts with the collection of pertinent data from these documents. The assemblage of this data and its compilation into a computer-processable data base is next.

An M.I.S. begins with a data base kept constantly up-to-date by the flow-through of orders, and the editing, whenever necessary, by a human operator. This is simple in a time-sharing mode. It would be very difficult on a conventional in-house basis.

The objectives of this data base are to provide current reports to management and whenever possible give them a "peek into the future."

Undertake the next few pages as a time-sharing user. Monitor the output as if it were your own. Imagine yourself as responsible for the month's movement of products. Does this output provide you with the necessary information to maintain surveillance of your business? Does it allow you to meet your objectives and to anticipate your problems?

The case presented is as simple and straightforward as possible. Specifically, it concerns the sale of a product to four sections of the country from three plants. Sales objectives for the month are established via budgeted goals.

The symbiotic relationship in this M.I.S. occurs at the start. The traffic clerks read the customer's order and check the mark-sense cards accordingly. This operation takes but a moment of their time. Their primary effort is devoted to order interpretation, product availability, plant scheduling, and shipping arrangements.

The traffic clerk accumulates mark-sense cards as he expedites the orders and billings. Once sufficient cards are accumulated, they are run through the mark-sense reader into the computer.

The output of orders and billings need not concern us. This is the mechanical part of the operation. Simultaneously, however, the computer is building several data banks. These are the heart of our M.I.S.

> DATA BASE I   —Open orders
> DATE BASE II   —Billings
> DATE BASE III   —The day's orders and billings

The orders and billings for the day have been written. Computer output like this is commonplace today. While this was being done, however, our M.I.S. data base was being constructed. Manipulation of this data base will provide our management information.

The first and most elementary step is to provide confirmation that the day's orders and billings have been processed. This is done by producing a daily order and billing report. This report confirms and identifies what orders have been initiated and what billings have been processed. It is output as in Figure 17.

These reports satisfy one of the current requirements of M.I.S. You will note they identify each transaction by:

1. Invoice number
2. Customer
3. Product
4. Plant
5. Receivable amount

This output provides the base point of the M.I.S. It confirms new orders in, invoices out. In between we are concerned with the movement of orders from placement to delivery, from sales to billing and "making budget." All data is now in our data base. Outputting meaningful information is now our objective.

ORDER REPORT   23 JAN
(GROSS VALUE BASIS—INCLUDING FRT. + INS., ETC.)

ORDER NO.	CUSTOMER	PRODUCT	PLA	GROSS VAL.	BASIS
692878	CHLANINTO	CONLOOGDIO	I	5629.92	CIF
692899	MODCHAMIR	CONLOOGDIO	I	451.14	CIF
699285	FRIEDBIGO	LONYLL	V	99.20	FAS
699293	CORKYAG	LOWANG PLEAD	V	1160.00	FOB
699294	CORKYAG	LOWANG PLEAD	V	290.00	FOB
692879	ILKO	CONLOOGDIO	I	4071.00	FOB
692879	ILKO	CANLAAGDIA	I	.00	FOB
692881	PRELIME	LOSAND	0	3381.00	FOB
692905	CINADOKEL	LINCO	0	7980.00	FOB
TOTAL				23062.26	

PLANT		DAILY TOTAL	MONTH TO DATE TOTAL	YEAR TO DATE TOTAL
NIAGARA	A	.00	467636.80	2856167.00
COLUMBUS	I	10152.06	1101243.66	12364129.66
ATLANTA	0	11361.00	147050.30	1918799.50
SUBTOTAL		21513.06	1715930.76	17139096.16
VERMONT	V	1549.20	437821.90	2753866.90
TOTAL		23062.26	2153752.66	19892963.06

YEAR TO DATE—THIS YEAR	17139096.16
YEAR TO DATE—PRIOR YEAR	17608673.00
PERCENTAGE	97.33

*

BILLING REPORT   23 JAN
(GROSS VALUE BASIS—INCLUDING FRT. + INS., ETC.)

ORDER NO.	CUSTOMER	PRODUCT	PLA	GROSS VAL.	BASIS
692879	ILKO	CONLOOGDIO	I	4071.00	FOB
692879	ILKO	CANLAAGDIA	I	.00	FOB
692881	PRELIME	LOSAND	0	3381.00	FOB
TOTAL				7452.00	

NET SALES ESTIMATES

PLANT		DAILY TOTAL	MONTH TO DATE TOTAL	YEAR TO DATE TOTAL
NIAGARA	A	.00	-3644.50	2990469.90
COLUMBUS	I	4071.00	771371.30	9679045.90
ATLANTA	0	3177.45	100531.75	1656286.85
SUBTOTAL		7248.45	868258.55	14325802.65
VERMONT	V	.00	102657.20	2186585.00
TOTAL		7248.45	970915.75	16512387.65

NET SALES ESTIMATES

YEAR TO DATE—THIS YEAR	14325802.65
YEAR TO DATE—PRIOR YEAR	15143567.00
PERCENTAGE	94.60

FIGURE 17   ORDER REPORT AND BILLING REPORT

This M.I.S. consists of five major reports:

   I. Current position compared to budget
  II. Weekly gross profit report
 III. Unbilled orders month-start
 IV. Unbilled orders midmonth
  V. Estimated net sales and gross profit

The three major bases are needed to output the above reports. Time sharing provides instant access to each for the daily editing, upkeep, revision, and corrections that are required.

All time-sharing services offer such editing capability. It is essential to the effectiveness of an M.I.S. system. The involved delays and revisions experienced by many computer setups would be intolerable in an interactive M.I.S. A current on-line system would hardly be acceptable if it dawdled over corrections the way your last credit card adjustment did.

The time-sharing user has complete and constant control over his data base. His data base is a viable and dynamic entity—always current, always ready for modification and adjustment; always, to use the jargon of the computer, ready for updating.

There is no question that this capability is one of time sharing's most important characteristics. Constant updating assures us that the reports output are accurate and current.

The first report, report I, is issued daily and accompanies the order and billing reports. Its purpose is to establish the sales position as of the day, the month and the year. To do this, the computer compares sales to budget on a daily basis. Based on B.F. Skinner's *Beyond Freedom and Dignity*, this would be the best possible way to keep a businessman's eye on the corporate objective—provide him with performance feedback on a daily basis.

This output comprises the third page of the daily report. It is generated by processing data base III.

NET SALES ESTIMATES

PLANTS	MONTH TO DATE PERCENTAGES		YEAR TO DATE PERCENTAGES
NIAGARA	63	100	101
ATLANTA	71	118	90
COLUMBUS	25	41	72
TOTAL	62	108	89
AREAS			
COASTAL	114	124	102
EASTERN	40	43	101
FAR WEST	90	98	68
SOUTHWEST	28	30	89

This example is the report, specifically, for the 18th of the month. It shows the current position of each plant and area in percent compared to its budgeted sales.

The first column of numbers compares the cumulated month's sales with the month's budget. These numbers reach 100 percent when month's budget is achieved.

The second column compares sales up to the present day of the month with budgeted sales for that day. To be on budget all month, would mean to read 100 percent all month.

The third column compares sales with those budgeted for the year to date. One hundred percent is on target; 90 percent means 10 percent below budgeted performance.

Emphasis here should be on the symbiotic nature of this information as made possible with time sharing. These percentages are the most important output of the daily order and billing report, yet they are produced solely as a byproduct of this activity. The flexibility and freedom to interact with the computer at any time makes it possible to maintain such a current data base and output system.

The remaining reports can best be described by going "on line." These reports are scheduled over a month's time. They are output to make the best use of the data. Their issuance is designed to keep the user current, and to give him a "peek into the future."

Report II, the month-start report, lists all open orders scheduled for shipment during the month. It reports on the first day of the month whether enough orders are on hand to make the month's budget. Time sharing is particularly appropriate for this report. Each month's different structure of weekends and closing dates affects scheduling. On time sharing the precise days of shipment can be selected.

COMPUTER	COMMENT	OPERATOR
	Dial 123-4567	
PLEASE LOG IN		HAP 103
READY		RUN DATES
WHAT AREA?		COASTAL
WHAT DATES?		01JUN,30JUN

You have now instructed the computer to review all open orders, and output these shipments scheduled for the month of June to the Coastal territory. Each area and time period is selected for output this way, and the final summary provides a thirty-day look at the estimated month's dollar sales:

COMPUTER   COMMENT   OPERATOR

REPORT II

Dates	COASTAL	EASTERN	FAR WEST	SOUTHWEST	Total
1. Over 1 month late	14,796	363,156	359,174	351,259	1,088,385
2. Last month	112,410	349,537	473,920	549,658	1,485,525
3. This month	254,161	254,758	498,652	924,546	1,932,117
TOTAL:	381,367	967,451	1,331,746	1,825,463	4,506,027
Monthly Budget	429,072	627,739	432,534	573,905	2,063,250
4. Next month through Dec.	171,893	1,208,955	2,323,364	2,600,432	6,304,644
5. Next year	–	–	–	–	–
6. Will advise	185,154	19,022	56,819	602,506	863,501

TOTAL UNBILLED ORDERS: . . . . $ 11,674,172

Report II provides an overview of all the business presently on the books. Also included are unscheduled shipments (Will advise). These are a valuable asset when seeking extra sales to meet the monthly budget.

The grand total of all open orders (the last line) provides a constant monthly indicator. This number fluctuates with open order input to provide a longer range (2 to 3 months) "peek into the future."

Report II, run on a changing, corrected and adjusted open order data base, satisfies most of the requirements of an effective M.I.S. Report II is also accompanied by a list of all orders and sufficient detail to identify each transaction.

CASE IN POINT: This report turned out to be an unexpected money-saver, and led to further time-sharing takeover of the order entry system.

Time–sharing was introduced on a modular basis. The M.I.S. reports were generated while manual order write-up was still taking place. This was before full symbiosis was achieved. The data from manually written orders and billings was manually extracted from documents and typed into the M.I.S.

Once the data was available to the computer, it checked the input from manual calculations against its own calculations. In the first month of operation, forty thousand dollars of variance was uncovered.

This was a strong point in the decision to expand the system to incorporate mark-sense input.

Report III emphasizes current position. Processing is weekly. The last week's billings are output and individual gross profits calculated on each transaction. This report keeps you current. The final objective of budgeting is to achieve budgeted goals. In report III the computer calculates and outputs detail and summary.

Report III tells us where we stand now, and tells us if our budgeted profit goals are being achieved. Here again a minimum of computer activity results in major output. Report III consists of a summary for the month and current profit details on last week's transactions.

COMPUTER	COMMENT	OPERATOR
	Dial 123-4567	
PLEASE LOG IN		HAP 103
READY		RUN PROFIT
GROSS PROFIT DETAIL AND SUMMARY?		YES
	A "NO" would request no detail, just a summary.	
	The summary for the month provides both weekly and cumulative output in dollars.	

DATES	Week's G/P	Cumulative G/P for the month	Cumulative Budget for the month
01 Mar.–07 Mar.	116,574.09	116,574.09	1st Wk. 200,000
08 Mar.–11 Mar.	91,379.02	207,953.11	
12 Mar.–13 Mar.	52,536.60	260,489.71	2nd Wk. 400,000
13 Mar.–14 Mar.	129,752.60	390,242.31	
15 Mar.–18 Mar.	45,215.83	435,458.14	3rd Wk. 600,000
19 Mar.–20 Mar.	69,749.18	505,207.32	
			TOTAL: 800,000

Report III keeps us current on our profit expectations. It flags any variations from the norm. On a weekly basis we have time to take corrective steps if profits fail to match budget.

Report IV is our next "peek into the future." This report summarizes all open orders scheduled for shipment prior to month-end. Again time sharing's interaction enables us to maintain a current data base. This in turn enables us to know precisely what's on hand as of a specific date.

The flexibility time sharing provides is critical at this point. This is not a blind computer processing of data. Each month is different. Work days are different. The month's budget is different. Our objectives for the month are different.

What we need to know at midmonth is "Will we achieve budgeted goals?" "Should we try to generate new business before month-end?" "Can we reorganize our delivery schedule to utilize next month's orders?" These questions can be answered if we query our data base astutely. When we have a firm grasp on our current situation two weeks before month-end, we can take action to meet our budgeted objectives. With these objectives in mind, we begin to massage our data base.

COMPUTER	COMMENT	OPERATOR
	Again, output for this report is simple, fast and specific.	
READY		RUN DATES
WHAT AREA?		COASTAL
WHAT DATES?	In this case we are looking not only for this month's open orders, but also to see if any orders have been unshipped from a previous month.	01JUN,20JUL
COASTAL 101,171		
WHAT DATES?	Computer now prints out "COASTAL" total.	21JUL,29JUL
COASTAL 66,487		
WHAT AREA?		EASTERN
WHAT DATES?		01JUN,20JUL
EASTERN 1,237,000		
	Here a weekend ends the month. No shipments can be billed after July 29.	
WHAT AREA?		EASTERN
WHAT DATES?		21JUL,29JUL
EASTERN 1,237,000	etc.	
	As these summations are output, the computer is also compiling a detail file.	

COMPUTER   COMMENT   OPERATOR

Two sources of informa-
tion are available when our
midmonth querying ends.
First, a summary of open
orders by plant and area in
dollars:

PLANTS	Unbilled orders as of above date	Unbilled orders prior to month-end	Month's billings to date	Predicted max. net sales tot.	BUDGET FOR THE MONTH
ATLANTA	282,845	381,484	129,145	739,474	759,674
COLUMBUS	40,282	18,300	3,720	62,302	186,001
NIAGARA	85,201	29,575	48,628	163,404	231,566
TOTAL	408,328	429,359	181,493	1,019,180	1,177,166
AREAS					
COASTAL	101,171	66,487	49,942	217,600	208,092
EASTERN	1,237,000	12,386	24,420	1,273,806	1,271,333
F. WEST	151,402	170,655	32,902	354,959	173,167
SO. WEST	67,661	150,690	29,308	247,659	293,083

Second, a detail file used to determine which orders can help us achieve budgeted goals. Figure 18 is one page of such a detail file.

Our current data base provided us with all the latest information. Our queries, unique to this particular day, month and year, provided us with summary information. Dependent upon our interpretation of that information we can take action.

We can take action because our detailed output gives the information we need to effect the order flow. It gives us this information *two weeks before month-end!* It gives us two weeks to change the pattern of events if we judge budgeted goals are in jeopardy.

Report V is a necessary, but less unique report. Report V summarizes the month's activities. Not exciting, but essential. In order to know where we are going, we must know where we have been.

Every business today summarizes the month's activities. As time passes, these summaries have been moved closer to month-end. However, it is not unusual for the computer summary to be completed one or two weeks after month-end.

SHIPMENTS SCHEDULED BETWEEN 01JUN and 20JUL
COASTAL TERRITORY

ORDER NO.	CUSTOMER	PRODUCT NAME	QUANTITY IN POUNDS	DOLLAR AMOUNT	DATE
C721904A	BERINGA	KALI	300000	35000	01JUN
C721909A	LOYENSEN	DUST	35770	12500	18JUL
C722203N	BORGENSO	SANDED ASH	8725	7300	17JUL
C722211C	LIENVAT	ISOL ASH	165000	32780	06JUN
C722355C	KLASSENS	FARI	29000	9875	17JUN
C722418N	BIANCON	SANDED ASH	9300	8576	15JUL
C722422C	LIENVAT	ISOL ASH	225000	52500	15JUL
C722425C	LIENVAT	ISOL ASH	277800	58430	13JUN
C272426A	BERINGA	KALLOS	800	560	07JUN
C722632C	WILLIANCO	KALI	43000	3756	22JUN

TOTAL ATLANTA PLANT   48060.00
TOTAL NIAGARA PLANT   15876.00
TOTAL COLUMBUS PLANT 157341.00
TOTAL AMOUNT BETWEEN 01 JUNE and 20 JULY   221277.00

FIGURE 18   OPEN ORDER DETAIL FILE

This time-sharing M.I.S. can output its month's summary the afternoon of the last day of the month. It has to, as tomorrow it is updated again by input from the first of the next month.

A summary report and detail report are output. This report provides managers with an immediate review of last month's activities. The request for this report is as direct as previous reports. Its output is as specific. The summary and the budget appear in Figure 19.

The foregoing has described a fully operating, interactive M.I.S. system. It performs not only the mechanical tasks of outputting order and billing documents, but also the more difficult task of outputting information.

A data base has been constructed while the day's orders and billings were produced. Time sharing's user interaction has enabled us to maintain the accuracy of this data base. This viable and dynamic condition has allowed us to extract pertinent and correct information on a predetermined or random time schedule—a schedule uniquely tailored to our requirements, not to those of the computer.

Finally, reports have been extracted that keep management current (I, II, V) and provided a peek into the future (III, IV).

MONTH'S SALES (N/S) AND GROSS PROFIT (G/P) IN DOLLARS

	ATLANTA		COLUMBUS		TOTAL A&C SALES	
	N/S	G/P	N/S	G/P	N/S	G/P
COASTAL	151,641.68	54,721.26	45,450.97	5,069.25	197,092.65	59,790.51
EASTERN	375,664.96	126,752.48	39,684.50	9,841.54	415,349.46	136,594.02
FAR WEST	141,973.86	29,061.81	29,046.61	121,217.01	171,020.47	41,278.82
SO. WEST	496,045.12	115,152.36	8,898.11	3,514.71	504,943.23	118,667.07
TOTAL:	1165,325.62	325,687.91	123,080.19	30,642.51	1,288,405.81	356,330.42

	N/S	G/P	
COASTAL	122,631.00	42,055.00	
F. WEST	38,252.00	13,944.00	GRAND TOTAL NET SALES . . . : $1,511,323.70 *
S. WEST	62,034.89	31,919.70	BUDGET . . . . : $1,366,267.00 *
TOTAL:	222,917.89	87,918.70	GRAND TOTAL GROSS PROFIT . : $ 444,249.12 *
			BUDGET . . . . : $ 410,733.00 *

FIGURE 19   MONTH'S SUMMARY AND BUDGET

7

GETTING TOP VALUE FROM THE
USER-INTERACTIVE TIME-SHARING M.I.S.

The crux of the computer paradox is that there are too many answers and not enough questions. The computer expert is always frustrated. He knows he can produce miracles with his hardware, but nobody asks him to perform. I frequently think, in his disappointment, he produces forty pounds of output just to emphasize his capabilities.

Which is the more intelligent approach? The architect builds a house and asks you to learn how to live in it, or you describe your dream house to the architect, and he builds it to your specifications? There is a great gulf between the user and the EDP technician. It is the user's fault. Until the user can describe what he wants, the technician will continue to output quantity instead of quality, data instead of information.

Time sharing will encourage the growth of the knowledgeable user. One who realizes he can demand any kind of service he needs. The time-sharing user should thrive on interaction with the computer. Hopefully, this familiarity will breed contempt that will strip the computer of its mystique. Once this aura of the unknown is gone, the user can concentrate on his real objectives.

First, the user must know what he wants. Then, the user must explicitly set forth his requirements. Finally, he must guide, direct and manage the computer and the computer people to the specific achievement of his goals.

How many times have you heard: "They are going to computerize my department. When they've built the system, they're going to tell me what to do"? "They" are always the computer experts, and "they" don't know as much about your department as you do. "They," however, are going to computerize it with or without your help. If you want to avoid catastrophe, you had better extend them a guiding hand. Remember, we're not talking about data processing (billings, debits and credits, payroll, etc.) but about information (M.I.S., simulations, etc.).

Time sharing lends itself perfectly to this approach. Use time sharing to provide you with computer know-how. Learn from time sharing the scope of computer capabilities. Once learned, guide, direct and manage the experts to *your* objectives.

In the preceding chapter we described an on-line, real-time, report-generating M.I.S. How can this be improved? Hopefully, you thought of several ways. Here is an improvement we can foresee.

The following dramatization is hardware and software possible now. It is the human element that is lacking. This M.I.S. contains a built-in, on-line, real-time, decision-making vice president "in the loop." Such time-sharing facilities are common, such knowledgeable vice presidents are rare.

Time sharing's greatest asset is user-computer interaction. Let's try to similate this interactive on-line situation by describing this computer package in dramatic form.

THE V.P.

A play in one act.

The Cast:

Mr. Paul Stans	Vice President
Miss Jensen	Secretary
Mr. Chuck Sims	Production Manager
Mr. Vince Finley	Marketing Manager
Mr. Sam Woods	Chicago Plant Manager
Mr. Jerry Rees	Controller
Computer	As itself

Time: 9:00 a.m., Monday, August 23.

Scene: V.P./Division manager's office.

A neat, efficient corner office. Businesslike yet spacious with an L-shaped desk, four or five comfortable chairs, and couch and coffee table across from the desk to complete the furnishings.

The only unusual piece of furniture is a CRT (cathode ray tube) unit and keyboard combination [Figure 20]. This is placed on a table directly behind the V.P.'s desk.

The V.P. enters followed a moment later by his secretary. He hangs up his coat, and as he approaches his desk turns for a moment to the console, selects a card from a file and inserts the card in a data phone.

Both he and his secretary sit down as the card he inserted activates the console.

Sec.:	Welcome back, sir. Did you have a pleasant trip?
V.P.:	About the same as usual. Lots of talk, little action.
Sec.:	I've left your calls on your desk, and assembled your mail for review.
V.P.:	Thank you, Miss Jensen, I'll get to those things a little later. What's on the agenda today?
Sec.:	This morning you have several meetings, and then a lunch with J.D. Wislo, Inc.
	(While they've been talking the card the V.P. had put in the data phone has activated the console. Throughout this dramatization the V.P. treats the console in a very casual fashion. He turns, pecks out a few numbers and then leans back, relaxes and watches the result appear on the screen.)

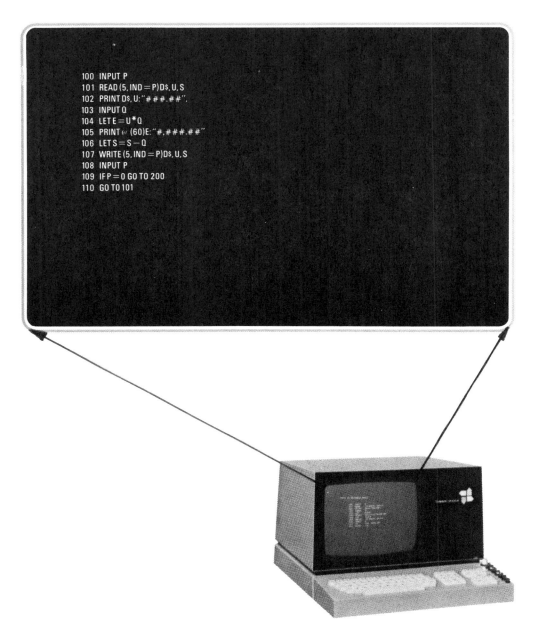

```
100  INPUT P
101  READ (5, IND = P) D$, U, S
102  PRINT D$, U: "###.##",
103  INPUT Q
104  LET E = U*Q
105  PRINT @ (60)E: "#,###.##"
106  LET S = S — Q
107  WRITE (5, IND = P) D$, U, S
108  INPUT P
109  IF P = 0 GO TO 200
110  GO TO 101
```

FIGURE 20   CATHODE RAY TUBE (CRT) TERMINAL

V.P.:   Before anything else, let me catch up on what's happened in the last two weeks.

Sec.:   Shall I call Mr. Wols? He mentioned he'd be glad to bring you up to date.

V.P.:   I'm sure he would, but I prefer to start my day from a more unbiased point of view. I'll just get it off the computer. What's the date?

Sec.:   Eight, twenty-three.

(The V.P. turns to the console and types: 8/23,%)

	SALES PERCENTAGES		Aug 23
	SALES COMPARED TO BUDGET FOR		
	THIS MONTH	THIS DAY, THIS MONTH	THIS DAY, THIS YEAR
PLANTS			
NEW YORK	41	72	117
LOS ANGELES	55	186	152
CHICAGO	11	37	99
TOTAL	41	141	137
AREAS			
EAST	38	129	88
MIDWEST	58	198	131
SOUTH	50	172	227
WEST	28	95	155

Sec.:   Sir, I don't pay much attention to the computer, but may I ask a question?

V.P.:   Certainly. Is something puzzling you?

Sec.:   Well, I'm not very mathematically minded.

V.P.:   (mumbling) I know, I know.

Sec.:   But even I can see that none of those columns either add up or average up to provide a total.

V.P.:   True, that's because the plants and areas are of different size. Los Angeles is our largest plant. Therefore its sales skew the totals.

Sec.:   I guess so.

V.P.:   Those results look pretty ragged. Chicago had better start producing. Let's look at today's order report.

(Types: 8/23, orders,S)

```
                          ORDER REPORT                          23 AUG
      ORDER NO.    CUSTOMER      PRODUCT        PLA    GROSS VAL.    BASIS
       692878     CHLANINTO     CONLOOGDIO       I       5629.92     CIF
       692899     MODCHAMIR     CONLOOGDIO       I        451.14     CIF
       699285     FRIEDBIGO     LONYLL           V         99.20     FAS
       699293     CORKYAG       LOWANG PLEAD     V       1160.00     FOB
       699294     CORKYAG       LOWANG PLEAD     V        290.00     FOB
       692879     ILKO          CONLOOGDIO       I       4071.00     FOB
       692879     ILKO          CONLOOGDIO       I          .00      FOB
       692881     PRELIME       LOSAND           O       3381.00     FOB
       692905     CINADOKEL     LINCO            O       7980.00     FOB

      TOTAL                                            23062.00
```

PLANT		DAILY TOTAL	MONTH TO DATE TOTAL	YEAR TO DATE TOTAL
CHICAGO	A	.00	467636.80	2856167.00
LOS ANGELES	I	10152.06	1101243.66	12364129.66
NEW YORK	O	11361.00	147050.30	1918799.50
SUBTOTAL		21513.06	1715930.76	7139096.16
VERMONT	V	1549.20	437821.90	2753866.90
TOTAL		23062.26	2153752.66	19892963.06

```
        YEAR TO DATE—THIS YEAR                      17139096.16
        YEAR TO DATE—PRIOR YEAR                     17608673.00
        PERCENTAGE                                         97.33
```

V.P.:   Orders about normal. However, do these monthly totals include the Nevada orders we've been expecting?

Sec.:   I'm not sure.

V.P.:   Don't worry. That was a rhetorical question.
          (Types: Nev; Orders, S)

ORDER NUMBER	CUSTOMER	PRODUCT	QUANTITY (LBS)	TOTAL BILLING
		NEVADA ORDERS		
682363	BOWSON	DANDON	27000.	29497.00
		SAND DUST	13500.	
		ASH DUST	13500.	
682380	LINDELCO	CONLOOGDIO	27000.	18330.00
682448	LINDSAYSON	LOSAND	1100.	970.00
682451	FIDELCHEM	LINCO	6675.	2636.00
682465	COSTROINT	LONYLL	21600.	2955.00
682466	LAGENCOM	CONLOOGDIO	4350.	1171.00
682570	BRINDON	CONLOOGDIO	11300.	793.00
682579	WILLIAMSON	LOSAND	9900.	3486.00
682627	CLARKSTON	ASH DUST	24.	840.00
682640	LEEUWINGEN	ASH DUST	66139.	35721.00

V.P.:   Nevada orders in! Now how about yesterday's billings?
            (Types: 8/22,BILLS,S)
Sec.:   What's the "S" for?
V.P.:   That command tells the computer to type out that portion of the
            Billing Report that sums the day's activities.
Sec.:   That's the part at the bottom that says "net sales estimates"?
V.P.:   Exactly.

(Computer outputs)

BILLING REPORT   22 Aug
(GROSS VALUE BASIS—INCLUDING FRT. + INS., ETC.)

ORDER NO.	CUSTOMER	PRODUCT	PLA	GROSS VAL.	BASIS
692879	ILKO	CONLOOGDIO	I	4071.00	FOB
692879	ILKO	CANLAAGDIA	I	.00	FOB
692881	PRELIME	LOSAND	O	3381.00	FOB
TOTAL				7452.00	

NET SALES ESTIMATES

PLANT		DAILY TOTAL	MONTH TO DATE TOTAL	YEAR TO DATE TOTAL
CHICAGO	A	.00	3644.50	2990469.90
LOS ANGELES	I	4071.00	771371.30	9679045.90
NEW YORK	O	3177.45	100531.75	1656286.85
SUBTOTAL		7248.45	868258.55	14325802.65
VERMONT	V	.00	102657.20	2186585.00
TOTAL		7248.45	970915.75	16512387.65

NET SALES ESTIMATES

YEAR TO DATE—THIS YEAR		14325802.65
YEAR TO DATE—PRIOR YEAR		15143567.00
PERCENTAGE		94.60

*

Sec.:   Sir, it seems to me that we had many more billings than that
            yesterday.
V.P.:   As I said, this is just the last few lines of billings. Those just
            before the summary.
Sec.:   There are more individual billings not shown?
V.P.:   Yes, but not enough according to that low Chicago total. Perhaps
            our plant is still not meeting its schedules. Let's print out our
            delinquent Chicago orders.
            (Types: 0,8/23,CHICAGO)

CHICAGO ORDERS AS OF AUGUST 23

ORDER NUMBER	CUSTOMER	PRODUCT	QUANTITY (LBS)	TOTAL BILLING
681362	WIERINGA	LINCO	100000.	3178.00
681881	BLINKERS	LOSAND	661392.	7100.00
682001	BAKSO	LONYLL	12000000.	72569.00
682088	COENDINGO	LINCO	352.	9152.00
682125	HOORNWEGAN	ASH DUST	330000.	29988.00
682143	SPALDINCO	ASH DUST	7500.	1853.00
			6500.	
682205	BROUWCHEM	CONLOOGDIO	33000.	2600.00
682210	INTENCHEM	LOSAND	110000.	14094.00
			TOTAL	170,534.00

Sec.:   You asked me to remind you to check on our Western sales.

V.P.:   I asked you that two weeks ago. Let's look at West through December end.
(Types: O,12/31,WEST)

WEST, SHIPMENTS SCHEDULED BETWEEN 23AUG AND 31DEC

ORDER NO.	CUSTOMER	PRODUCT NAME	QUANTITY	AMOUNT	DATE
702339	PONDERING	LIPP	300,CWT	2570.	15NOV
710456	HANDBROS	LIPP	220,CWT	2651.	29AUG
710588	TENOVRE	SANDDUST	360,CWT	2628.	15NOV
710589	TENOVRE	SANDDUST	360,CWT	2628.	13DEC
710868	CORDERY	LIPP	330,CWT	3300.	01NOV
711284	MARGARITA	PPTS	12,MT	2012.	21OCT
711285	MARGARITA	PPTS	12,MT	2012.	27AUG
711442	CENDINGLO	LINK ASH	95,ST	1799.	01OCT
711443	CENDINGLO	LINK ASH	95,ST	1799.	04OCT
711444	CENDINGLO	LINK ASH	95,ST	1799.	06OCT
711445	CENDINGLO	LINK ASH	95,ST	1799.	08OCT
711732	ONOLINDA	MOLFRAM	550,ST	120637.	15NOV
711733	ONOLINDA	MOLFRAM	550,ST	120637.	15DEC
711731	ONOLINDA	MOLFRAM	550,ST	120637.	14OCT
711804	HENKRIHM	SANDDUST	5,CWT	404.	29OCT
711826	SOAPAFRI	PPTS	2,CWT	324.	01NOV
TOTAL WEST	388636.				

Sec.:   Would you like me to make a note of these orders?

V.P.:   No thanks, the computer can always retrieve them if I need them. In fact, let's look at those percentages again.
(Types: 8/23,%)

	SALES PERCENTAGES		AUG 23
	SALES COMPARED TO BUDGET FOR		
	THIS MONTH	THIS DAY, THIS MONTH	THIS DAY, THIS YEAR
PLANTS			
NEW YORK	41	72	117
LOS ANGELES	55	186	152
CHICAGO	11	37	99
TOTAL	41	141	137
AREAS			
EAST	38	129	88
MIDWEST	58	198	131
SOUTH	50	172	227
WEST	28	95	155

V.P.:   I still don't like those Chicago numbers. Ask Sam Woods to step in here.

Sec.:   Yes sir.

(The secretary picks up the telephone and calls Mr. Woods.)

Sec.:   He says he'll be right up. Oh, there are the month's results again.

V.P.:   Yes, given a little thought, it's remarkable how little note taking we need with a good data bank.

Sec.:   You mean once you can call for information via the computer there is no need for a desk full of papers?

V.P.   Exactly. I'll be calling up all kinds of information today. I don't need hard copies, since if I want to see it again, I can call it up again.

Sec.:   Where does that leave me?

V.P.:   Continuing to misspell the important letters to our customers. Unfortunately, we haven't built a vendor-buyer "mad bank" yet.

Sec.:   Mad bank, sir?

V.P.:   Mutually Accessible Data Bank.

Sec.:   I'm not sure I like this no-notes system.

V.P.:   It's called "paperless communication," and an interesting dissertation on it by Mr. F.R. Sheldon appeared several years ago in *Data Processing Magazine.* [Figure 21]

(The V.P. turns to the CRT and studies the percentages still on the screen. Mr. Woods enters the room, and Miss Jensen leaves.)

Chi. Mgr.:   Hello, Paul, welcome back. Had a nice trip?

V.P.:   Pretty good, Sam. Cleared up a few things. How did it go here?

Chi. Mgr.:   Fantastic, fantastic. I'm sailing right along.

V.P.:   I'm glad to hear that, but look at those sales percentages. Doesn't Chicago look a little low? Only made 11% of the month's budget? That's only 37% of where we should be, as of today.

PAPERLESS COMMUNICATION*
By Fred R. Sheldon

In the future, forward-looking, advanced corporations will have eliminated all intra-company memoranda, reports, and similar internal means of correspondence. Most of the hardware and technical advances for such an achievement already exist and the development of "paperless communication" requires only pioneering by innovating entrepreneurs.

With a paperless communications system, internal memoranda and the like would be "written to file," i.e., entered into a central data processing computer from a remote console. The primary recipients of messages and their "carbon copy" receivers will be appropriately designated, and the computer will automatically make the communications available to memory registers assigned to these individuals. Executive and key management personnel will have individual desk display screens to which they can call all communications addressed to them since they last examined their "incoming file." Suitable controls at desk display units will allow temporary or permanent filing of communications, removal from an individual's register, or even generation of hard copy (for study during commuting or other travel). Since an individual will have access to all messages addressed to him as soon as they are written, mail and messenger delays and costs will be eliminated, as will the costs of many files and of manual filing itself.

Groups of middle and lower middle managers will be served by a single display unit, and will operate from a common, group register. The size of individual or group registers will be determined on a statistical basis according to message frequency, the computer adjusting register sizes as needed. In fact, efficiency of the system can be improved constantly from automatically computed audits that will monitor types and frequency of messages, the number of responses, and the time required for them. Such internal audits, carefully used, could provide a valuable guide toward individual productivity and performance.

Selective messages

Some key executives will have access to data in all registers, while others will be limited to single or group registers as their positions and company functions dictate. Where company activities warrant it, central data acquisition will be on a real-time basis with up-to-the-minute facts available to operating personnel in either tabular or graphical form. Some personnel may be authorized to change data registers by means of keyboard input or light pen attachments to their display units.

Higher company executives will probably be more concerned with averages and trend data than with real-time data in their planning and long-term corporation guidance. To assist them in this most important function, the central computer will contain a library of simulation models reflecting all aspects of the company's business, including major markets served. Thus, using internal data, government statistics, external market projections, and innovative thinking, key executives will use the central data processing facility and its stored simulation models to test strategic decisions and to plan the successful course of the corporation through time, all without generating mountains of paper.

Datamation

*Reprinted by permission of *Data Processing Magazine,* April 1965.

FIGURE 21

Chi. Mgr.:   Oh, that's O.K. I've got business in the pipeline. That little old number will be jumping up any day now.

V.P.:   By the end of the month?

Chi. Mgr.:   Well, yes. I suppose so. Lots of orders are coming in. You'll definitely see an improvement.

V.P.:   Do you know how many open orders you have on hand?

Chi. Mgr.:   Not exactly, the situation changes constantly . . .

V.P.:   I checked the delinquent orders just now. I hope we'll have them out by month-end.

Chi. Mgr: No question about it.

V.P.:   Let's sum up all the business we have on the books before the 31st.

(Types: O,8/31,CHICAGO)

ORDER NO.	CUSTOMER	PRODUCT NAME	QUANTITY	AMOUNT	DATE
C712973I	REVERS	SADSOLFD COR	800,CW	6000.	12JAN73
C722031I	MIGNOSUTO	CON DU CAR	42,CW	2883.	8JAN73
C722140I	MIRCIS	SOPP	462,CW	5082.	4JAN73
C722358I	JEMEIDAT	OOPA	199.99,MT	44798.	1JAN73
C722641I	PRUQOIM	TOLKO	220,CW	2222.	11JAN73
C722739N	HEUKEL	FOREDON	10000,LB	30000.	10JAN73
C722824N	CEEPERORGA	ETHIAL	35000,LB	51100.	2JAN73
C722818I	MIGNOSUTO	OOPA	23.99,MT	5799.	3JAN73
C722887I	TAMPEROL	OOPA	9.93,MT	2017.	3JAN73
C722866I	GROFCISRO	SAMP	1,CW		8JAN73
C722866I	GROFCISRO	SOPP	3,CW		8JAN73
C722866I	GROFCISRO	TOLKO	25,CW		8JAN73
C722866I	GROFCISRO	OOPA	50,CW	808.	8JAN73
C722869I	HORZEG	CON DU RAC	952.66,KG	1486.	4JAN73
C722888I	KISMIS	SADSOLFD COR	9.07,MT	1565.	8JAN73
C722817I	PONWOLBRO	FFOSBROMILSO	4.40,CW	82.	1JAN73
C722892I	GROFDIMRO	OOPA	30,CW	276.	8JAN73
C730036I	TONNENTBRI	CON DU CAR	3992,KG	5828.	8JAN73

SO AM   159946.03 GROSS SALES (RECEIVABLES)
NOT INCLUDING "WILL ADVISE" SHIPMENTS.

V.P.:   Not enough, Sam.

Chi. Mgr.:   By the end of the month? Oh, no sir, not unless we really get on the stick. That's what we plan to do.

V.P.:   It'll really take some pushing.

Chi. Mgr.:   We'll get right on it. I think if we drop everything we can bring it up by month-end.

V.P.:   That's encouraging, Sam. Do you want to get after it right now?

Chi. Mgr.:   You bet. Will you excuse me, sir?

V.P.:   Certainly, Sam. Will you ask Miss Jensen to come in as you leave? (The Chicago Manager leaves. A moment later the V.P.'s secretary re-enters.) (V.P. types: COLEVER, O, G/P)

| ALL SHIPMENTS | | | | | | |
ORDER NO.	CUSTOMER NAME	PRODUCT NAME	QUANTITY IN LBS	PLANT NET	DOLLARS UNIT	EST GP%
722205	COLEVER	DUST	200000.	9.40	CWT	5.3
722464	COLEVER	KALI	100000.	11.73	CWT	5.0
722578	COLEVER	FARA	40000.	8.43	CWT	11.6
722527	COLEVER	ISOL ASH	194660.	21.94	ST	27.8
722371	COLEVER	LEODINAC	800.	15.97	CWT	27.2
722461	COLEVER	KALLOS	3220.	46.43	CWT	36.7
722438	COLEVER	LOKO BULK	40700.	8.50	CWT	8.2
722487	COLEVER	CAN LOR CHOS	7700.	2.20	CWT	25.0
722498	COLEVER	KALLOS	6900.	47.09	CWT	37.6
722564	COLEVER	FARA	40000.	7.93	CWT	5.0
722579	COLEVER	KLAS DICA	24200.	16.39	CWT	32.6
722619	COLEVER	SANDED TECH	1500.	1.45	LB	58.6
722736	COLEVER	BIOKALIKAN	40800.	49.67	CWT	32.2
722737	COLEVER	BIOKALIKAN	4500.	55.86	CWT	39.7
721782	COLEVER	SODCARFD	10000.	4.12	CWT	17.7
722662	COLEVER	BIOKALIKAN	11100.	47.15	CWT	28.6
722663	COLEVER	CYANOLUM	250.	56.45	CWT	56.1
722668	COLEVER	BIOKOLIKON	3300.	59.00	CWT	37.1
		BIOKALIKAN	1500.	59.00	CWT	42.9

TOTAL PLANT NET   325362.65
TOTAL TRANSFER COST   245961.22

TOTAL GROSS PROFIT   79401.43   AVE. G/P PERCENTAGE   24.4

V.P.:   Good. Colever orders are beginning to come in, and I see we didn't sacrifice profits to get the contracts.

Sec.:   Ever since they increased the printout speed to 2,400 characters per second I can't even follow this stuff.

V.P.:   I know, I know. Would you kindly check the book on my credenza. What's Colever's code?

Sec.:   Here it is. File "CCLL5."

V.P.:   Thanks. I'm going to merge Colever into our budget.

Sec.:   You're increasing our budget this late in the year?

V.P.:   To be quite honest, the Colever business is a windfall. It was unbudgeted last year. If we started recording these sales now we would skew our percentages badly.

Sec.:   Of course, and everyone would be thinking they had achieved budget when they hadn't.
               (V.P. types: "CCLL5" MERGE "CURRENT YEAR.' ")

	TODAY	YEAR END
YEAR'S BUDGET	15156251 MERGED	17312502
ACTUAL SALES (EX COLEVER)	20764064 PROJECTED	28446767
COLEVER SALES	25645 AS BUDGETED	2156251
TOTAL AT YEAR END		30603018

SALES COMPARED TO BUDGET FOR

8/23%

	THIS MONTH	THIS DAY, THIS MONTH	THIS DAY, THIS YEAR
PLANTS			
NEW YORK	41	72	117
LOS ANGELES	55	186	152
CHICAGO	11	37	99
TOTAL	41	141	137
AREAS			
EAST	38	129	88
MIDWEST	58	198	131
SOUTH	50	172	227
WEST	28	95	155

V.P.:   So, I add the Colever business to our budget, and we're again seeing a true picture of our operation.

Sec.:   Why isn't there a bigger change in the numbers?

V.P.:   The Colever sales are phased in. The new budget won't start impacting sales for several weeks.

Sec.:   So, where do we stand now that you've changed things so?

V.P.:   Look at the screen. I typed "8/23,%" and the revised percentages are right under the budget numbers.

Sec.:   That's less change than we see from day to day.

V.P.:   Quite true.

Sec.:   I see, you budgeted very little Colever business this month.

V.P.:   Since Colever is just now beginning to impact sales, its effect is minimal. If we didn't do this now, however, each day's Colever sales would distort the picture more.

Sec.:   We're still 137% over budget. That's very good!

V.P.:   No, that's not good. That's bad budgeting.

Sec.:   It's better than being under budget!

V.P.:   I guess so.—Don't I have a meeting on our new product this morning?

Sec.:   Yes, sir. Mr. Sims is outside now.

V.P.:   For a production manager Sims is remarkably prompt, but where is my marketing manager?

Sec.:   I'm sure Mr. Finley is here now. They both were anxious to talk to you.

V.P.:   Would you show them in?

(The secretary leaves. The V.P. blanks the screen. Mr. Vince Finley and Mr. Chuck Sims enter. They exchange pleasantries and sit down.)

V.P.: Chuck, would you review the status of this new product for Vince and me?

Prdt. Mgr.: Certainly, sir. We're very fortunate. This new product can be manufactured for about one-tenth our present product cost. We've run plant costs and production averages, and settled on numbers we have considerable confidence in.

V.P.: How are the plant plans progressing?

Prdt. Mgr.: Splendidly. I've had all the data loaded in the computer as you requested. It's available under "CALL PLANT."

V.P.: Thanks, Chuck. Now Vince, I know you've not even started your market penetration studies, but off the top of your head . . . ?

Mkt. Mgr.: I'll try. I understand this could be an 8,000,000 unit market. Let's figure we move 1,000,000 the first year, and increase that by about 75% each year thereafter.

V.P.: Let's put this together and see what we've got.

Mkt. Mgr.: My initial guess—one million year one, seventy-five percent increase yearly thereafter.

V.P.: Let's merge plants and markets and output quantities. Here goes. (Types: "CALL PLANT" USE 1000000,.75,10)

YEAR	MARKET AT 75% INCREASE	PRODUCTION*	PLANT COST ADJ.%
1	1000000	1000000	0
2	1750000	2000000	0
3	3062500	4000000	0
4	5359375	5000000	0
5	9378100	8000000	10
6	16413075	8000000	25
7	28722881	8000000	55
8	50265041	8000000	276
9	87963823	8000000	335
10	153936690	8000000	585

*PLANT COST 1256842

Mkt. Mgr.: Boy, I really blew that estimate!

Prdt. Mgr.: I wish you were right. I wouldn't mind increasing my plant by a factor of 6.

V.P.: Do your figures really show you can produce such a production jump? Going from 8 million to 154 million for only a six-fold plant cost increase?

Prdt. Mgr.: We designed this plant with a minimum capacity of 10 million.

V.P.: Yes, I notice you can go to sixteen million four with only 25 percent plant cost increase.

Prdt. Mgr.: Furthermore, there is some high-speed equipment we can't justify at the eight million per year level.

V.P.:   I'm glad you built its specs into your model, however, it's very useful knowing the outside parameters. I didn't even know we could gear one plant up to 154 million.

Mkt. Mgr.: Actually, I wasn't too far off, if you look at the five-year numbers.

V.P.:   I presume you're looking for full market saturation in five years.

Mkt. Mgr.: Exactly. I think Chuck set things up that way.

Prdt. Mgr.: As you know, Paul, my plant estimates are on a modular basis.

V.P.:   I know, Chuck, those numbers under "production" are your maximum outputs for each year.

Prdt. Mgr.: That's right. Production equipment and raw materials set those limits.

V.P.:   Well, although I'd like to see such growth, past experience tells us eight million is maximum.

Mkt. Mgr.: Furthermore, we can't attack the market faster.

V.P.:   In the past our increase introduction expenditure didn't justify faster penetration.

Prdt. Mgr.: You're saying that my plant production and output increase is about where you want it?

V.P.:   Yes, we really might as well gear sales to your production figures.

Mkt. Mgr.: With the stipulation that if this product's growth pattern is different we reconsider.

V.P.:   Of course.

Mkt. Mgr.: What now?

V.P.:   Looks like we'll have to reestimate.

Mkt. Mgr.: My market penetration number is too high. Try 60%.
          (V.P. types: 1000000,.6,5)

YEAR	MARKET AT 60% INCREASE	PRODUCTION	PLANT COST ADJ.%
1	1000000	1000000	0
2	1600000	2000000	0
3	2560000	4000000	0
4	4096000	5000000	0
5	6553600	8000000	0

-1000000,.65,5

YEAR	MARKET AT 65% INCREASE	PRODUCTION	PLANT COST ADJ.%
1	1000000	1000000	0
2	1650000	2000000	0
3	2722500	4000000	0
4	4492125	5000000	0
5	7412006	8000000	0

V.P.:   Sixty-five percent should do it.

Prdt. Mgr.: How certain are we of any of these numbers?

V.P.:   Not very. Nobody's going to call you on these estimates. We've just built the bare skeleton.

Mkt. Mgr.: It's up to us, Chuck, to put some meat on these bare bones.

V.P.:   We've just roughed out our targets. Now you two can detail it.

Mkt. Mgr.: If we decide we're conservative on our penetration numbers?

Prdt. Mgr.: We'll firm it up. We can always revise our plant size estimates to accommodate a firm number.

V.P.:   You'll be able to work together for the next several weeks. Put your results in the computer. Let's have another session two weeks from today.

           (The Production and Marketing Managers leave and the secretary enters.)

Sec.:   Mr. Johnson called. You'd think as president of this company we'd hear from him more often.

V.P.:   The only time he calls is when he has questions.

           (V.P. picks up telephone and dials, as the secretary leaves.)

V.P.:   Good morning, sir. Yes, the trip was fantastic. No, the office didn't miss a beat. I'm all caught up on the last two weeks. No, sir, it's not too early to review the month's business.

           (As he talks he holds the telephone with one hand and types with the other.) (V.P. types: MONTH'S, BILLS)

COMPUTER TYPES: AREAS, PLANTS OR STATES?

V. P.:   Yes, sir, I know you've been particularly interested in plant output recently.

           (V.P. types: PLANTS, $)

COMPUTER OUTPUTS:

N.Y.	180312	72
L.A.	927388	186
CHI	80960	37

V.P.:   Chicago is a bit low at $80,960, but Los Angeles is 86% over budget as of today. Sorry, sir. I know you don't like percentages.

           (V.P. types: PROJ,MO-END,$)

COMPUTER OUTPUTS:

	ACTUAL CURRENT	PROJECT TO MONTH'S END	MONTH'S BUDGET
N.Y.	180312	324561	450780
L.A.	927388	3030572	1656050
CHI	80960	264960	736000
TOT	1188661	3944364	3293206

V.P.:   New York is at $180,312, Los Angeles at $927,388, and Chicago at $80,906. Projected, the one really in trouble is Chicago at $264,960 by month-end. Stateswise, we're in very good shape.

          (V.P. types: MONTH'S BILLS)
COMPUTER OUTPUTS: AREAS, PLANTS OR STATES?
          (V.P. types: STATES)
COMPUTER OUTPUTS: ?
          (V.P. types: CAL)
COMPUTER TYPES: 876507

V.P.:	California has been very strong this month. In the neighborhood of $900,000.

          (V.P types: PROJEX)
COMPUTER TYPES: 1200000

V.P.:	I'd estimate we'll exceed our $1,100,000 budget by at least $100,000 this month.
	Yes, sir, we're pretty much on target everywhere. There's that weakness in Chicago, but I've got Woods on that already.
	Thank you. Have a nice California trip. Good-bye!
	(Secretary returns with coffee.)
V.P.:	Thank you. Has Mr. Rees completed his budgeting for next year?
	(As the V.P. looks at his mail, Miss Jensen telephones Mr. Rees.)
Sec.:	Good morning Mr. Rees, Mr. Stans will be able to see you now
	Yes, he'd like to discuss budgeting. Good-bye!
	(Turns to Mr. Stans.)
Sec.:	Mr. Rees will be here in a moment.
V.P.:	Thank you, send him right in.
	(Miss Jensen leaves, and Mr. Stans blanks the CRT screen. A moment later Mr. Rees enters.)
V.P.:	Good morning, Jerry. How's the budgeting business?
Contr.:	I'm all ready for you. Want to go on the tube and see what I've got?
V.P.:	Wait a minute, Jerry. I've been away two weeks, remember? I know I asked you for a more positive way to build budgets, but review things a little so I can get oriented.
Contr.:	Certainly Paul. You'll recall we questioned our present methods of budgeting from the bottom up. That is, the lowest echelon submits the expected sales for next year.
V.P.:	Oh yes. I was worried that a cautious salesman could underestimate, and be able to make his year's budget by June first.
Contr.:	Cautious or clever?
V.P.:	True, but is there a better way?
Contr.:	Not until computers. There's so much paper work involved we had to start at the bottom. Each man estimated his area and we built it up piece by piece.
V.P.:	Of course, we provided supervision. Each link in the chain attempted to pass on guidelines.

Contr.:	Of course, but what if we recommended a ten percent increase and when the budget was assembled we didn't like the result?
V.P.:	Don't remind me. We tried that once, and the screams of anguish were horrendous.
Contr.:	We never did succeed. Nobody "had any more time" or they were away on trips.
V.P.:	Spare me the details. What have you got now?
Contr.:	Something I call "Top-Down Budgeting." We've built a program into the computer that models our complete product line. This consists of 107 products from three plants, distributed to four major areas.
V.P.:	I hope you're not asking me to make decisions on all 107 product lines.
Contr.:	No, no, let me explain, then I'll give you a demonstration.
V.P.:	You have the floor.
Contr.:	Top-down budgeting works like this. You provide the computer with what you feel is a desirable growth (or no-growth) percentage for each area next year. The computer applies this to all plants and areas and outputs a result. You review this and determine if the answers are reasonable. You might go through three, four or five such guesses until you're satisfied with the results. Once you're satisfied, you call in the sales and marketing managers.
V.P.:	I'd better, unless I want a revolt on my hands.
Contr.:	Any changes they want to make we make right at the console. Rerun the program, and you've got a new budget, but this time it includes their thinking!
V.P.:	You mean I cycle through this budget until I'm satisfied? Then I cycle through while consulting with sales and marketing until we're all satisfied?
Contr.:	Precisely.
V.P.:	Let's get a look at this budget.
Contr.:	Just call "BUDGET."
	(V.P. types: BUDGET)

	LOS ANGELES		CHICAGO		TOTAL	
	NET S.	GROSS P.	NET S.	GROSS P.	NET S.	GROSS P.
NEW YORK	.000	.000	.000	.000	1607.090	634.365
EAST	972.612	234.876	577.750	131.884	1550.362	366.160
MIDWEST	3014.638	860.583	900.680	276.570	3915.318	1137.154
SOUTH	1329.206	313.161	120.515	28.133	1449.721	341.294
WEST	3018.044	853.870	102.085	21.172	3120.129	875.042
TOTAL	8334.50	2262.49	1701.03	457.76	11642.62	3354.61

NET SALES,　YEAR 0 IN $0000s

V.P.:	Year zero?
Contr.:	We use the current year as zero. Next year is year 1, and so forth.
V.P.:	I recognize this year's budget. How do I project it for five years at 5.0% a year?
Contr.:	Simply ask for "PROJECT BUDGET," 1.
V.P.:	(making notes) What does "1" mean?
Contr.:	This program is built on five levels. Level 1 means you are providing only five growth figures, a growth figure for each year.
V.P.:	What other options do I have?
Contr.:	Level 2 is fifteen percentages, one for each of three plants for five years. Level 3 is thirty percentages, one for each area and New York for five years. Finally, we can crank in five times the 107 products, or 535 input percentages.
V.P.:	Who inputs that data?
Contr.:	After you have decided on the broad growth levels, the computer outputs the details. These are then distributed to the appropriate salespersons. They review this information, and modify it to reflect their own best judgment.
V.P.:	I see, instead of asking, "How much are you going to sell this year?"
Contr.:	Which rather puts us in their hands.
V.P.:	We're going to say: "Can you hit these targets next year?"
Contr.:	Right, and we're going to provide them with product-by-product targets!
V.P.:	Very neat. Now, how do I produce a five-year budget, growing at five percent a year?
Contr.:	Simply type the program name "PROJECT BUDGET" when the computer asks for "LEVEL" type "1."
V.P.:	Done. Now it has typed "DETAILS."
Contr.:	Type "NO" and five 5s separated by commas.
V.P.:	"NO" means we don't want details for this run, and fives are the growth rate for five years?
Contr.:	Correct.

	LOS ANGELES		CHICAGO		TOTAL	
	NET S.	GROSS P.	NET S.	GROSS P.	NET S.	GROSS P.
NEW YORK	.000	.000	.000	.000	1607.090	634.365
EAST	972.612	234.876	577.750	131.884	1550.362	366.160
MIDWEST	3014.638	860.583	900.680	276.570	3915.318	1137.154
SOUTH	1329.206	313.161	120.515	28.133	1449.721	341.294
WEST	3318.044	853.870	102.085	21.172	3120.129	875.042
TOTAL, YR0	8334.50	2262.49	1701.03	457.76	11642.62	3354.61
NEW YORK	.000	.000	.000	.000	1687.444	666.083
EAST	1021.243	246.620	606.637	138.478	1627.883	335.098
MIDWEST	3165.370	903.620	945.714	290.399	4111.084	1194.011
SOUTH	1395.666	328.819	126.541	29.540	1522.207	358.359
WEST	3168.946	896.563	107.189	22.231	3276.135	918.795
TOTAL, YR1	8751.22	2375.61	1786.08	480.65	12224.75	3522.35

V.P.:   We only got one year!

Contr.:   Hit the "ROLL" button. The rest will come up.

            (V.P. strikes "ROLL" button, and the remainder of the output rolls up on the screen. The first year disappears off the top.)

| | LOS ANGELES | | CHICAGO | | TOTAL | |
	NET S.	GROSS P.	NET S.	GROSS P.	NET S.	GROSS P.
NEW YORK	.000	.000	.000	.000	1771.817	699.387
EAST	1072.305	258.951	636.969	145.402	1709.274	404.353
MIDWEST	3323.638	948.793	993.000	304.919	4316.638	1253.712
SOUTH	1465.450	345.260	132.868	31.017	1598.317	376.277
WEST	3327.394	941.392	112.549	23.343	3439.942	964.734
TOTAL, YR2	9188.79	2494.40	1875.39	504.68	12835.99	3698.46
NEW YORK	.000	.000	.000	.000	1860.408	734.357
EAST	1125.920	271.898	668.818	152.672	1794.738	424.570
MIDWEST	3489.820	996.233	1042.650	320.165	4532.470	1316.397
SOUTH	1538.722	362.523	139.511	32.567	1678.233	395.091
WEST	3493.763	988.461	118.176	24.510	3611.939	1012.971
TOTAL, YR3	9643.23	2619.11	1969.15	529.91	13477.79	3883.39
NEW YORK	.000	.000	.000	.000	1953.428	771.075
EAST	1182.216	285.493	702.259	160.306	1884.475	445.799
MIDWEST	3664.311	1046.044	1094.782	336.173	4759.093	1382.217
SOUTH	1615.658	380.649	146.487	34.196	1762.145	414.845
WEST	3668.451	1037.884	124.085	25.735	3792.536	1063.620
TOTAL, YR4	10130.64	2750.07	2067.61	556.41	14151.68	4077.56
NEW YORK	.000	.000	.000	.000	2051.099	809.628
EAST	1241.327	299.768	737.372	168.321	1978.698	468.089
MIDWEST	3847.527	1098.346	1149.521	352.982	4997.043	1451.328
SOUTH	1696.441	399.682	153.811	35.906	1850.252	435.587
WEST	3851.874	1089.779	130.289	27.022	3982.163	1116.801
TOTAL, YR5	10637.17	2887.57	2170.99	584.23	14859.26	4281.43

V.P.:   Nice! You know, Jerry, simply multiplying the gross numbers by 5% doesn't really budget anything.

Contr.:   There's lots more to this program than multiplying totals by 5%, Paul. Although you are looking at totals, every single product has also been projected on a 5% basis.

V.P.:   Of course, I'm only interested in totals but eventually we'll need those details.

Contr.:   Correct: You make your adjustments at this level. When we need details we'll simply instruct the computer to type them out.

V.P.:   Let's try this again. Can we project at any level we want?

Contr.:   Of course, try again.

V.P.:   Let's be bold. Let's grow at 10, 20, 30, 40 and 50% for the next five years!

            (V.P. types: PROJECT BUDGET.)

COMPUTER TYPES: LEVEL

            (V.P. types: 1)

COMPUTER TYPES: DETAILS

            (V.P. types: Yes, 10, 20, 30, 40, 50)
Contr.:   Why the "YES" requesting details at this time?
V.P.:   Two reasons: First, how long does it take, second, it's such an ambitious project, I just know there's something I'm going to want to look at.
Contr.:   O.K. After the summary comes up, change the name of the detail file to something else.
V.P.:   Why is that?
Contr.:   Each time the program is run with this option it overwrites any detail file present. By changing the name you effectively save the detail file you have just produced.
V.P.:   Yes, and later I'll have it output from the high-speed printer and we can look at it product by product.
Contr.:   Very good, Let's call it "PROJ 50."
            (The CRT starts to output.)
V.P.:   Here comes the summary. Let's see [glancing at his watch] that took about a minute to process.
Contr.:   The time it takes is, of course, dependent on how many others are using this service at this moment.
V.P.:   Yes, and ten o'clock is a pretty busy time.
Contr.:   Busy and therefore expensive. Once this program is firmed up we should plan this type of "in-the-loop" activity on off hours if possible.
V.P.:   What's the cost differential?
Contr.:   A good 50%. Well, there's two years of your output!

	NET S.	GROSS P.	NET S.	GROSS P.	NET S.	GROSS P.
NEW YORK	.000	.000	.000	.000	2736.852	1273.468
EAST	1727.605	560.928	753.295	167.601	2480.899	728.529
MIDWEST	2475.530	718.752	761.862	275.625	3237.392	994.377
SOUTH	1615.887	280.551	443.937	161.866	2059.824	442.477
WEST	3177.641	905.426	322.536	103.761	3500.177	1009.787
TOTAL, YR0	8996.66	2465.66	2281.63	708.85	14015.14	4387.98
NEW YORK	.000	.000	.000	.000	3010.537	1334.815
EAST	1900.365	617.020	828.624	184.361	2728.989	801.381
MIDWEST	2723.083	790.627	838.049	303.188	3561.132	1093.815
SOUTH	1777.476	308.606	488.330	178.052	2265.806	486.658
WEST	3495.406	995.969	354.789	114.137	3850.195	1110.106
TOTAL, YR1	9896.33	2712.22	2509.79	779.74	15416.66	4826.77
NEW YORK	.000	.000	.000	.000	3612.645	1601.778
EAST	2280.438	740.425	994.349	221.233	3274.787	961.658
MIDWEST	3267.700	948.752	1005.658	363.825	4273.358	1312.577
SOUTH	2132.971	370.327	585.996	213.663	2718.967	583.990
WEST	4194.487	1195.163	425.747	136.964	4620.234	1332.127
TOTAL, YR2	1875.59	3254.67	3011.75	935.69	18499.99	5792.13

(V.P. strikes the "ROLL" button.)

	NET S.	GROSS P.	NET S.	GROSS P.	NET S.	GROSS P.
NEW YORK	.000	.000	.000	.000	4696.438	2082.311
EAST	2964.569	962.552	1292.653	287.603	4257.223	1250.155
MIDWEST	4248.009	1233.378	1307.356	472.973	5555.365	1706.351
SOUTH	2772.862	481.425	761.795	277.761	3534.657	759.187
WEST	5452.833	1553.711	553.472	178.054	6006.304	1731.765
TOTAL, YR3	15438.27	4231.07	3915.28	1216.39	24049.99	7529.77
NEW YORK	.000	.000	.000	.000	6575.013	2915.236
EAST	4150.397	1347.573	1809.715	402.644	5960.112	1750.217
MIDWEST	5947.213	1726.729	1830.298	662.162	7777.512	2388.891
SOUTH	3882.007	673.996	1066.513	388.866	4948.520	1062.862
WEST	7633.966	2175.196	774.860	249.275	8408.826	2424.471
TOTAL, YR4	21613.58	5923.49	5481.39	1702.95	33669.98	10541.68
NEW YORK	.000	.000	.000	.000	9862.520	4372.853
EAST	6225.596	2021.359	2714.572	603.967	8940.168	2625.325
MIDWEST	8920.820	2590.094	2745.448	993.242	11666.267	3583.336
SOUTH	5823.010	1010.993	1599.770	583.299	7422.780	1594.292
WEST	11450.948	3262.794	1162.290	373.913	12613.239	3636.707
TOTAL, YR5	32420.37	8885.24	8222.08	2554.42	50504.97	15012.513

Contr.:   Why don't you change the name now?
            (V.P. types: Change "DETAIL" to "PROJ50")
Contr.:   Those later years look like sheer fantasy.
V.P.:   True, but that first year at 10% looks very possible. What if we
            just use 10% as our growth rate?
            (V.P. types: PROJECT 1.)
Computer types: LEVEL?
            (V.P. types: 1)
Computer types: DETAILS?
            (V.P. types: Yes, 10,10,10,10,10)
Contr.:   You've asked for details again.
V.P.:   Yes. I'm always sure I'll find something I want to study more
            closely.
Contr.:   For the sake of economy, may I suggest you look at the results?
            Then if you are still interested it's cheaper to rerun.
V.P.:   That's assuming I'll only be interested in details of about every
            third guess I make.
Contr.:   That's a pretty fair guess. Anyway it's easier to make a note of
            the percentages you want and we'll rerun the program and print
            it out—all on the high-speed printer, on off hours, of course.
V.P.:   Spoken like a true controller!
Contr.:   I guess we're both true to type!
V.P.:   I'll ignore that. Here comes my 10% output now.
            (CRT begins to output)

	NET S.	GROSS P.	NET S.	GROSS P.	NET S.	GROSS P.
NEW YORK	.000	.000	.000	.000	2736.852	1213.463
EAST	1727.605	560.928	753.295	167.601	2480.899	728.527
MIDWEST	2475.530	718.752	761.862	275.625	3237.392	994.377
SOUTH	1615.887	280.551	443.937	161.866	2059.824	442.417
WEST	3177.641	905.428	322.530	103.761	3500.177	1009.187
TOTAL, YR0	8996.60	2465.66	2281.63	708.85	14015.14	4387.98
NEW YORK	.000	.000	.000	.000	3010.537	1334.815
EAST	1900.365	617.020	828.624	184.361	2728.989	801.381
MIDWEST	2723.083	790.627	838.049	303.188	3561.132	1093.815
SOUTH	1777.476	308.606	488.330	178.052	2265.805	483.655
WEST	3495.406	995.969	354.789	114.137	3850.195	1110.105
TOTAL, YR1	9896.33	2712.22	2509.79	779.74	15418.68	4826.77
NEW YORK	.000	.000	.000	.000	3311.591	1468.296
EAST	2090.402	678.722	911.488	202.797	3001.888	881.520
MIDWEST	2995.391	869.690	921.854	333.506	3917.245	1203.196
SOUTH	1955.223	339.467	537.163	195.857	2492.388	535.324
WEST	3844.946	1095.566	390.268	125.551	4235.214	1221.116
TOTAL, YR2	10885.96	2983.44	2760.77	857.71	16958.32	5309.45
NEW YORK	.000	.000	.000	.000	3642.750	1615.126
EAST	2299.442	746.595	1002.635	223.077	3302.077	969.672
MIDWEST	3294.930	956.659	1014.039	366.857	4308.969	1323.516
SOUTH	2150.745	373.413	590.880	215.443	2741.625	583.850
WEST	4229.441	1205.122	429.295	138.106	4658.736	1343.228
TOTAL, YR3	11974.56	3281.79	3036.85	943.48	18654.16	5840.40
NEW YORK	.000	.000	.000	.000	4007.025	1775.638
EAST	2529.386	821.254	1102.898	245.384	3632.284	1065.639
MIDWEST	3624.423	1052.325	1115.443	403.543	4739.866	1455.857
SOUTH	2365.820	410.755	649.968	236.987	3015.788	647.742
WEST	4652.385	1325.634	472.225	151.916	5124.609	1477.551
TOTAL, YR4	13172.01	3609.97	3340.53	1037.83	20519.57	6424.44

Contr.: Do you realize how much work you've done in the last five minutes?

V.P.: Sure, I've typed three strings of numbers and three sets of one-word instructions. About thirty seconds, I guess.

Contr.: At a conservative estimate, you've had the computer do about 25,000 calculations.

V.P.: Oh, boy, that's going to cost me!

Contr.: About $4.75.

V.P.: That's reasonable.

Contr.: Reasonable! Even under the best of conditions it would take a man two days to do one set of those calculations, not to mention checking and assembling them into meaningful output!

V.P.: I gather you're telling me I just did two days' work.

Contr.: I'm telling you that you just got three looks at possible company futures that you wouldn't have gotten without time sharing.

V.P.:	You're right. I wouldn't have allocated six man-days to those three outputs.
Contr.:	In short, you've just been given several perspectives on this business you wouldn't normally have.
V.P.:	Right, and I'll need several more now that this tool is available.
Contr.:	At a cost of $5.00 per shot I guess the corporation can afford it!
V.P.:	O.K. you've given me a new toy. Now how do I impact the rest of the corporation with it?
Contr.:	By leading them, not following them.
V.P.:	I'm sure it would say something like that in my V.P. manual, if I had one.
Contr.:	Remember, this is called top-down budgeting. By selecting a budget output, let's say the 10% one, you have set the corporate goals.
V.P.:	But I don't expect every one of our products to increase yearly by 10%.
Contr.:	Exactly, that's when we start down. To check with those on the spot whether individual product goals are possible.
V.P.:	I check with whom?
Contr.:	There are four levels. Level one, we have agreed, is the 10% output established by you. Level two is the sales and plant managers. Level three are the area managers, and level four are the salesmen.
V.P. (indignantly):	I talk to the salesmen!
Contr.:	No, no. You confer with level two. They in turn interact with levels three and four.
V.P.:	How?
Contr.:	You confront the sales and plant managers with the 10% summary, and ask, "Can we achieve these goals?"
V.P.:	Or can we better them?
Contr.:	Of course. Then they offer changes, corrections, modifications and adjustments based on their knowledge of plant capacity and sales potential.
V.P.:	What about all the individual product idiosyncrasies?
Contr.:	We'll get to them. They are handled at level four.
V.P.:	I hope so.
Contr.:	After you have agreed on all changes, the projection is recycled.
V.P.:	How's that?
Contr.:	Specifically, we simply change the numbers in the projection. The computer then converts these changed numbers to percents. It considers this as the percentage input for further projections.
V.P.:	If I input "YES, 10,10,10,10,10," I'll get what we now have up on the screen.
Contr.:	Correct. You can now change those numbers based on your staff's advice.

V.P.:   Like this.
            (V.P. types and changes the year one total from 9896.3 to 9446.4.)

Contr.:   Good, now type PCT.
            (V.P. types: PCT.)

Computer types: 5,10,10,10,10

Contr.:   Now you can rerun the program with these percentages, and get
            your revised projection.

V.P.:   So I cycle this way based on the revisions I receive from the sales,
            marketing and plant managers.

Contr.:   Naturally, you will be querying them on their reasons for any
            changes.

V.P.:   Yes, and my interaction with them should give them some insight
            into their interaction at lower levels.

Contr.:   Exactly. Once the goals have been reviewed and modified, a new
            projection is output. You set the first goal at level one. The goals
            established after your consultation are level two.

V.P.:   This revised projection is now printed out, I gather, and supplied
            to those at level three.

Contr.:   Yes, to the plant managers, to confirm they can supply what is
            required, and to the area managers to use as their goals.

V.P.:   They then can request changes and adjustments if they note any
            discrepancies.

Contr.:   Yes, and remember, these changes, if valid, are still adjustable
            quickly through the program.

V.P.:   What about history?

Contr.:   We have the last five years' sales set up in the same format.
            Everyone should have copies.

V.P.:   I can see this conferring and recycling taking place fairly quickly
            After all, we're still only dealing with that single page of printout.

Contr.:   Yes, and while you're doing the thinking the computer is doing
            all the clerical work.

V.P.:   Also, there shouldn't be these one- or two-day delays while
            someone reorganizes the numbers.

Contr.:   I've three printouts showing just which level is concerned with
            what data. Here they are labeled.
            Level 1—V.P.
            Level 2—V.P. with sales and plant managers
            Level 3—Area and plant managers
            [See Figures 22, 23 and 24]

V.P.:   So we get through these three levels. Now what?

Contr.:   Here is where we lead rather than follow. The computer now
            prints our product detail. This is output for each area and plant.

V.P.:   For this year and five years out? Is this the computer output
            level 4 worksheet? [Figure 25]

Contr.:   Exactly, as per the consensus of levels one to three.

V.P.:   Each salesman then gets this detail for his area.

Contr.:   The salesman is requested to agree or disagree with the numbers provided.

V.P.:   Some of those numbers are going to look pretty silly. What about discontinued items for next year?

Contr.:   The salesman would not have included them in his conventional bottom-to-top budgeting. He merely deletes them from this budgeting.

V.P.:   He'll have to increase sales elsewhere to accommodate that loss.

Contr.:   This is exactly what he would have done, if he had been initiating the budgeting.

V.P.:   So what do we do with all the changes the salesman might make?

Contr.:   The output to the salesman looks like this:

	BUDGET YR. LBS.	1973 $	1974 $	1975 $	1976 $	1977 $
ROXIDE	11745.	12919.	14211.	15633.	17196.	18915.
OXIDE	14960.	16456.	18102.	19912.	21903.	24093.
SULFLKE	34960.	39456.	42302.	46532.	51185.	56303.
SULEDSOLD	28600.	31460.	34606.	38607.	41873.	46061
ONTIUM CARB	84000.	92400.	101640.	111804.	122984.	135283.
63	172440.	189684.	208652.	229512.	252469.	277716.
90	24750.	27225.	29947.	32942.	36236.	39860.

Contr.:   He then overwrites exactly what changes he requires.

V.P.:   Now we're asking him to agree or disagree with our numbers.

Contr.:   Furthermore, these changes are monitored by his superior.

V.P.:   His superior will already have participated in this so he'll have the benefit of an overall view.

Contr.:   Note that we don't waste the salesman's time by asking him to scramble around finding last year's numbers.

V.P.:   Yes, I note all levels can spend their time thinking, not paper-shuffling.

Contr.:   The manual labor comes at the end, and at the clerical level. Once all the sales estimates are assembled, they are keypunched in and recycled.

V.P.:   What if the results show a 3% increase instead of the 10% we started out with?

Contr.:   Very doubtful. Remember, all levels were making best estimates. The salesman's task is to juggle his product line. Some up, some down, so that the goals set will be met.

V.P.:   Just what he does anyway, but this time with a definite goal.

Contr.:   Rather than going through the same juggling act with no goal in mind, and letting the results be a surprise.

BUDGET PROJECTION, LEVEL 1

BUDGET PROJECTION

	PLANT #1		PLANT #2		TOTAL	
	NET S.	GROSS P.	NET S.	GROSS P.	NET S.	GROSS P.
PLANT #3	.000	.000	.000	.000	2739.584	1218.932
AREA 1	1727.605	560.928	753.295	167.601	2480.899	728.529
AREA 2	2475.530	718.752	761.862	275.625	3237.392	994.377
AREA 3	1615.887	280.551	443.937	161.866	2059.824	442.417
AREA 4	3177.641	905.426	322.536	103.761	3500.177	1009.187
1972 TOTAL	8996.66	2465.66	2281.63	708.85	14017.88	4393.44
PLANT #3	.000	.000	.000	.000	3013.542	1340.825
AREA 1	1900.365	617.020	828.624	184.361	2728.989	801.381
AREA 2	2723.083	790.627	838.049	303.188	3561.132	1093.815
AREA 3	1777.476	308.606	488.330	178.052	2265.806	486.658
AREA 4	3495.406	995.969	354.789	114.137	3850.195	1110.106
1973 TOTAL	9896.33	2712.22	2509.79	779.74	15419.66	4832.79
PLANT #3	.000	.000	.000	.000	3314.897	1474.908
AREA 1	2090.402	678.722	911.486	202.797	3001.888	881.520
AREA 2	2995.391	869.690	921.854	333.506	3917.245	1203.196
AREA 3	1955.223	339.467	537.163	195.857	2492.386	535.324
AREA 4	3844.946	1095.566	390.268	125.551	4235.214	1221.116
1974 TOTAL	10885.96	2983.44	2760.77	857.71	16961.63	5316.06
PLANT #3	.000	.000	.000	.000	3646.386	1622.398
AREA 1	2299.442	746.595	1002.635	223.077	3302.077	969.672
AREA 2	3294.930	956.659	1014.039	366.857	4308.969	1323.516
AREA 3	2150.745	373.413	590.880	215.443	2741.625	588.856
AREA 4	4229.441	1205.122	429.295	138.106	4658.736	1343.228
1975 TOTAL	11974.56	3281.79	3036.85	943.48	18657.79	5847.67
PLANT #3	.000	.000	.000	.000	4011.025	1784.638
AREA 1	2529.386	821.254	1102.898	245.384	3632.284	1066.639
AREA 2	3624.423	1052.325	1115.443	403.543	4739.866	1455.867
AREA 3	2365.820	410.755	649.968	236.987	3015.788	657.742
AREA 4	4652.385	1325.634	472.225	151.916	5124.609	1477.551
1976 TOTAL	13172.01	3609.97	3340.53	1037.83	20523.57	6432.44
PLANT #3	.000	.000	.000	.000	4412.127	1963.102
AREA 1	2782.324	903.380	1213.188	269.923	3995.513	1173.303
AREA 2	3986.866	1157.557	1226.987	443.897	5213.853	1601.454
AREA 3	2602.402	451.830	714.964	260.686	3317.366	712.516
AREA 4	5117.623	1458.198	519.447	167.108	5637.070	1625.306
1977 TOTAL	14489.22	3970.96	3674.59	1141.61	22575.93	7075.68

FIGURE 22   LEVEL 1, BUDGET PROJECTION

GETTING TOP VALUE FROM THE USER-INTERACTIVE TIME-SHARING M.I.S.

139

BUDGET PROJECTION, LEVEL 2

BUDGET PROJECTION

	PLANT #1		PLANT #2		TOTAL	
	NET S.	GROSS P.	NET S.	GROSS P.	NET S.	GROSS P.
PLANT #3	.000	.000	.000	.000	2739.584	1218.932
AREA 1	1727.605	560.928	753.295	167.601	2480.899	728.529
AREA 2	2475.530	718.752	761.862	275.625	3237.392	994.377
AREA 3	1615.887	280.551	443.937	161.866	2059.824	442.417
AREA 4	3177.641	905.426	322.536	103.761	3500.177	1009.187
1972 TOTAL	8996.66	2465.66	2281.63	708.85	14017.88	4393.44
PLANT #3	.000	.000	.000	.000	3013.542	1340.825
AREA 1	1900.365	617.020	828.624	184.361	2728.989	801.38
AREA 2	2723.083	790.627	838.049	303.188	3561.132	1093.815
AREA 3	1777.476	308.606	488.330	178.052	2265.806	486.658
AREA 4	3495.406	995.969	354.789	114.137	3850.195	1110.106
1973 TOTAL	9896.33	2712.22	2509.79	779.74	15419.66	4832.79
PLANT #3	.000	.000	.000	.000	3314.987	1474.908
AREA 1	2090.402	678.722	911.486	202.797	3001.888	881.520
AREA 2	2995.391	869.690	921.854	333.506	3917.245	1203.196
AREA 3	1955.223	339.467	537.163	195.857	2492.386	535.324
AREA 4	3844.946	1095.566	390.268	125.551	4235.214	1221.116
1974 TOTAL	10885.96	2983.44	2760.77	857.71	16961.63	5316.06
PLANT #3	.000	.000	.000	.000	3646.386	1622.398
AREA 1	2299.442	746.595	1002.635	223.077	3302.077	969.672
AREA 2	3294.930	956.659	1014.039	366.857	4308.969	1323.516
AREA 3	2150.745	373.413	590.880	215.443	2741.625	588.856
AREA 4	4229.441	1205.122	429.295	138.106	4658.736	1343.228
1975 TOTAL	11974.56	3281.79	3036.85	943.48	18657.79	5847.67
PLANT #3	.000	.000	.000	.000	4011.025	1784.638
AREA 1	2529.386	821.254	1102.898	245.384	3632.284	1066.639
AREA 2	3624.423	1052.325	1115.443	403.543	4739.866	1455.867
AREA 3	2365.385	410.755	649.968	236.987	3015.788	647.742
AREA 4	4652.385	1325.634	472.225	151.916	5124.609	1477.551
1976 TOTAL	13172.01	3609.97	3340.53	1037.83	20523.57	6432.44
PLANT #3	.000	.000	.000	.000	4412.127	1963.102
AREA 1	2782.324	903.380	1213.188	269.923	3995.513	1173.303
AREA 2	3986.866	1157.557	1226.987	443.897	5213.853	1601.454
AREA 3	2602.402	451.830	714.964	260.686	3317.366	712.516
AREA 4	5117.623	1458.198	519.447	167.108	5637.070	1625.306
1977 TOTAL	14489.22	3970.96	3674.59	1141.61	22575.93	7075.68

FIGURE 23   LEVEL 2, BUDGET PROJECTION

BUDGET PROJECTION, LEVEL 3

BUDGET PROJECTION

	PLANT #1		PLANT #2		TOTAL	
	NET S.	GROSS P.	NET S.	GROSS P.	NET S.	GROSS P.
PLANT #3	.000	.000	.000	.000	2739.584	1218.932
AREA 1	1727.605	560.928	753.295	167.601	2480.899	728.529
AREA 2	2475.530	718.752	761.862	275.625	3237.392	994.377
AREA 3	1615.887	280.551	443.937	161.866	2059.824	442.417
AREA 4	3177.641	905.426	322.536	103.761	3500.177	1009.187
1972 TOTAL	8996.66	2465.66	2281.63	708.85	14017.88	4393.44
PLANT #3	.000	.000	.000	.000	3013.542	1340.825
AREA 1	1900.365	617.020	828.624	184.361	2728.989	801.381
AREA 2	2723.083	790.627	838.049	303.188	3561.132	1093.815
AREA 3	1777.476	308.606	488.330	178.052	2265.806	486.658
AREA 4	3495.406	995.969	354.789	114.137	3850.195	1110.106
1973 TOTAL	9896.33	2712.22	2509.79	779.74	15419.66	4832.79
PLANT #3	.000	.000	.000	.000	3314.897	1474.908
AREA 1	2090.402	678.722	911.486	202.797	3001.888	881.520
AREA 2	2995.391	869.690	921.854	333.506	3917.245	1203.196
AREA 3	1955.223	339.467	537.163	195.857	2492.386	535.324
AREA 4	3844.946	1095.566	390.268	125.551	4235.214	1221.116
1974 TOTAL	10885.96	2983.44	2760.77	857.71	16961.63	5316.06
PLANT #3	.000	.000	.000	.000	3646.386	1622.398
AREA 1	2299.442	746.595	1002.635	223.077	3302.077	969.672
AREA 2	3294.930	956.659	1014.039	366.857	4308.969	1323.516
AREA 3	2150.745	373.413	590.880	215.443	2741.625	588.856
AREA 4	4229.441	1205.122	429.295	138.106	4658.736	1343.228
1975 TOTAL	11974.56	3281.79	3036.85	943.48	18657.79	5847.67
PLANT #3	.000	.000	.000	.000	4011.025	1784.638
AREA 1	2529.386	821.254	1102.898	245.384	3632.284	1066.639
AREA 2	3624.423	1052.325	1115.443	403.543	4739.866	1455.867
AREA 3	2365.820	410.755	649.968	236.987	3015.788	647.742
AREA 4	4652.385	1325.634	472.225	151.916	5124.609	1477.551
1976 TOTAL	13172.01	3609.97	3340.53	1037.83	20523.57	6432.44
PLANT #3	.000	.000	.000	.000	4412.127	1963.102
AREA 1	2782.324	903.380	1213.188	269.923	3995.513	1173.303
AREA 2	3986.866	1157.557	1226.987	443.897	5213.853	1601.454
AREA 3	2602.402	451.830	714.964	260.686	3317.366	712.516
AREA 4	5117.623	1458.198	519.447	167.108	5637.070	1625.306
1977 TOTAL	1,4489.22	3970.96	3674.59	1141.61	22575.93	7075.68

FIGURE 24   LEVEL 3, BUDGET PROJECTION

SUMMARY BY N/S

PRODUCTS	BUDGET YR. LBS.	1973 $	1974 $	1975 $	1976 $	1977 $
ROXIDE	11745.	12919.	14211.	15633.	17196.	18915.
OXIDE	14960.	16456.	18102.	19912.	21903.	24093.
SULFLKE	34960.	38456.	42302.	46532.	51185.	56303.
SULEDSOLD	28600.	31460.	34606.	38067.	41873.	46061.
ONTIUM CARB	84000.	92400.	101640.	111804.	122984.	135283.
63	172440.	189684.	208652.	229512.	252469.	277716.
90	24750.	27225.	29947.	32942.	36236.	39860.
NACID	27008.	29709.	32679.	35947.	39542.	43496.
BORATE	4979.	5476.	6024.	6627.	7289.	8018.
2 50	204001.	224401.	246841.	271525.	298678.	328546.
PEROXIDE	7000.	7700.	8470.	9317.	10249.	11273.
RSULPHATE	6000.	6600.	7260.	7986.	8785.	9663.
ACETIC ACID	4000.	4400.	4840.	5324.	5856.	6442.
XERSULPHATE	24216.	26638.	29302.	32232.	35455.	39001.
XPOLYSULFIDE	11832.	13015.	14317.	15748.	17323.	19056.
LID	12642.	13906.	15297.	16827.	18509.	20360.
SSH	5151.	5666.	6233.	6856.	7542.	8296.
PROD	8415.	9256.	10182.	11200.	12320.	13552.
KTU	8668.	9557.	10512.	11564.	12720.	13992.
OMSED	2200.	2420.	2662.	2928.	3221.	3543.
S ACID	89318.	98250.	108075.	118882.	130770.	143848.
PLT	196512.	216163.	237780.	261557.	287713.	316485.
PST	51612.	56773.	62451.	68696.	75565.	83122.
PSART	390000.	429000.	471900.	519090.	570999.	628099.
TLL	46375.	51013.	56114.	61725.	67898.	74688.
TLS	25456.	28002.	30802.	33882.	37270.	40997.
PARN	49519.	54471.	59918.	65909.	72500.	79750.
XSUL ANHY	12546.	13801.	15181.	16699.	18369.	20205.
AXASH	44176.	48594.	53453.	58798.	64678.	71146.
QUI	8800.	9680.	10648.	11713.	12884.	14172.
MTV	20750.	22825.	25107.	27618.	30380.	33418.
YLOCHLO	33165.	36481.	40130.	44143.	48557.	53413.
HYL CAR	16000.	17600.	19360.	21296.	23426.	25768.
STF	5250.	5775.	6352.	6988.	7687.	8455.
140	5896.	61486.	67634.	74398.	81837.	90021.
AA	20506.	22557.	24813.	27294.	30024.	33026.
BOT	9056.	9962.	10958.	12054.	13259.	14585.
ONSM	82124.	90337.	99371.	109308.	120239.	132263.
ONL35	10608.	11669.	12836.	14119.	15531.	17084.
MON	7177.	7895.	8685.	9553.	10509.	11559.
YLNALCOHOL	404800.	44528.	48981.	53879.	59267.	65193.
H	142800.	157080.	172788.	190067.	209073.	229981.

END OF AREA 1   BUDGET SUMMARY

STOP

FIGURE 25   SALES BUDGET WORKSHEET

V.P.:	Yes, and then defending that with great zeal. You never know whether he is always right the first time, or merely hates to rebudget.
Contr.:	The latter, I'm afraid.
V.P.:	Jerry, this looks very interesting. Now tell me what's wrong with it.
Contr.:	I'm afraid it has a major flaw.
V.P.:	Now he tells me. What is it?
Contr.:	It forces people to think!
V.P.:	And worse still, to think systematically!
Contr.:	With this serious disadvantage it can only start at the top. That's why I hope you will undertake this effort.
V.P.:	It is worth a try. We'll go with it. I'm tired of having the tail wag the dog.
Contr.:	Any further questions?
V.P.:	Yes, why wasn't this done before?
Contr.:	We never had an interactive computer time-sharing system before!

(END)

SUMMARY

There is only one valid epilog to this play: The user does the thinking, the computer does the work.

8

HOW TO DESIGN YOUR OWN
TIME-SHARING INFORMATION SYSTEMS

Time sharing offers such specific answers to a manager's problems that it is difficult to describe its benefits in generalities. When a chapter on information systems was considered, the question arose, "Is it pertinent in a book on time sharing?" The answer is "Yes" when the chapter's emphasis is on "building" rather than "using."

Time sharing, M.I.S. and computers are all new tools. Those who have started to employ them successfully must resist the temptation to exhort. Thus, this chapter will concentrate on describing how time sharing may be used. The value, the new capabilities and the expanded insights provided can only be evaluated by the user who can follow the examples, not as ends in themselves, but as guideposts to applying time sharing to his own specific situation.

Time sharing opens up a whole new dimension in computer/user interaction. This is impossible in the conventional in-house EDP environment. Once the third generation of computers offered user/computer interaction, the generation of the user arrived. The EDP establishment became the mechanic and the manager/user can assume the role of driver.

Each business, each scientific endeavor, each educational problem can be approached by considering its individual and unique properties. The computer can now be used to develop unique insights into individual situations.

In years past computer payroll and order entry programs could be transferred lock, stock and barrel from business to business. Whether the payroll was for a plumbing business, a shoe factory or a retail operation, the payroll activities were the same.

Time sharing offers much more. Time sharing can be tailored to the unique situation; patterned to reflect specifically the needs of the user at any level of activity. It can accommodate the management needs at the top level, the requirements of the traffic department or the projections of the corporate staff. Furthermore, it can be used to consolidate and coordinate all these disparate activities simultaneously.

The responsibility of designing a computer-based information system lies entirely with the users. Ground rules should be:

1. No one knows your needs better than yourself.
2. The computer can do anything you can precisely define.
3. Don't waste time asking "What can the computer do?" Ask "What do I need?"

The first step in a comprehensive time-sharing program design undertaking is to define the problem precisely. If this is done well, programming, input and implementation will be routine.

CASE IN POINT: The personnel department of any company with more than five hundred employees has considered the computer. Unfortunately, they are usually limited to what can be conveniently extracted as a byproduct of payroll.

Time sharing offers a variety of personnel library package programs specifically designed for use by the personnel people.

One personnel department of a large milling company had despaired of ever knowing "who we have working for us." They felt they were last on the list of the EDP establishment. Finance, sales, marketing and production all had first call on the computer. Their entreaties were all greeted with the familiar reply: "Sure, we can do it, but that's about three years out."

Their present manual system involved files, clerks, and endless retyping and updating of records. They felt like the Red Queen in "Alice in Wonderland"; they had to run at full speed just to stay in the same place.

Time sharing put them directly in touch with their own information. Adopting one of the library programs, similar to that described below, they built their own personnel information system.

The result "put them in touch with their people." Thousands of dollars of clerical hours were eliminated for hundreds of dollars of time-sharing efficiency.

Two program designs follow. They should be viewed as examples of the type of thinking you should be applying to your own requirements.

A Personnel Information System

The Company: A medium-sized company consisting of twenty plants and fifteen hundred employees.

The Objective: To be able to screen the work force to assure the proper application of personnel skills, equitable pay scales and advancement opportunities.

Program Purpose: 1. To screen the work force for specific abilities.
2. To monitor the work force for compensatory status.
3. To select personnel by special characteristics.
4. To output individual histories.
5. To output advancement profiles.
6. To organize and summarize workers by division, national area, department and plant.

Note that these objectives make no mention of the computer. When developing any information system, the user should only consider his needs. Be confident that computer processing can take care of itself.

The specific output, reports and searches is the next order of business. What questions are you going to ask? What reports do you need? What specific requests do you want answered?

Design the output in minute detail. Ennumerate each detail of each report. Set up the specific headers required. Detail precisely and efficiently each question to be asked.

The erroneous approach is "First list all the elements you will need captured in the data base." This advice leads to three major difficulties.

1. You can't know what you need in your data base until you know precisely what output is required.
2. The effort to specify every imagined detail required can become so complex that the user despairs of ever completing the task.
3. Finally, such an approach frequently generates a data base full of information never needed. Once established, however, the additional input must be processed for each new data input. Incidentally, this type of programming frequently accounts for those ridiculously detailed questionnaires we have all filled out.

Design of output is not an easy task. The user must live with this output. The user should know precisely what he needs. Productive and usable report design is the critical phase of time sharing from the user's viewpoint. The user must work with these reports every day. He should be prepared to describe these needs in detail.

Let's undertake the design of a report that outputs the work force of a specific plant. Broadly, this might be in two parts.

1. A summary of the plant details
2. A listing of individual workers and their skills.

Such a report might look like this:

PERSONNEL REPORT

Plant: Branden Plant, Waukeegan, Ill.
Force: 1,500
Payroll: $9,000,000
Exempt: 1,250
Nonexempt: 250

NAME	YEARS	GRADE	SALARY	POSITION	SKILLS
Abelard, J.L.	5	7	9,500	12	1,7,3
Attenbal, T.E.	12	5	7,270	7	2
Baltree, C.E.	7	12	14,700	3	9,15,5
Bustra, T.Y.	22	8	10,600	5	1,4,12

As soon as we have formatted the report, the data base requirements become obvious. Furthermore, additional types of programming are suggested.

First, data base requirements:

1. Employee name
2. Coded grade, position and skills
3. Year of employment
4. Salary
5. Plant identification
6. Exempt/Nonexempt status

Secondly, the report suggests that it should provide selectivity. Trying to find skill #19 in a listing of 1,500 employees would be time-consuming in itself. Thus, the program might ask, "Ranking by what category?" A response of 1 to 6 would command ranked output by name, years, grade, etc. We cycle and build this new requirement into our design.

PERSONNEL REPORT

PERSONNEL REPORT WITH GRADE 5 REQUESTED

NAME (1)	YEARS (2)	GRADE (3)	SALARY (4)	POSITION (5)	SKILLS (6)
Attenbal, T.E.	12	5	6,970	7	2
Ally, S.K.	7	5	7,000	7	2,4
Cacta, F.I.	5	5	6,800	6	2,7
Eval, S.O.	5	5	7,100	8	2,3,5

This design suggests further modification. Should output be alphabetical or by salary? Should it be fixed or optional? Perhaps it should be by position.

Time sharing was never advertised as easy. Again the user/designer cycles, redoes his work, and tries to improve and restructure his output. This interactive thought and speculation continues until every detail of process and procedure can be delineated. Such designing, building and structuring may take several days. It is safe to say, however, that whatever the time, it would have been longer and less productive if the user attempted to assign this responsibility to another.

The final test of the design is documenting each step as if it were on the computer. The final design step would simulate actual computer functioning. A final written simulation might look as follows:

COMPUTER	COMMENT	OPERATOR
	Dial 123-4567	
PLEASE LOG IN		HAP 103
READY		RUN PERSONNEL
WHAT PLANT?	All plants are identified by a number.	7
RANK BY?	Each column header is numbered. In this case we will request ranking by salary, column 4.	4
EXTRACT COLUMN?	We require all employees of the same grade output, grade 5, in this case.	5
	Our output then becomes:	

PERSONNEL REPORT

PLANT   :   Branden Plant, Waukeegan, Ill.
FORCE   :   1,500
PAYROLL   : $9,000,000
EXEMPT   :   1,250
NONEXEMPT: 250

NAME (1)	YEARS (2)	GRADE (5)	SALARY (4)	POSITIONS (5)	SKILLS (6)
Eval, S.O.	5	5	7,100	8	2,3,5
Ally, S.K.	7	5	7,000	7	2,4
Sargi, B.O.	9	5	6,990	7	2
Attenbal, T.E.	12	5	6,970	7	2
Cacta, L.E.	5	5	6,800	6	2,7
Tanta, O.L.	3	5	6,600	7	2,4

AVE. YRS. 6.8   AVE. SALARY 6,910

The above simulation is a critical part of program design. In the time-sharing environment both people and computer time is expensive. The user can save lots of both by determining in advance precisely what he wants.

It is impossible to emphasize enough the importance of meticulous attention to detail. Such preplanning is the one advantage and control that the user/manager has over his project. Thousands of good computer applications have been lost when the user fails to control the direction of the project. Careful preplanning keeps the control in the user's hands.

These admonitions to the user are not intended to fault the programmer. It is the responsibility of the user to provide the programmer with clear and concise descriptions of his requirements. The programmer should not be asked to fill in the gaps in the user's thinking. Anything left to chance falls under that ubiquitous business law, "If something *can* go wrong, it will."

The above description encompasses only one aspect of a personnel program. Programs to output various personnel aspects can be added. The data base requirements would cover not only this program, but others. The above merely covers the initial approach, the delineation of a single program in a personnel package that may include one data base and a dozen interacting programs.

One of the most fertile fields for time sharing is in the financial area. Computers entered the business world through the controller's department. Naturally, after solving the clerical problems of payroll and order entry, the controller's department was satisfied.

User/computer interaction to manipulate, project and analyze a company's financial past, present and future is ideally suited to time sharing. It enables the knowledgeable user to put himself "in the loop" and inspect option after option of the company's financial future.

A Financial Analysis

The Company: A one-billion-dollar company consisting of twenty divisions in widely diversified markets.

The Objective: To evaluate various financial options. To evaluate individually and in combination, each division's financial performance and efficiency.

Program Purpose: 1. To output the financial statement of each division of the corporation.

2. To add, subtract or rearrange divisions and output individual and combined financial statements.

3. To project and manipulate division financial statements by product line.

The finance man has already structured his output to conform to mathematical manipulation. Sometimes, once the routine financial tasks were computerized, the job was considered done. Forty-three clerks had been replaced, the profit and loss statement and the balance sheet were being computer output. Why do more? Time sharing can do much more. It can put the finance man "in-the-loop." A properly devised program should allow him to project, revise, and speculate with this financial model of his company.

We won't approach this program as we did the previous personnel program. Outlining and detailing a complex financial program could take months. Again the question is not what we put *in,* but what we want *out.*

For this financial model example, let's assume the program is written and available. Let's approach the terminal with certain specific objectives in mind, and run the program to develop the information we require.

The company, the program objectives and the program purpose is as described on the previous page. The specific purpose, at this session, is to determine if corporation profits, present and future, can be increased by elimination of certain unprofitable product lines.

For purposes of clarity, more questions than absolutely necessary will be asked. Keep in mind that programs of this nature are designed for the knowledgeable user. It is not expected that anyone without intimate financial knowledge of the corporation would design, develop and use such a program.

As this program is conceived, a detailed data base is required. A partial list of the data required is as follows:

1. Past five years' balance sheets of the twenty divisions comprising the corporation.
2. Past five years' profit and loss statements by division.
3. Past five years' sales by product line by division.
4. Property, plant and equipment relationships to product line.
5. Sales and administration related to product line.
6. Interrelationships of product lines, if any.
7. Product phase-in, phase-out times.

Yes, this is complicated. This is sometimes the tragedy of time-sharing. A few quick words to a technician will not result in a financial model. Only the user knows or can detail what he wants. Until recently, a financial manager sometimes took weeks to explore one future corporate option. Today, many still do. At a time-sharing console a dozen can be explored in one afternoon.

CASE IN POINT: Earlier, an example was provided of time sharing's application to profitability studies. The same large chemical company, after success with this program, undertook to put on time sharing the major portion of the whole sixty-page A.F.E. study.

The results were astonishing. After insertion of 100 basic pieces of raw data, a complete A.F.E. study, sensitivity analysis and projection was output. One hundred pieces of raw data were organized, converted, projected and printed out for sixteen dollars per run. Manually such an evaluation was estimated in the thousands of dollars.

A further asset developed. Many options could now be explored. The effect of various accounting methods (LIFO, FIFO) could be applied and results on the model explored in minutes.

The management man-hours saved, and the multiple options that could be reviewed by management were of incalculable value. Multiple looks at a project's future were now possible.

COMPUTER	COMMENT	OPERATOR
	Dial 123-4567	
PLEASE LOG IN		HAP 103
—READY		RUN FINANCE
—READY	This command requests the last five years' P & L statements	CORP P & L 0,-4
	NOTE: Year zero is the current year.	

CORPORATION IN $000,000s

INCOME: YEAR	-4	-3	-2	-1	0
SALES	500	610	820	928	1009
OTHER INCOME	6	8	10	8	9
COST AND EXPENSES					
COST OF SALES	386	475	645	708	781
S & A	60	61	84	98	105
R & D	9	14	18	21	24
TAXES	24	33	40	52	47
NET INCOME	27	35	43	57	61

COMPUTER	COMMENT	OPERATOR
CONTINUE?	Commands five-year projection	PROJECT CORP P & L 0, + 5

COMPUTER		COMMENT		OPERATOR	

CORPORATION IN $000,000s

INCOME: YEAR	0	+1	+2	+3	+4	+5
SALES	1009	1170	1300	1430	1545	1660
OTHER	9	13	11	13	15	20
COST AND EXPENSES						
COST OF SALES	781	886	1055	1083	1188	1269
S & A	105	159	165	175	185	210
R & D	24	28	29	31	34	36
TAXES	47	47	64	56	70	75
NET INCOME	61	63	74	77	83	90

CONTINUE?   DIVS P & L A, D, F1

DIVISIONS IN $000,000s

INCOME: YEAR	A	D	F
SALES	68	111	46
OTHER	0	0	0
COST AND EXPENSES			
COST OF SALES	50	84	33
S & A	10	14	8
R & D	1	2	0
TAXES	3	4	2
NET INCOME	4	7	3

CONTINUE?

Keep in mind this program is being run by a knowledgeable user. He has now output the background data for his evaluation.

Now he can turn his attention to his specific problem. As mentioned earlier, this is to determine if elimination of certain marginal product lines in divisions A, D and F would improve their earnings.

The lowest product line profits are known to be product lines PI and PT of division D.

CONTINUE?   This command makes   DIV. D

COMPUTER	COMMENT	OPERATOR
	available all data on division D.	
ACTION?	This command instructs deletion of lines PI, PT.	DELETE PI,PT
CONTINUE?		DIV. P & L D,O

DIVISION YEAR 0, $000,000s

INCOME	
SALES	106
OTHER	0
COST AND EXPENSES	
COST OF SALES	80
S & A	13
R & D	2
TAXES	4
NET INCOME	7

Note, that although some difference is apparent, no real impact on profitability has been made.

To check this analysis, a P & L statement five years out for both cases is requested.

CONTINUE?   DIV D AS IS, LESS PI,PT

YEAR + 5, $000000s

INCOME	AS IS	LESS PI,PT
SALES	144	141
OTHER	0	0
COST AND EXPENSES		
COST OF SALES	108	106
S & A	18	17
R & D	4	4
TAXES	5	5
NET INCOME	9	9

The previous five outputs took ten minutes. To provide this information the computer has processed and projected the corporate model four times. Not just the numbers printed out, of course, but all the detailed data. This would include twenty divisions and their respective 200 product lines. It is difficult to imagine the complexities the computer can handle today. Five to six thousand calculations can be made, while the user is following one of the above ten line printouts.

This description is not advanced to impress you with the marvels of the computer, but to emphasize that any equivalent manual investigation has been close to impossible before time sharing became available. Not only was such a review difficult, but so time consuming that the user easily lost the thread of his investigation when presented with each option several days apart.

To return to our evaluation: We have determined that elimination of product lines PI and PT in Division D do not materially change the division's profits. We'll explore a different avenue.

COMPUTER	COMMENT	OPERATOR
CONTINUE?	Let's first look at five years of division F.	DIV. P & L F,0-4

YEAR $000,000s

	-1	-2	-3	-4	0
INCOME					
SALES	30	36	40	43	46
OTHER	0	0	0	0	0
COST AND EXPENSES					
COST OF SALES	22	25	29	31	33
S & A	6	6	7	7	8
R & D	0	1	0	0	0
TAXES	1	2	2	2	2
NET INCOME	1	2	2	3	3

Product line K is in a highly competitive field. An old plant is operating inefficiently.

CONTINUE?		DIV F
ACTION?		DELETE K,0-4
CONTINUE?		DIV. P & L F

YEAR $000,000s

	-1	-2	-3	-4	0
INCOME					
SALES	29	34	39	42	45
OTHER	0	0	0	0	0
COST AND EXPENSES					
COST OF SALES	20	22	25	27	30
S & A	5	5	5	6	6
R & D	0	0	0	0	0
TAXES	1	1	2	2	2
NET INCOME	3	6	7	7	7
O.E.R.					

COMPUTER	COMMENT	OPERATOR
	Comparing the above with the previous output, the deletion of product K appears desirable.	

If you are a reader like many, you may have skipped some of the above. If this is so, a rhetorical explanation of what you have just missed diagrammatically seems necessary.

Time sharing provides the opportunity to hold a complete model of a system, to interact dynamically with it, to allow any thought or speculation about the system to be instantly realized. Many good ideas and options are lost because they are "too complicated." That is, it would force someone to spend several hours tediously calculating their way through the option. Would you ask your accountant to prepare twenty profit and loss statements? Would you request he produce ten balance sheets at month's end?

Without realizing it, we have been screening out options. The business mind is conditioned to balance usefulness against cost. This cost has always been in man-hours. Ten balance sheets have always been too costly and tedious unless the objective was sufficiently "important." Ten projections of balance sheets was too time-consuming. The boredom usually meant a disgruntled accountant. The prize was not worth the price. Today, on time sharing, all this can be done in a half hour for less than ten dollars.

Unfortunately, the fact that it can be done does not mean it is done. Old habits are hard to change. Unless the individual is farsighted and innovative, the old thinking persists.

Time sharing offers unique and comprehensive opportunities, but it isn't easy. If these possibilities can be foreseen, they are obviously worth the effort. Too often the initial effort of designing, programming and data input discourage the novice user. The only way to overcome this is to emphasize the return. A unique financial model of your company is not easy to construct. Once constructed, however, it can be put to a multitude of uses, and provide a many-faceted insight into operations.

Full appreciation of this type of in-the-loop activity is a new concept. Those who explore it will profit. This is emphatically not an encouragement for the newcomer to sit down at a time-sharing terminal and model his company. Rather, it is a picture of where he might go after he has acquainted himself with the enormous interactive potential that time sharing offers.

Almost daily new generalized report-building programs are being offered by time-sharing companies. These bypass the necessity to do your own programming. Time-sharing companies have anticipated the need for financial programs, for programs for use in education, science and manufacturing. Learning, familiarization and activation of these programs is not easy, but far simpler than direct programming. Rather than building the house, you are merely being asked to furnish it. Learning to take a computerized look at your problems is the most difficult. Once into time sharing, opportunities will open up faster than you can design for them.

Time sharing opens up whole new orders of magnitude in your approach to problem solving. It makes modeling and simulation totally interactive. It puts you, the user, in complete charge of the computer.

Designing the program to meet your requirements is the most critical phase of time sharing. Structuring the operations so you can generate specifically what you need determines whether the computer will perform for you or not. The success or failure of your time-sharing effort, at the sophisticated level of information systems modeling and simulations, depends entirely on the initial design by you, the user.

9

HOW AND WHEN TO BUILD A
TIME-SHARING DATA BANK

The computer belongs to the scientist/technician. Programs belong to the systems analyst/programmer. Only the data bank belongs to the user!

"Data base" or "data bank" refer to a collection of data stored in the computer. This data base is then used by the computer as a source of information. Reduced to its barest essentials it looks like this illustration in Figure 26.

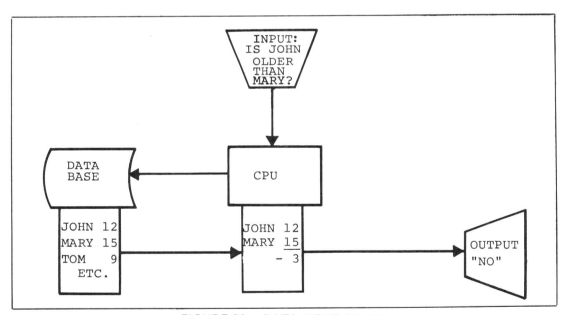

FIGURE 26   DATA INPUT CHART

1. The computer is asked a question.
2. The computer searches its data bank for the information it needs to answer the question (John's and Mary's ages).
3. Once the data is located, the computer manipulates the data (subtracts John's age from Mary's age) to obtain the answer.
4. The computer outputs the answer.

The data base is the viable and dynamic entity in any computer package. Programs once written remain static. All processing procedures and output formats

155

have been anticipated in the design and programming phase. However, the data base, that portion the programs process, should be as flexible as possible.

Daily input to the data base is common. The changing data base provides the timeliness to any information system. This distinguishes it from static information systems such as written records or card files. New information is input, old information is removed and current information may be corrected. Unlike a filing system or a manual record, all information in the computer data base can be current and correct.

Time sharing enhances the versatility of any data base because it provides continuous access and correction. This need for flexibility and versatility dictates that any time-sharing system selected have a sophisticated, easy-to-use editing mode (method of operation).

Regardless of the skill of the user, if the information being acted on is old, inaccurate or nonexistent, the output will be wrong. This logic brings us face to face with the oldest, and perhaps the truest of computer cliches, "GIGO"—Garbage In, Garbage Out.

To assure that computer output satisfies the user's needs, the data base must be accurate, complete and current. These requirements can only be satisfied by the most careful and meticulous design of the data base. All essential data must be included and all nonessential data must be screened out.

There is nothing mysterious about a data base. It should contain every element that will be needed by the computer to answer whatever questions may be asked by the computer programs run against it. The normal data bank is an assemblage of carefully structured information. Each individual entry might consist of from one to one hundred or even one thousand pieces of data. What makes the data base complex is that it contains thousands of these individual entries. Of course, these entries are not held by the computer numerically or alphabetically. They have been reduced to machine language as binary bits. To the user, of course, this is unimportant. At any time the computer can be instructed to convert its binary information and print it out in alphanumeric configuration (plain English).

Everyone is familiar with credit cards. Our present credit card economy would be impossible without computers and their data banks. A credit card data base might look like that shown in Figure 27. Ten thousand or one hundred thousand of these entries would make a respectable data base.

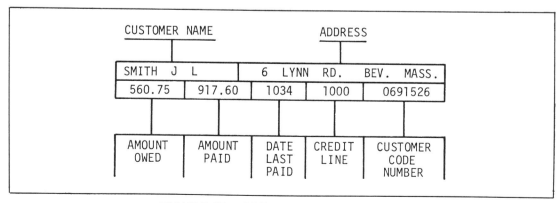

FIGURE 27   CREDIT CARD DATA BASE

Time sharing rarely uses a 100,000 entry data base. At that level it would be easy to justify in-house equipment. Time sharing is more likely to deal with smaller and much more flexible data bases—those that change constantly, output data and reports daily, and require a high degree of user interaction. Such a data base requires great care and planning. Since input will be almost continuous, each piece of data is critical, and each user/computer interaction must be meaningful.

Thus, the data base is truly the heart of any interactive time-sharing package. In the initial problem-solving phase of time sharing, inputting several numbers for a projection is a simple, one-time use of a specific data base. However, as the use of time sharing expands and becomes more sophisticated, more elaborate data banks become essential.

The qualities of a data base closely parallel the characteristics of any information system. Viewed from the aspect of data base construction, the five characteristics of an M.I.S., defined in chapter 6, might be applied as follows:

1. Symbiotic—The data base should be constructed with as little interference as possible with normal operations. Avoid extra data extractions, listings or key punching.
2. Dynamic—The data base should be continuously updated.
3. Viability—The data base should be correctable, adjustable and expandable at any time.
4. Timeliness—The data base should reflect all current information.
5. Peek into the Future—The data selected for the data base should provide information that will allow the computer to project trends and cycles and allow modeling and simulation.

Since the data base is the heart of any information system, it is not surprising that its attributes should be the same.

There are two levels of data base use. If we want to be highly specific, problem-solving data, inserted one time only, could be defined as a "data base." Credit card type information, kept and maintained in a separate computer file for years, could be called a "data bank." The distinction is academic and "bank" and "base" are now used interchangeably.

Time sharing is an excellent medium for problem solving. Programs such as those described in chapter 4 are examples of this type.

Each time sharing company maintains a library of programs. Many of these programs are self-contained. That is, when activated their first request is for input information. The simplest input might be a series of numbers for a calculation. For example:

COMPUTER	COMMENT	OPERATOR
	DIAL 123-4567	
LOG IN		HAP 103
READY	The program "ship" is designed to provide a delivered price for a shipment from the U.S. to a foreign destination.	RUN SHIP

COMPUTER	COMMENT	OPERATOR
INPUT DATA?	The various elements necessary to calculate a CIF price are inserted for this single calculation.	12.50, .07, 42.50, WM, .8, 100, 101, 1.3,
	Without further delay, using the program "ship" and the eight data elements just input, the computer calculates and outputs the answer.	
C.I.F. 14.96/100 LBS READY		LOG OUT

In the above example the data base consists of just eight elements and must be input each time an answer is needed. Whole libraries of programs are available this way. They provide an important resource for any time-sharing company. This type of data input is always the first with which the new time-sharing user acquaints himself.

As familiarity with time sharing grows, additional requirements develop. Great complexity can be built into time-sharing programs. Finally, there comes the day when you find yourself typing the same information in over and over. Better still, before that point, you realize that the data being input is repetitious. When this occurs, it is time to start thinking in terms of a permanent data file, base or bank.

Dynamic operation consists of processing a data file that is kept permanently updated. A data base of personnel where "New Hires" and "Fires" are input and/or deleted on a daily basis is an example. Also, a customer file (another way of saying customer data base) may be updated daily by adding new customers. Or, an open order file may be written that contains the vital elements of each order placed.

The specific nature of such data banks requires great care in construction. The most effective visualization of this concept is to picture a giant cube. It may contain a thousand or one hundred thousand pigeonholes. Each pigeonhole contains one element of information.

The computer complexity of this concept, and the programming machinations to handle these data files need not concern the user. Time sharing uses two ways to seek information in a data base.

1. Sequential
2. Random access

"Sequential" means that the computer starts reading its data base from the beginning and reads until it finds the required data. "Random access" means that the request itself (such as a customer code number) contains sufficient information so the computer can go directly to the spot where the data is stored.

Sequential files (data base) are easier to program. Random access files allow faster and cheaper access to information. Once the data base grows large, only random access files can find the data fast enough.

Graphically a sequential data base "search" might look like the illustration in Figure 28.

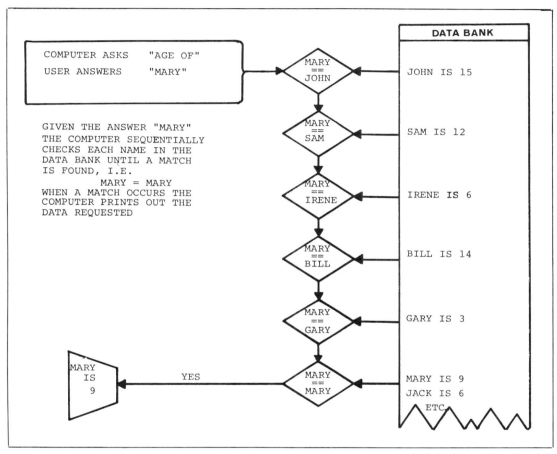

FIGURE 28   SEQUENTIAL COMPUTER SEARCH

Random access is more complicated and difficult to explain, both in theory and in fact. The user, however, need not be concerned with either, merely that random access is faster. Using the same structure as in the sequential example, random access may be visualized as in Figure 29.

In terms of computer speeds, search of a:

1. Sequential data base is *slow*.
2. Random access data base is *fast*.

The sophisticated data base is dynamic. Data is constantly being input, updated, revised, corrected and deleted. This flexibility can only be achieved by constant user/computer interaction. Once this timeliness is engineered into the data base, skillful program design can extract the needed information.

To use a facetious example, picture the data base as a baloney divided into

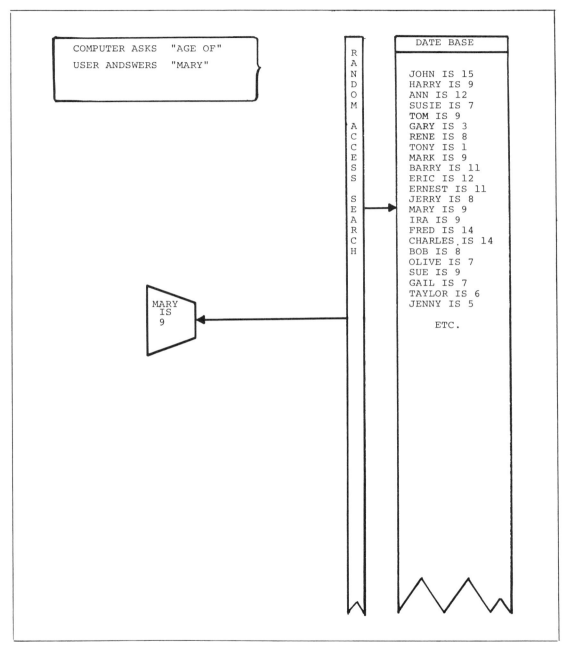

FIGURE 29   RANDOM COMPUTER SEARCH

pigeonholes. Each pigeonhole can contain a single piece of data. Like-numbered pigeonholes contain the same kind of data. That is, all #1 pigeonholes might contain order numbers; #2 pigeonholes selling prices and so on.

The programs are then written to slice this baloney in different ways. All the information is contained in the data base at all times. Program A, however, might read and output just that contained in pigeonhole #6. Program B might slice from a different angle and output data in several pigeonholes.

It is obvious that if a variety of informational requirements are to be met, all data must be organized in the data base for ready accessibility.

Furthermore, constant interaction to keep the data current is provided by time sharing's editing mode. Thus, the data bank's value lies not only in its stored data, but also in the flexibility time sharing provides to update this data continuously—to have the "baloney" always ready for an informational "slice." Visually, this simile may be pictured as in Figure 30.

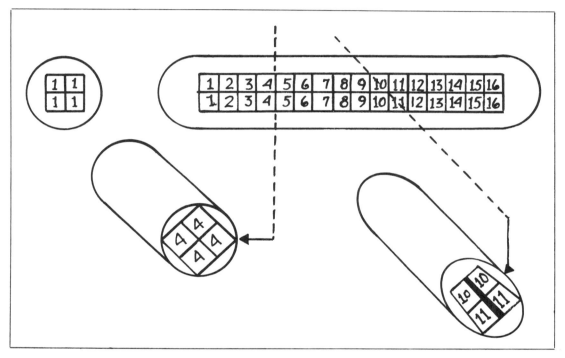

FIGURE 30   DATA BASE BALONEY

The selection of data for your data base is critical. Any sizable project, when first approached, seems to contain so much data that you might despair of collecting it all. Don't be discouraged. This is never true. First, computer hardware is so powerful today that only the most esoteric projects exceed its capability. Such disciplines as meteorology, advanced chemistry and physics might fit this category.

It takes considerable thought and study to realize the data that is needed in a particular data bank. One example will serve to illustrate this point. A company dealing in world trade had constructed and was operating an M.I.S. This package of programs was designed to output management information of the following types:

1. A daily report on all incoming orders and outgoing billings.
2. A weekly gross profit report.

3. A monthly financial summary.

4. A monthly sales summary.

To accomplish this the data base consisted of twenty elements, each extracted as the billing was written by the computer.

This M.I.S. had been running for three years when a new law was passed to stimulate international trade. As with most bureaucratic ventures, it required tedious and involved reporting of the beneficiaries' affairs. Once done, the international trader was entitled to a tax rebate.

An initial survey of the law showed how complicated it was. To receive the maximum benefit, each invoice had to be processed separately. Several tax options were available on each sale. Each sale required individual inspection and calculation to determine if tax option 1, 2 or 3 applied.

In the case of this particular exporter, several avenues of approach were open:

1. Assign an accountant to the task of writing up each month's tax exemptions. (It was estimated this would take about a week of his time each month.)

2. Arbitrarily apply the tax relief only to major sales. (It was estimated this would cover about 60% of the month's business.)

3. Apply the least effective tax option to all sales, and work only with the gross sales. (This would entail a single tax estimate calculation at month's end.)

4. Put it on the computer.

Obviously, we are interested in determining whether it could be put on the computer. In fact, any normal businessman will skim through the first three options in the blink of an eye. Unfortunately, he may find that putting it on the computer isn't very easy.

Remember, we are dealing with a structure (the new tax law) built entirely outside the company. It was built to serve purposes and end uses never envisioned by the company. It complies with a law adhering to various legal principles, political policies and national interests quite divorced from routine business activity.

Upon studying the tax law, it was found that it required a listing of all transactions, a determination of profit via two options (actual and a specified percent of gross sales), and allowances for marketing and operating costs.

The tax report, when complete, would consist of data and calculations, but they could all be extracted from the data base information. The data bank contained twenty-six elements of information. For the tax program only ten were needed, specifically:

1. Plant	6. Gross Sales
2. Product Group	7. Ocean Freight
3. Product	8. Selling Price
4. Order Number	9. Cost of Sales
5. Country	10. Commission

There is still more. The report, the accountants say, must be by product. All products must sum, and subtotals and totals must be provided. Here again, time sharing's flexibility becomes apparent. All time-sharing companies have programs that sort lists. These sort programs reorder either numerical or alphabetical data. By combining a program specifically written for this tax situation with a packaged sort program, it was possible to meet the tax requirements promptly.

How this was done will be detailed in chapter 10. The critical factor that made it all possible, however, was data base design. When the law was reviewed, it was found that all the elements necessary for its implementation were already resident in the company's data base.

The Domestic International Sales Corporation (D.I.S.C.) Act was passed by Congress in 1971, and went into effect in 1972. Since then it has been possible to determine how a number of international companies coped with this law.

Three actual examples investigated, of about the same size, reported the following: Company A was able to put it on time sharing as described above. Their first report was output within one month. Company B elected to process the data manually. The year's work involved about a four man-month effort. Company C attempted to handle it in-house, but the enormous initial data input (invoice by invoice) was unsuccessful. After eighteen months, a manual effort is continuing until they "get the bugs out."

> CASE IN POINT: The following program description is a generalization. In a specific instance, a similar effort was undertaken by a large New York exporter. Reducing their experience to its basics, their D.I.S.C. program was also built on time sharing.
>
> For a one-time programming charge of $2,000 and a "run" charge quarterly of $150.00, they have met their D.I.S.C. commitments. The equivalent effort manually would have cost a minimum of $5,000 annually.
>
> Another company has to date spent $15,000 attempting in-house operation and is still trying to get "D.I.S.C. on the system."

There is no substitute for meticulous planning when designing a data base. This means that each report must be constructed in advance. Try to make your errors and omissions before programming begins. Making a list of all data elements needed will not work. This technique leads to excessive data storage. The whole time-sharing exercise is undertaken to accomplish one thing. Since this is the case, the time spent to design and format this information had best be spent at the beginning. This phase of time sharing is tedious, but critical. If data cannot be organized into a usable format, no data base or computer program should even be attempted.

The data bank design phase is critical in determining whether your concept can, in fact, be computer implemented. If you are aiming at predicting future growth, plant feasibility or economic expansion, do you have sufficient information to predict trends? Thus, the first rule when using time sharing is to be sure where you are going before you take off. To avoid "GIGO," be sure the elements in your data base are tested and reliable *before you start the programming phase.*

There are several other dangers in data base building. Don't include redundant information. For example, don't input a man's age and his date of birth. The computer can always calculate his age from his birth date. Don't store the results of computer calculations. Frequently, computer processing time is cheaper than computer storage. Distinguish between dynamic and static data. If programs are only run once a month or less, perhaps both the data base and the program should be stored outside the time-sharing system.

Time sharing is dynamic. Constant update, input, processing and output are the characteristics best suited to time sharing. Any data base used for time sharing should reflect these characteristics.

Not only storing information, but editing and updating are critical to a viable data base. Here again, time sharing provides the constant user/computer interaction that is essential in a data bank environment that must be constantly undateable.

A viable data base is essential for any time-sharing package. The program, once written, remains the same. The user remains with a static program and a viable and dynamic data base. The input, update and editing of the data base by the user thus determines the value of the whole package.

To recapitulate, if you, the user, must live with your data base, make sure at the start it is sound. The five points to remember are:

1. Symbiotic input
2. Avoid redundancy
3. Good editing capability
4. Reliable information
5. Viable data

10

HOW TO GET YOUR TIME-SHARING COMPUTER PROGRAMS WRITTEN

Proprietary programs are time sharing's greatest asset. The sophisticated user demands programs uniquely tailored to his needs. To achieve this objective, the user must originate and design these programs himself.

Program building proceeds in three steps:

1. Design
2. Interaction with the systems analyst (chapter 11)
3. Interaction with the programmer (chapter 12)

Program design can never be too complete. Nothing should be left undetailed. Sullivan's law, "If something can go wrong, it will," must have been written for program design.

Program design is a frame of mind. Don't think in terms of the computer. Avoid intruding into the field of the programmer. Simply and clearly specify the data available, the manipulations to be made, and the output required. Once this is done systems analysis and programming are mechanical operations, as they should be. Furthermore your design then becomes the track on which the project runs. You remain in command of the project.

Programming efforts rarely fail because the computer fails. Primarily such efforts fail because people fail. Sound design puts the user in charge.

Program writing consists of three phases.

1. The User's Design
2. The System Analyst's "Blueprint"
3. The Programming

The more complete the user can make his design, the more efficiently program writing will proceed.

As mentioned in chapter 9, several years ago Congress passed an export incentive bill (D.I.S.C.). It provided a tax refund for sales made to foreign customers. To take full advantage of this tax benefit, it was necessary to make precise calculations of each individual transaction. Here is how one company went about it.

The accountants issued a report outlining the specific requirements of the new law. Here is where the real work begins—with the format of the final document, the final output. Design has nothing to do with systems analysts, programmers or computers. It begins with what you, the user, want. It describes your final objective in detail. This is not done with exposition or explanation, but by precisely defining the final document. Column headers, final numbers, details and all calculations are delineated to produce an exact reproduction of the finished output.

First the column headers are defined:

COLUMNS 1-5C

COLUMN 1	COLUMN 2	COLUMN 3	COLUMN 4	COLUMN 5A	COLUMN 5B	COLUMN 5C
DIVISION GROUP AND PRODUCT DESCRIPTION	ORDER NUMBER	FOREIGN COUNTRY	GROSS SALES	OCEAN FREIGHT	OTHER CHARGES	NET SALES

COLUMNS 6-10

COLUMN 6	COLUMN 7	COLUMN 8	COLUMN 9	COLUMN 10
MANUFACTURING COST	SELLING EXPENSES	ALLOCATED OVERHEAD	ADDITIONAL OVERHEAD	COMMISSION

COLUMNS 11-15

COLUMN 11	COLUMN 12	COLUMN 13	COLUMN 14	COLUMN 15
TAXABLE INCOME	PERCENT OF THE NET SALES PRICE	GREATER OF COLUMNS 12 & 14	FIFTY PERCENT OF TAXABLE INCOME	ALLOWABLE COMMISSION

Now the contents of each column must be defined. The more detail the better, including the variables, the format and the calculations.

Variables are assigned at this point so you may later be able to identify them in the program text. Your assignment of variables provides a bridge between you and the programmer. It establishes a means of communication.

The format detail governs the size and type of output. It controls the type and size of information in each column. By defining this you check to see whether your data will fit the output you are requesting.

The calculation detail is the user's sole responsibility. It covers the processing and manipulation of all the data supplied. Such detailing might look like the following:

COLUMN 1:
 VARIABLES: DIVISION, GROUP & PRODUCT = TG
 OUTPUT = PRINT TG
 CALCULATIONS = SUBTOTALS BY
           DIVISION & GROUP (T)
 FORMAT = 2A, 3A3

COLUMN 2:
 VARIABLE: ORDER NUMBER = XJ
 OUTPUT = PRINT XJ
 CALCULATIONS = NONE
 FORMAT = I6

COLUMN 3:
 VARIABLE: COUNTRY OF DESTINATION = A
 OUTPUT = PRINT A
 CALCULATIONS = NONE
 FORMAT = 2A3
 ... And continue for the full sixteen columns.

All the critical details have now been assembled. At this point it is desirable to list the variables assigned. Those used in columns 1, 2, and 3 would include, for instance:

A = Country
TG = Division, Group and Product
XJ = Order Number

Additional data of a one-time nature is also required. In this case they are percentages to be applied against the data being processed. They might be coded as:

Percentage A = PCTA
Percentage B = PCTB
Percentage C = PCTC

To digress for a moment, note that this example has one unique feature worth emphasizing. One of the major problems of a user is where to get his information and how to insert it into the data bank. On massive input programs, this job can sometimes be horrendous. Take one recent example I encountered: foreign exchange rates between the U.S. dollar and twelve selected foreign countries, daily, from 1950 to date.

The D.I.S.C. example was chosen because it avoided this problem. The company had maintained an integrated data base of the export activities for several years. When Congress passed its export incentive bill, all required information was already resident in the company data bases. Availability of this data made this programming job possible. The alternative would have been manual extraction from invoices and keypunch input, an enormous undertaking since seven thousand invoices were involved representing 308,000 pieces of data in two major data banks.

A single piece of invoice data, consisting of five lines, looks like this:

Line 1 AOLACKERA, 500, ST, FRANCE
Line 2 IAN, LEPOIS,0,721096,3159,0
Line 3 29856.72,0,852.91,LMV,5906.25,0,0,290.62
Line 4 1224.30,0,722.63,596.75,0,72.55,0,0
Line 5 1224.30,8279,436.45,0,0,72.55

Two data banks of this complexity must be merged. Different data from each must be selected. Finally, a single data bank must be created. This data bank contains only the data required by the D.I.S.C. calculations. In this example it will be 9,000 lines long (multiple product invoices create additional lines) and contain 90,000 data elements. It should be noted that this is not considered a large file manipulation by in-house EDP standards. However, in the highly interactive time-sharing environment this is a respectable task.

The exercise up to this point has consisted of organizing and identifying the data elements to be used in the D.I.S.C. package. No computer activity has as yet been undertaken. Two major data bases have been reviewed. A determination has been made that ten data elements are required and available within these two files. A further conclusion has been reached, namely that three percentages, i.e. PCTA, PCTB and PCTC are required. The above evaluation has accounted for all necessary data. We can now address ourselves to extracting and manipulating it. This will proceed in three steps:

1. Extract pertinent data from the two primary data banks.
2. Assemble it in the required order.
3. Manipulate it and output it in the outlined format.

Column 1 requires "subtotals" by group. This requires a sorting of the data. To save additional programming space and expense, a library sort program will be used. The decision to use a library sort program thus further dictates how the new data base should be formatted. For convenience, the data to be sorted should be first. Thus the division and the product group will be first, the product name second. The remaining data will follow. One line containing all ten elements will be created.

The first phase of the program will read the two data bases and extract the pertinent information. The user should precisely indicate the data bases to be read and the data to be extracted. The desired variables should be indicated.

Both data bases are read side by side, the pertinent data elements are selected and the final summation precisely defined as follows:

Data Base Name: ONELINE
Contents: Division Product Group and Product Name, Order Number, Country of Destination, Gross Sales, Ocean Freight, Net Sales, Cost of Manufacture, Commission
Example: INAOLACKERA,721096,France,31590,756,29856,20856.75,72.55

We now have designed a data base specifically built for a sort program. The library program can read the merged data bank and sort on the first eleven characters. The result of this single sort will organize the data into three categories:

1. Division
2. Product Group
3. Product

A data base is now available that, when processed, can be output as desired. Now the second phase of the program will read the sequenced data base and output the final D.I.S.C. report with its fifteen columns of data and attendant calculations. From this point on it is in the hands of the systems analyst and the programmer. There will be a great deal of interaction, but it should be for clarification, not expansion.

It is satisfying when a carefully documented program is finally complete. In spite of the complexity of design, the final result is simple. Here is how the final package runs.

D.I.S.C. PROGRAM

COMPUTER	COMMENT	OPERATOR
	Dial 123-4567	
PLEASE LOG IN		HAP 103
READY		
—		RUN DISC
HAVE YOU SORTED ONELINE YET?		NO

COMPUTER	COMMENT	OPERATOR
	This program runs in three phases. Phase 1 - Extract data from two data banks. Phase 2 - Sort data. Phase 3 - Output D.I.S.C. results.	
	This reply informs the computer Phase 1 is to be implemented, i.e. merge data banks 1 and 2.	
STOP	The program is completed, a file named "ONELINE" has been written.	
	A portion of the "ONE-LINE" file might look like this:	

READY				TYPE ONELINE TO TEL		
ICKTXTAA	711872CHILE	936.62	141.01	718.05	551.62	.00
OWSODA	712512CANAD	2108.98	.00	2108.98	1518.77	.00
IDSOLSULFD	720056VIESO	7020.03	310.79	6541.34	2257.20	224.40
OSKPERSULPH	720161CANAD	3334.62	.00	3334.62	2904.00	.00
ISSODPERSUL	720161CANAD	3596.58	.00	3596.58	2688.00	.00

Phase 1 is complete. The ONELINE data base represents single product sales invoice by invoice. These must now be sorted by division, product group and product. This information is in the first eleven fields.

In the preceding example of ONELINE text, the first eleven fields are:

ICKTXTAA____

I = DIVISION
C = PRODUCT GROUP
KTXTAA = PRODUCT

Thus, by sorting on the first eleven fields, the full 90,000 pieces of data are sequenced by division, product group and product.

Returning to the terminal, we utilize the sort command:

COMPUTER	COMMENT	OPERATOR
—		SORT/ONELINE/1.11/R72/SORTLINE/

COMMUTER	COMMENT	OPERATOR
THE FILE SORTLINE HAS BEEN WRITTEN.		
—	We output a few lines to check the results:	
—		TYPE SORTLINE TO TEL

COMMUTER	COLUMN				
IAALITOA720425CANAD	1109.22	.00	1109.22	849.80	53.26
IABALLIS721875PUERI	3149.00	709.76	2352.00	22300.00	134.10

COMMUTER	COMMENT	OPERATOR
	Phase II is completed.	
	Summation, calculation and output of the final D.I.S.C. report can now be implemented.	
	The D.I.S.C. program is now run again. The second option is selected.	
—		RUN DISC
HAVE YOU SORTED ONELINE YET?		YES
	Phase III requires additional data, which the computer requests.	
INPUT PCT,PCTB,PCTC		
	These three numbers are provided by the accountants. Since they may be changed from run to run, they are input from the terminal.	
		.5,.015,.0
FILES DISC 1, DISC 2 AND DISC 3 ARE CREATED		
STOP		
—	The first page looks like this:	TYPE DISC 1 TO TEL

COLUMN 1 DIVISION GROUP AND PRODUCT DESCRIPTION	COLUMN 2 ORDER NUMBER	COLUMN 3 FOREIGN COUNTRY	COLUMN 4 GROSS SALES	COLUMN 5A OCEAN FREIGHT	COLUMN 5B OTHER CHGS	COLUMN 5C NET SALES
OD ADIPOL BC	720344	CANAD	908.26	.00	.00	908.26
OD KRONOX S	720651	MEXIC	8243.25	.00	.00	7782.45
TOTAL GROUP D			9151.51	.00	.00	8690.71
OE DAC	720360	JAPAN	1466.61	71.00	.00	1383.61
OE DAPON 35	720508	NETHE	92.00	48.15	.00	37.84

OE DAPON 35	720315	GERMA	1900.00	.00	.00	1883.10
OE DAPON M	720377	GERMA	90.00	.00	.00	89.66
TOTAL GROUP E			3548.61	119.15	.00	3394.21
OF DAIPMON	720506	UKGB	850.63	17.00	.00	788.63
OF DAPMON	720388	CANAD	1147.79	.00	.00	1147.79
OF DAPMON	720491	BELGI	1170.00	.00	.00	1170.00
OF DAPMON	720367	SWEDE	90.55	54.93	.00	22.62
OF DAPMON	720452	CANAD	1373.43	.00	.00	1369.87
TOTAL GROUP F			4632.40	71.93	.00	4498.91

This ends Phase III

As usual, a detailed description complicates the actuality. After familiarity with the package is achieved, it becomes direct and straightforward.

COMPUTER	COMMENT	OPERATOR
	Dial 123-4567	
PLEASE LOG IN		HAP 103
READY		RUN DISC
HAVE YOU SORTED ONELINE YET?		NO
STOP		
READY		
STOP		SORT/ONELINE/1.11/R72
		/SORTLINE/
—		RUNDISC
HAVE YOU SORTED ONELINE YET?		YES
INPUT PCTA,PCTB,PCTC		.5,.015,.0
DATA BANK DISC 1, DISC 2, DISC 3		
ARE CREATED		
STOP		

What has this exercise accomplished? By sheer accident, an interesting insight into time sharing's value was highlighted six months after the program was initiated. The first two months' output was issued, but the data banks not saved. Six months later when new percentage figures were devised, there was no way to rerun the first two months. It was estimated that the new numbers would save the company $20,000 to $30,000 per month.

The accountants decided to do the job manually. Two months' manual D.I.S.C. processing required four accountant weeks to complete! The remaining four months (with the saved data) was processed through the system for $80.00 per month!

The preceding user detail is required no matter how the system analysis and programming are implemented. Four program-building routes are open to the time-sharing user.

1. In-house
2. Outside contract

3. Time-sharing company assistance
4. Do your own programming

In all cases, sound design is essential. Each method has its own advantages and disadvantages. Unfortunately, the user often has no choice. Circumstances beyond his control may dictate which option he must use.

IN-HOUSE

Many companies maintain resident systems analysts and programmers. These people maintain and operate the company's computers. Their skills can also be applied for writing programs to be used on time sharing. If this capability is available to the user, he is fortunate. He can work with people he knows. He can participate closely in program implementation, and a minimum of outside costs should be incurred.

Unfortunately, there are drawbacks. In-house programming leads to people problems, priority problems and implementation problems. Success requires leadership and tact on the part of the user. He must develop a comfortable and easy relationship with his programmer. Their working together will be critical to the success of the venture. In all cases, careful program objectives are essential; for in-house programming they are critical.

OUTSIDE CONTRACTS

There are many companies available for software work (programming). They review the program requirements and, for a fee, write the program or programs required. Contact can be made with these firms or individuals through computer-oriented periodicals, consultants or your time-sharing company.

Once contacts are made, the user's job is to select the company best suited for his purpose. There are several criteria, such as:

1. Design.
2. Familiarity with the language.
3. Familiarity with the subject.
4. Compatibility with the programmer.
5. Economics.
6. Method of operation.
7. Familiarity with the time-sharing company to be used.

DESIGN

Prepare your program design in detail before you even attempt to let an outside contract. First, a complete design will help you decide what type and style of programming skills you require. A simple program might not require outside help. A program package using the time-sharing company's library programs might best be written by them.

A program design can sometimes require strong emphasis on large files. In this case, your time-sharing company might be weak. Thus, your design would indicate not only an outside programmer, but also another time-sharing service.

> CASE IN POINT: In a large corporation just such a situation occurred. A highly interactive M.I.S. program was built outputting forty management reports each month. This system was built on an XDS 940, noted for its efficient and effective interactive operation. At the end of the month, a one-hundred page summary of the month's activities was required.
>
> The XDS 940 was slow and inefficient when processing this amount of data. Result: At month-end the data was edited on the XDS 940, then taped out. The tape was then input to another time-sharing company's IBM 360. The 360 processed the data in minutes and output the result at a high-speed terminal. The job took fifteen minutes instead of hours.

Both you and your contractor need a complete design to make an estimate on costs. Let's imagine we are to build a house. You call in a contractor. "Build me a house," you say. "How many rooms?" he asks. "I don't know," you reply. Any cost estimate you get after that exchange you deserve!

In the context of house building this seems ludicrous. With programming it happens all the time. Programmers frequently voice a very valid complaint: "I can't program what I don't know." It is the user's job to communicate his requirements. Until or unless his design is complete, all other activities are a waste of time.

FAMILIARITY WITH THE LANGUAGE

Most time-sharing companies offer a choice of several languages. The two most popular are FORTRAN and BASIC. Whatever the language, make sure the contractor assigns a programmer familiar with the language. It may not be difficult for a programmer to learn a new language. However, you should not tolerate on-the-job learning when you are paying for it. No amount of quick study will make up for experience. When seeking a software contract, people are likely to exaggerate their capabilities.

FAMILIARITY WITH THE SUBJECT

Software companies specialize in different fields. One may have gained expertise in engineering, another in accounting. During the initial interview, attempt to determine with which areas the candidate company is familiar.

There is no assurance that you will find a company specializing in your field of interest. However, some effort should be made to select a firm that will not find your objectives totally foreign to their past efforts.

COMPATIBILITY WITH THE PROGRAMMER

When contracting for outside programming, make sure you meet the programmer.

Once negotiations are complete and the contract signed, your only contact will be with him. Compatibility and rapport with the programmer will assure the success of your effort.

Like horses, changing programmers in midstream is inadvisable. The programmer employment market is a highly volatile one. Get what assurance you can that the programmer who initiates your project will remain long enough to finish it. This is not a minor point. I have had four programmers in four months on one project. One and one-half months would have done the job.

Programmers each have their own style. It is unfair and costly to ask a programmer to finish another's program. First, they must review it to learn what the other has done. Second, they must modify their approach to accommodate what the other has initiated. Frequently, the programmer will prefer to start again, rather than pick up in the middle. All this is costly and time-consuming.

ECONOMICS

Contract programming is a most amorphous subject. There are no hard and fast rules. Costs break down into two major categories: computer time and programmer time.

Computer costs can escalate dangerously if not rigidly restricted. The debugging phase is the most dangerous. To avoid this, costs should carefully be defined. Maximum charges for programming, debugging and running should be established.

Estimates from several contract programming services should be solicited. Cross checking and discussion of their proposals should be a must. Your design will serve as the foundation of these estimates. That's why it must be comprehensive.

Approach these negotiations prepared to use all the business acumen and experience you can muster. Loopholes left open will come back to haunt you later. It would take a separate book on contract negotiations to give this subject its due. A checklist of dos and don'ts will have to suffice here.

1. Approach the negotiations with a final design.
2. Don't modify or add to your requirements during program writing.
3. Establish a firm price for the job.
4. Don't authorize changes in the design casually. Understand the full implication of each change.
5. Set cost and time parameters for the programming and debugging phases.
6. Restrict programming work on the computer to a cost-definable area. Check costs being generated frequently.
7. Devise a formula to cope with computer overcharges, if they should occur.
8. Establish a clear turnover procedure.
9. Do not pay for a program until all the bugs are out.

METHOD OF OPERATION

The mechanical process of programming may be handled in a number of ways.

Each has its advantages and disadvantages. The best mode of operation is the simplest. Have the program written, compiled and debugged completely outside your time-sharing environment. This technique assures that your contract costs are your actual costs.

It is impossible to estimate how much computer time is required to write, compile and debug a program. One programmer might write a 500-line program and it will run the first time. Another will run the program fifty times before all the bugs are out. If this debugging occurs at your expense, charges can get away from you. Once the program is in the debugging phase, you are committed. As a user you can only point out what is wrong, not how to correct it.

Every program situation is different. It is impossible to list all the pitfalls that may occur. One frequent error is to get involved in the debugging. This starts when the programmer calls you up and says, "It's all finished, go ahead and run." You start the program and it bombs out! The programmer is informed, he calls back ten minutes later, and says, "I've fixed it. Run it again." Five lines beyond the first error you crash again. You call the programmer. This process can go on all day. What's actually happening is that you are doing the debugging!

These are the two extremes: Either you don't touch the program until it runs, or you get involved in the debugging.

FAMILIARITY WITH THE TIME-SHARING COMPANY TO BE USED

Outside contracts may be written with a firm or individual recommended by your time-sharing company. This has several advantages. First, it is in the best interests of both you and your time-sharing service to get programs up and running promptly. Second, they will usually recommend someone already familiar with their service. This avoids on-the-job learning at your expense.

Should you contract with a firm or individual unfamiliar with your time-sharing service, take certain precautions.

1. Have a representative of your time-sharing company participate in some of your discussions.
2. Insist that the programmer familiarize himself with your time-sharing service.
3. Encourage a high degree of interaction and cooperation between programmer and time-sharing service.

CASE IN POINT: An extreme example emphasizes the need to select a cooperative time-sharing company. It may tarnish time sharing's image slightly, but should serve as a caution when selecting a time-sharing company.

A program was written in cooperation with a contract time-sharing company. The job was not well done, and after extensive debugging trials, in-house personnel took over and completed it. Certainly it was a jury-rigged system—half done in-house, half outside.

Several years later, a minor improvement was contemplated. The time-sharing company was solicited for assistance. They replied that they were sorry, they were not familiar with the final version. Their only offer was programming assistance—available at $200 per day.

TIME-SHARING COMPANY ASSISTANCE

Essentially the same factors apply here, as mentioned above. The advantage is that familiarity with the service will expedite program writing. The disadvantage is that a programmer may not be assigned exclusively to your job. In this case, the demands of his other responsibilities may distract him. A crisis in the office (and time-sharing companies have their share) may take him off your job for a week. This is controllable. Your contract (and its cost) should reflect the priority you assign to the undertaking. If low priority, allow intermittent work on the program and expect a lower cost. If priority, specify one programmer exclusively and pay accordingly.

DO YOUR OWN PROGRAMMING

It is unusual for a user to have a computer programmer on his staff. The time-sharing user's emphasis is on operation and output. Programming is an intermittent activity.

Programming ability can be an asset to a user. It provides an additional insight into the problems of the system analyst and the programmer. Programming knowledge gives the user a feel for what can and cannot be done.

During the design phase a feel for programming restrictions may limit or expand a designer's (user's) requirements. Take the D.I.S.C. program described earlier. The use of a library program was incorporated into the package. This was suggested by the designer to reduce additional programming time and effort.

Programming skill is not essential to the user. However, if the user feels comfortable in this discipline, he can profit by learning it. There are three ways a user can learn to program:

1. Interactively via time-sharing instruction programs.
2. With PI (programmed instruction) texts.
3. In regular time-sharing classes.

Time-sharing companies encourage programming skills. The best source of information on any of the above is your time-sharing company.

Interactive Programming

Library computer programs are available to teach the user programming. The program outputs questions, the user replies. The question-and-answer interchange leads the user through the learning process. These programs employ the most modern teaching techniques. For many people they are a quick and highly effective teaching method.

P.I. (Programmed Instruction)

This method merely substitutes a book for the terminal. The series of questions are printed, rather than computer output. Again, as the user answers each question, he is guided through the learning process.

Regular Classes

Time-sharing companies encourage their customers to learn programming. They frequently schedule classes for this purpose. Check with your time-sharing company for this service; in most cases they will be happy to oblige. This type of instruction is usually gratis, involves small classes, and can be scheduled fairly easily.

Outside Instruction

Every city today has computer schools. Three- to eleven-month courses range from $500 to $1,800. Usually if you have initiated time sharing such outside instruction is not necessary.

Don't undertake such courses as a prerequisite to time sharing. First, get your feet wet in a time-sharing environment, then plan the type of instruction you require.

SUMMARY

Design is the key to effective time sharing. The user should exert every effort to detail his requirements before the technicians are called in. Design controls the programming effort. Design provides the economic, personnel, input, calculation and output control of the endeavor. A sound design is the single most important tool and control for the user.

11

FACILITATING USER INTERACTION
WITH THE SYSTEMS ANALYST

There are four ways a time-sharing user can get a computer program written.

1. Use in-house systems analysts and programmers.
2. Use the time-sharing company's in-house personnel.
3. Do the systems analysis and programming himself.
4. Contract outside.

Of course, combinations of the above are possible. The user designs the program, someone else encodes it.

In other chapters the design, structure and implementation of a program are explored. However, as in any endeavor, interaction between people is critical. To get his program written, the user must lead the way. He must establish the objectives and maintain control of the project.

Let's return to our house building metaphor. You consult with your wife and family. Together you decide where to build the house, how many rooms, what utilities and how to furnish it. You then call in the architect for design and blueprints. Later you hire a builder for construction. You consult, review and discuss all phases of the project with the architect and builder, but you never lose sight of the fact that they are building your house. Long after they have gone on to build other houses, you will be living in whatever they left behind.

By this analogy you, the user, are building the program, the systems analyst is the architect, the programmer is the builder. Don't be intimidated by "all them spinning wheels and blinking lights." You don't have to know how to operate a bulldozer to insist you need a ten-foot deep foundation.

The user's role is to use not only the computer to achieve his goal, but also the personnel to build the software for attaining his objective. The user must work with and direct two very new disciplines: systems analysis and programming.

THE SYSTEMS ANALYST

Systems analysis is a very new skill. It involves a way of looking at things in a more organized fashion. The concept recognizes that things don't happen in a fragmentary way; all activities are interconnected and interrelated.

Two hundred years ago a drop of water was nothing more than a drop of water.

Then Leeuwenhoek invented the microscope. Suddenly a whole world of interrelated activity appeared. A whole system of plants and animals were discovered living and growing in a drop of water.

Take a sneeze, for instance. A sneeze is a sneeze is a sneeze. But is it? Looked at from a systems point of view, it's a whole chain of events.

1. A tickle in the nose.
2. A pause in what you are doing.
3. A stab for your handkerchief.
4. A race between hand and nose.
5. An explosion of noise and germs.
6. Who won? Nose or hanky?
7. A branch point for the system.
    a. Hand won—hanky washed.
    b. Nose won—somebody else's system catches a cold.
8. And the systems go on.

Systems analysis is a means of detailing activities so they may be organized in the most effective fashion. Since computers are logical and efficient machines, any problem they work on must be presented logically. Thus, to create a program for the computer, you first must meticulously define the problem. This is the system analyst's job: to sit down with you, the user, and define precisely what you want.

If done properly, the user will come away with a much better insight into his own activity than he ever had before. After a productive systems session, such comments as the following are common:

"I never knew there was so much detail in this business."
"I really never looked at this problem that way before."
"That's the first time I learned anything new about this business in years."
"There's a lot going on here I never really paid any attention to."

The systems analyst provided these insights. The user had all the knowledge of the system, but never systematized it before.

Like the sneeze, however, once you start detailing the procedures new insights almost inevitably develop. A systems analyst speeds up program design with his experience. All the information used, however, must come from the user.

Today any clearly definable job in business, education, science or government can be handled on the computer. "Clearly definable" is the catch. "Clearly definable" should be the objective of user/system analyst interaction.

It is during these interactions that the user must spell out precisely what he wants. It is at these sessions that the user frequently discovers he doesn't know what he wants. It is at these sessions that the sneeze must be broken down into individually identifiable activities. Frequently the user learns more than the systems analyst!

These sessions develop into the feasibility study. Assuming the results are positive, they continue through a series of steps. Systems analysis and design consist of:

1. The feasibility study.
2. Cost analysis.

3. Input data evaluation.
4. Input-output record design.

THE FEASIBILITY STUDY

Is a proposed time-sharing effort worth its salt? The feasibility study determines if usefulness, effectiveness and timeliness warrant the systems, programming and the computer effort involved. It takes into consideration:

1. Availability of data.
2. Reliability of data.
3. Input of data
4. Timeliness of data.
5. Personnel requirements.
6. Hardware capability.
7. Usefulness of output.

Availability of Data

Time sharing's greatest asset is timeliness. Time-sharing programs are usually characterized by frequent input to a data bank, and frequent output in the form of reports.

The collection and assemblage of data is always the responsibility of the user. Although this has nothing to do with programmers or computers, it is the absolutely essential ingredient in making the whole time-sharing effort productive.

CASE IN POINT: The feasibility study must determine whether the data necessary to achieve the user's objectives is available. A large N.Y. company experienced a concrete example of this during the early phases of computer development in the early sixties. Like most large and progressive companies, they instituted computer output of payroll and order/billing during the first generation of computer introduction. When this was completed, the EDP establishment proposed a market report for sales. It was not difficult to design the market report per se. Obviously, a sales effort needed information on its sales area, customer and product, by month and year to date.

With enthusiasm born of inexperience on the part of the programmers, and indifference born of ignorance from sales, a program was designed and written. It worked fine. Unfortunately, the market report never reached the sales department until twenty-eight days after month-end. It took twenty-six days to make the data available for input to the computer and two days to input, run and make copies for distribution.

Availability of data was handled manually. The data was calculated and extracted from the face of each individual customer invoice. These invoices were only available for this purpose after accounting had processed them for the financial reports.

The data required for the market report was not actually shown on the face of the invoice. All attendant documents were required so specific calculations could be made. Such charges as inland freight, cost of sales, and so on had to be ferreted out and entered in separate boxes at the bottom of the invoice accounting copy. All these calculations and separate charges had to be reconciled with the gross receivables amount as it appeared on the face of the invoice. Manual processing of one invoice might require six or eight documents.

Thus, this whole procedure required the collection of all pertinent papers; completion of all accounting processing; extraction of all pertinent information from substantiating documents; calculation of all charges pertinent to the sale; cross check of this data; manual recording of charges in thirty-two boxes at the bottom of the accounting copy; keypunching of this information into a data base; running the program. Furthermore, all this was done by a centralized accounting and EDP group who had numerous additional demands and commitments.

This system failed for several reasons.

1. It tied up too many people in the effort of making data available for the program.
2. The complexity of the collection system made it almost impossible to make changes or correct errors.
3. The complexity itself generated errors at the collection, accounting and keypunching points.

At the low point of the effort, no one in sales knew who to contact in EDP to make corrections in the output!

Some time-sharing programs are started before it is determined if the information is available at all. Sometimes a projection program is designed and written before it is determined whether any historical information is available!

The systems analyst can help delineate what data is required. He will expect the user to make the data available when it is required. The user must develop the in-house data flow.

Reliability of Data

All the computing power in the world will never change this fact: During the earliest stages of any feasibility study determination of data reliability is critical. A case might reluctantly be made regarding "availability" on the basis of "better late than never." No such aphorism will excuse misinformation, however. The computer even serves to exaggerate this situation. People are inclined to believe what they see in print. They are inclined to believe computer printouts.

> CASE IN POINT: A simple time-sharing program was devised by an exporter. It was designed to allow the salesmen to input details of a shipment and the computer to output a profit estimate. The program worked fine. One day the sales manager, in a routine review of sales, noticed an exorbitant profit on a sale—a profit totally at variance with past performance. When the salesman was queried, his answer was, "Well, that's what the computer reported. You wouldn't want me to argue with the computer, would you?"
>
> He then confidently went to his files, and proudly produced the time-sharing readout. He righteously pointed to the last line that confirmed his profit.
>
> His manager, just as righteously, pointed to the first line—input typed in by the salesman himself. This line contained a cost-of-sales figure at variance with actual by a factor of ten. It could have been at this point that "GIGO" entered the English language.

The need for reliable data is obvious if productive results are to be achieved. In the rush to get the computer to work on a problem this is sometimes overlooked. It is self-evident that this is solely the user's responsibility. Every effort should be made to assure that only reliable information enters the system.

Time sharing offers several unique features to assist the user in maintaining high data reliability. The primary asset is the high degree of user/computer interaction. Data can be input at any time. Data can be edited at any time. Data can be output and reviewed at any time.

This is, of course, in contrast to in-house EDP facilities. These usually have a heavy workload, tightly scheduled processing commitments, and a work regimen that requires input sheet preparation, keypunch input and scheduled operation.

In the market report example given earlier, there were multitudinous errors. Nevertheless, it took weeks to assemble them and more time to organize, format and keypunch these corrections. Finally, additional time passed while a slot between other jobs could be found to run corrective programs.

Once the program was available on time sharing, any corrections could be made in minutes. No input preparation, no keypunching, no scheduling was necessary.

Input of Data

If time sharing's first greatest asset is timeliness, its second is interaction—the ability of the user to gain access to the computer at any time; to input data at a moment's notice; to type in data, call his program and output information.

Assuming the availability and reliability of the data is sound, its input must also be carefully thought out. The preceding market report example is one case. There are several input traps that should be avoided.

1. Voluminous manual input for little and infrequent output.
2. Complex or repetitious interaction.
3. Unnecessary input.
4. Inefficient methods of input.

If a program requires voluminous input from a terminal, consider whether in-house EDP wouldn't be better. Time sharing's value is in its interaction with the user. If the user does all the "action" perhaps this data input would input better via the keypunch route.

There are always exceptions, but the user should keep time sharing for interaction. Voluminous manual input is for conventional EDP processing. They have the staff and equipment; the skills and schedules. Complex or repetitious interaction is another matter. This is entirely within the control of the user and systems analyst.

A large bank had devised a project evaluation program. This was designed so input of an income stream would output a percentage called the profitability index. It was customary to generate ten or fifteen parallel income streams, run a "P.I." on all and compare the results.

A single income stream might consist of ten to twenty numbers. Each represented one year's income. The first number represented initial investment.

Data would look like this:

Option	Initial Investment	Years: 1	in $000,000s 2	3	4	5	6	7	8	9	10
#1	5	2	3	3	3	3	3	3	3	3	3
#2	7	1	2	4	5	5	5	5	5	5	5
#3	11	3	3	4	5	6	6	6	6	6	6

etc.

With five or ten of these options, the user would approach the terminal and face the following.

COMPUTER	COMMENT	OPERATOR
	Dial 123-4567	
LOG IN		HAP 103
—		RUN PI
DO YOU WISH PAYOUT IN YEARS?		YES
DO YOU WISH PAYOUT AS P.I.?		YES
NAME OF PROJECT?		RX 2
DO YOU WISH RESULTS TO FILE OR TO TEL?		TEL
DO YOU WANT TOTAL PROJECT INCOME?		YES
HOW MANY PROJECT YEARS?		10
HOW MUCH WAS THE INITIAL INVESTMENT?		5
INPUT 10 YEARS INCOME		2,3,3,3,3,3,3,3,3,3
	Almost instantly the calculations are made and the answer given.	
2 YEARS, P.I. 30.0, PROJECT INCOME 29		
DO YOU WISH ANOTHER RUN?		YES
DO YOU WISH PAYOUT IN YEARS?		YES
DO YOU WISH PAYOUT AS P.I.?		YES
NAME OF PROJECT?		RX 3
DO YOU WISH RESULTS TO FILE OR TO TEL?		TEL
DO YOU WANT TOTAL PROJECT INCOME?		YES
HOW MANY PROJECT YEARS?		10
HOW MUCH WAS THE INITIAL INVESTMENT?		7
INPUT 10 YEARS INCOME?		1,2,4,5,5,5,5,5,5,5
3 YEARS, P.I. 20.0, PROJECT INCOME 42		
	And for run number three.	

COMPUTER	COMMENT	OPERATOR
DO YOU WISH ANOTHER RUN?		YES
DO YOU WISH PAYOUT IN YEARS?		YES
DO YOU WISH PAYOUT AS P.I.?		YES
NAME OF PROJECT?		RX 4
DO YOU WISH RESULTS TO FILE OR TEL?		TEL
DO YOU WANT TOTAL PROJECT INCOME?		YES
HOW MANY PROJECT YEARS?		10
HOW MUCH WAS THE INITIAL INVESTMENT?		11
INPUT 10 YEARS INCOME?		3,3,5,5,6,6,6,6,6,6

3 YEARS, P.I. 18.0, PROJECT INCOME 52

Ten runs like this can drive any user right up the wall. You will note the computer requests "How many project years?" in question seven, and then instructs the user "input *10* years income." The computer is quite capable of counting the income stream numbers themselves after they are input. The only reason for question seven is to ask question nine!

Without elaborating on the many obvious faults in the above, here is how it should be done.

COMPUTER	COMMENT	OPERATOR
	Dial 123-4567	
LOG IN		HAP 103
—		RUN PI
DATA?		5,2,3,3,3,3,3,3,3
		7,1,2,4,5,5,5,5,5,5
		11,3,3,5,5,6,6,6,6,6,
2 YEARS, P.I. 30.0, PROJECT INCOME 29		
3 YEARS, P.I. 20.0, PROJECT INCOME 42		
3 YEARS, P.I. 24.0, PROJECT INCOME 52		
CONTINUE?		NO
—		LOGOUT

Watch this: Avoid this type of designing. Keep firmly in mind that this is the milieu of the user. The design of the program should not only solve the problem, but it should be easy and efficient to operate.

If this advice is not heeded your users will desert you. To save the program, costly redesign may be necessary.

Time sharing relieves tedious work. The user will frequently slip back to his manual technique if the computer demands too much of him.

A poorly designed program may provide the answer, however, if it is difficult to initiate, the user may prefer a longer but more relaxed procedure, i.e. the old manual method.

A further aggravation is questions so badly phrased or worded the intent is obscure. An example from the above is the query, "Input data to tel?" Does this mean you are to give the data to the computer, or is the computer asking whether you want it to type something?

Again, the user gets what he asks for—either well thought-out questions or questions left to someone else. For piece of mind, considerable care should be devoted to this subject.

Time sharing is not a continuous activity. Computer output, such as questions developed casually during programming, may appear quite ambiguous when returned to after a month's absence.

Input direct from the terminal to the computer is not the only input means. The user and system analyst must decide which is most appropriate. Several alternatives might be:

1. Input to a file.
2. Paper tape.
3. Tab cards (keypunch).
4. Magnetic tape.

Each has its own advantages. Input first to a computer file allows for easy editing and changes in data between runs. Paper tape allows off-line typing, which avoids on-line charges during the typing of a large file. Tab cards permit the keypunching of voluminous data bases, for instance, outside the time-sharing environment. Magnetic tape can store data cheaply off-line, but have it ready for input promptly when required. Large data bases updated quarterly might fall into this category.

Timeliness of Data

The computer has increased our ability to process information a thousandfold. In the market report example cited earlier, we couldn't economically produce such a document in the fifties. In the following decade we produce it and complain because it's twenty-five days late!

Like it or not, however, computer output is like the daily paper. If it's one day old, it's out of date. There's still some leeway with computer printouts, but the more current they are, the more valuable they are.

Time sharing improves by another order of magnitude the timeliness of reports. Continuous access to the computer accounts for this. Constant interaction with the computer both for input and output provides this capability. The user should make every effort to capitalize on this time-sharing characteristic. The planning for data input should be as continuous as possible.

The output of reports should be as current as possible. There will always be some competitiveness between in-house and time-sharing services. Timeliness is one of time sharing's built-in advantages. Input and output should be designed to reflect this. Collection, revision and update of data should be patterned to take advantage of this.

This advantage functions at two levels.

1. Individual Problem Solving.
2. Report Generating.

Such programs as regression analysis, financial evaluation and acquisition studies are one-time shots. You collect your data, feed it into the computer, and walk away with the results.

When your data is ready, you want to run it. You, the user, are not interested in having it "scheduled." You are not interested in having it first "reformatted" or "keypunched." Time sharing takes in the data whenever you supply it and outputs your answers then and there.

Report-generating programs usually process a large data bank and output reports. The reports are as current as the last information input. If this data is input once a month, some reports, when issued, are a month late. Time sharing provides continuous access to these data bases. Daily updating can become routine. If the data bank is current, the reports are current.

At a large New York concern a current file of invoices is maintained. On the first of each month each area and division manager receives a listing of each transaction for the preceding month, and a net sales and gross profit summary. Since the file is current (based on daily input), the reports are current.

Personnel Requirements

During the feasibility study, considerable time and effort must be devoted to two phases of the personnel picture.

1. What type of personnel is required for the time-sharing effort?
2. Can the effort replace existing personnel, or will it be directed to developing new information sources?

Time sharing is new enough so that specific personnel characteristics have not been defined.

We probably all have observed that some people take to computers, while others can't abide them. Training, familiarization or psychology will not change this.

Time sharing, for the next few years, at least, will have to be staffed by volunteers. You know how to select volunteers; they're the fools who step forward when everybody else steps back.

Fortunately, there is one further technique—a screen for the volunteers, if you will. This one rarely fails. Sit the person at a terminal, and tell him what to do. One person will take the experience comfortably, another will agonize. I've seen it happen many times, the initial reaction at the terminal is indicative of future performance. Certainly no one should be employed without some checkout in the time-sharing environment.

Replacing existing personnel with time-sharing activities is quite possible. One New York exporter replaced a six-member order and billing write-up group with a terminal and one time-sharing terminal operator. These situations are so unique, however, that they are difficult to identify. There is enormous power in time-sharing; it is up to the user to put it to its best advantage.

Hardware Capability

In an in-house feasibility study, hardware governs the direction of the computer effort. Fortunately, in time sharing, if the hardware isn't available from one time-sharing company, it will be from another. The time-sharing user has great flexibility in this area, sometimes even using two time-sharing companies to produce a single report.

A large textile concern in New York was using a time-sharing company in Philadelphia. Although there were plenty of New York time-sharing companies, the text editor and input/output mode particularly suited this firm's requirements. However, when the monthly summary was due, it required a high-speed printer. The only one available was in New York. The solution was to extract the data base from the Philadelphia computer on magnetic tape. Input this to a local New York time-sharing company. Then run the report on the local high-speed printer and walk three blocks to pick up the printout.

There is one area of restriction on the time-sharing user—his input/output devices. If you have a 10 cps (characters per second) machine, don't expect to output a 500-page report. It would take one work-week!

In the hardware area, the time-sharing user selects services to meet his requirements. He may use several services if their hardware suits his needs.

Choosing your time-sharing service is therefore an integral part of your feasibility study. The feasibility study for project "A" might indicate time-sharing company "K." For the next project nothing will prevent you from selecting company "L" if the hardware better suits your purpose. Time sharing no doubt provides greater hardware flexibility than any other computer approach.

Usefulness of Output

The feasibility study must determine that all this activity will result in the output of useful information. Since the time-sharing user is frequently the user of its output, this should be easy, but this is not always so.

Time-sharing information frequently elicits a long route list. Some are people who really need it, some are people who think they need it, and some are people who think they should be on the route list.

Newspapers frequently wonder if a comic strip is actually being read. To find out, they simply don't print it for a week. If readers complain, they reinstate it. If no response is forthcoming, they drop it. This is the best way to determine if a report is being used. Output it, but don't issue it. If no one calls to ask for it, it can't be of much value.

COST ANALYSIS

Cost analysis is an integral part of the feasibility study, since with an unlimited budget anything is possible. The purpose of cost analysis, run concurrently with the feasibility study, is to determine if you are getting your money's worth.

1. Is the cost of input worth the output?
2. Will the information output be used?
3. Is a one-shot job worth the program building cost?
4. Is it really a time-sharing job?

The user must answer these types of questions during the cost analysis. The same type of criteria should be applied to a time-sharing cost analysis as to any other business evaluation.

Computer cost analysis, however, has yet to be well defined. If your company has developed a cost assignment procedure it is probably as good as any other. The present "state of the art" is far from perfected. Common sense is the best guide.

DATA COLLECTION, STUDY AND RECORDING

The third phase of the feasibility study concerns data collection, study and recording. The user and systems analyst must resolve the following questions:

1. What data is available?
2. How will it be processed?
3. How will it be output?

The user must depend heavily on the systems analyst. The user knows what and where the information is. The systems analyst must organize and format it for computer use, processing and output. It is in this area that the value of the systems analyst becomes apparent. It is also here where the user is called upon to describe his data sources and operations in depth. Failure at either level can jeopardize or misdirect the project. If the user can define his requirements precisely, the systems analyst can design the program accurately.

INPUT-OUTPUT DESIGN

Input-output design determines whether the system will efficiently serve the user's needs, or become a millstone around his neck. Once the job is done, input-output is the user's responsibility. Input-output is the house you finally live in. Once the house is built, the user is responsible for the results.

The user's activities will then center on this input-output function. Once the program is finished, it is buried in the computer. The user's actions revolve around his interaction with the program. The user's responsibility now becomes:

1. To develop sources of data.
2. To assemble the data for input.
3. To substantiate the data for accuracy.
4. To input the data.
5. To output the data.
6. To feed back corrections to the data.

The user's interaction with the systems analyst sets the tone, pace and style of everything that comes afterward. This is where all problems should be anticipated and solved. This design phase is the user's last chance to make changes and adjustments.

Systems analysis is the architectural phase of program design. From here on changes not only become difficult, but costly and hazardous as well.

12

USER INTERACTION WITH THE TIME-SHARING PROGRAMMER

Meticulous interaction with the systems analyst is necessary if it is to result in a blueprint for the programmer. The analyst's output can take a number of forms:

1. Verbal description of requirements to the programmer.
2. A written description or outline.
3. A flowchart.
4. A combination of all three.

Don't rely on verbal descriptions. These are the most tempting to use, and the most catastrophic to implement.

First, unless you attend each analyst/programmer session, you have no fix on the direction and thrust of program development. Second, you have no check on how effective your interaction with the systems analyst has been. Finally, even if you attend these analyst/programmer sessions, they are likely to be conducted in an EDP goobledygook completely foreign to a user.

Scratch option number one.

A written description or outline is frequently used. This technique helps the user find out what he has been talking about and the programmer what he is supposed to do. The degree of detail will depend on the systems analyst, but the accuracy will depend on how well you, the user, review his efforts.

A written description may well be the only one you feel comfortable with. Keep in mind this will be the only way you can change, modify or correct the program in the future.

Don't regard this written summary simply as confirmation of your conversations with the systems analyst. This is the blueprint of your program. The final design of your house. Study and review it as you would the final drawings of your home. If you find no mention of an air conditioner, there will be none in the final structure. If there is no mention of storage space (literally, in the home *or* the program), none will be included.

Personally, I distrust written descriptions. The English language simply is not precise enough to do justice to computer requirements.

CASE IN POINT: Many dollars can be lost unless the programmer is provided with a clear chart of his direction. Reprogramming to correct faulty descriptions can be very costly. For instance, at a large commodity house a time-sharing program was written and

189

SYSTEM FLOWCHART SYMBOLS

PROCESSING A major processing function.	**INPUT/ OUTPUT** Any type of medium or data.
PUNCHED CARD All varieties of punched cards including stubs.	**PERFORATED TAPE** Paper or plastic, chad or chadless.
DOCUMENT Paper documents and reports of all varieties.	**TRANSMITTAL TAPE** A proof or adding machine tape or similar batch-control information.
MAGNETIC TAPE	**DISK, DRUM, RANDOM ACCESS**
OFFLINE STORAGE Offline storage of either paper, cards, magnetic or perforated tape.	**DISPLAY** Information displayed by plotters or video devices.
ONLINE KEYBOARD Information supplied to or by a computer utilizing an online device.	**SORTING, COLLATING** An operation on sorting or collating equipment.
CLERICAL OPERATION A manual offline operation not requiring mechanical aid.	**AUXILIARY OPERATION** A machine operation supplementing the main processing function.
KEYING OPERATION An operation utilizing a key-driven device.	**COMMUNICATION LINK** The automatic transmission of information from one location to another via communication lines.
FLOW ◁ ▷ ▽ △	The direction of processing or data flow.

FIGURE 31   FLOWCHART TEMPLATE

tied to certain in-house EDP runs. It functioned perfectly and produced meaningful information specifically designed for sales and marketing.

After several months of operation, the in-house people requested a "hash total." To them, this meant a total number of all units processed. It was meaningless to sales, since it amounted to adding up apples, oranges and pineapples. To EDP it was a necessary computer check on throughput.

Result: Programming charges of several thousand dollars to meet a nonuser, but essential, requirement.

Unfortunately, some people never quite get the hang of a flowchart. This is unquestionably the best form of communication between user, systems analyst and programmer. It is the computer equivalent of the architectural blueprint.

If you are comfortable with flowcharts, they can be used in a multitude of ways to assist your time-sharing activities. The full spectrum of time-sharing operations is susceptible to flowcharting. There are a number of flowcharts that can be used:

1. Broad brush flowcharts.
2. Detailed flowcharts.
3. System flowcharts.
4. Program flowcharts.
5. Procedural flowcharts.
6. Documentation flowcharts.

BROAD BRUSH FLOWCHARTS

The initial outline of a package of programs may be diagrammed in this way. No detail is included; only the flow of generalized activities is laid out. The procession of the data through several programs is described. A flowcharting template is used to draw these symbols.

Templates, Figure 31, are available from a number of sources. Several computer companies, including IBM, supply these free to their customers. There is the International Organization for Standardization (ISO), which recommends standardized symbol usage.

In fact, the user may select symbols for his own convenience, or follow those recommended on the template. Those used to describe a broad brush flowchart might be as in Figure 32.

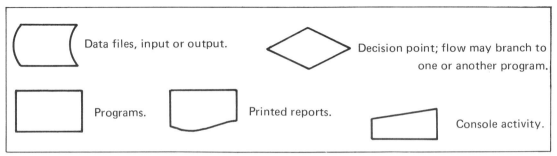

FIGURE 32 TEMPLATE SYMBOLS

For broad brush flowcharts only the input, output and interaction are indicated; no details are shown (Figure 33). This guide is then used to maintain control of the sessions with the systems analyst and the programmer.

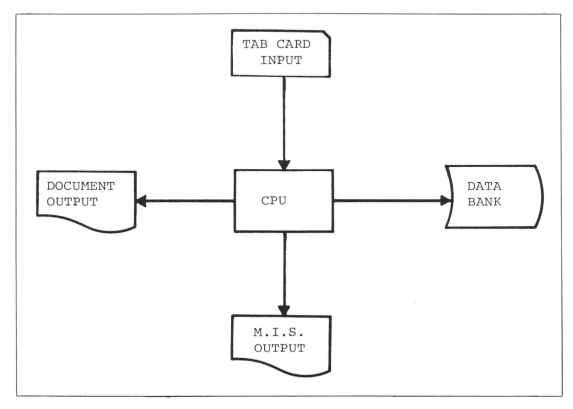

FIGURE 33   BROAD BRUSH FLOWCHART

The broad brush flowchart keeps you on the track. It tells you where you have been, where you are and where you are going. When the package of programs is completed, it then serves as a guide when you run the whole package. It is your roadmap through the package of programs being created.

DETAILED FLOWCHARTS

Just as the name implies, all details of a system can also be delineated. Drawn up by the systems analyst, this flowchart will not only confirm your discussions with him, but highlight any breakdown in logic if such has occurred.

A detailed system flowchart would describe the input and output element by element. Each piece of data contained in a file would be listed, each source of data spelled out, and each report header fully developed. This type of detail is frequently overlooked. It is better to encounter problems at this stage than discover such omissions partway through the programming.

Common sense should guide you at this stage. The urge to "get on with the programming" is great. Mistakes at this level can be corrected with an erasure. Omissions uncovered during or after the programming phase can be very costly. The detailed flowchart should account for every piece of input and output.

SYSTEM FLOWCHARTS

These charts have nothing to do with the computer per se. They are concerned with the flow of information up to input and after output. All this flowcharting concerns itself with is the manual effort involved in the systems work. This documentation not only serves in laying out the program, but later will serve as a guide to the manual input phase of the operation.

Complex program packages require precise and extensive input organization. This is what a system flowchart details.

PROGRAM FLOWCHARTS

The systems analyst's communication with the programmer can best be achieved with program flowcharts. The user should consider these as the final result of his interaction with the systems analyst.

Program flowcharts should not be given just a cursory glance by the user. He should be able to follow them through step by step. Every input, every logic loop, every output should be confirmed within the design.

The day of the grandiose instruction to the programmer is past. The program flowchart is the nitty-gritty of the systems effort. "Write me a program to output invoice totals" is a request that shirks the user's responsibilities. It is the type of request that results in the computer horror story everyone has shuddered at. The eight months' effort that was abandoned as too complicated, too involved, or too expensive. If the effort is, in fact, any of these, it should be uncovered during the flowcharting phase, not after six months of programming.

Program flowcharts become the track on which the total effort runs. All details of data handling, mathematical formulation, and output can and should be anticipated and indicated.

Once user and systems analyst have agreed on the detailed flowchart, the job of the programmer is straightforward, a simple job of translation.

The reasons for this attention to detail is twofold:

1. What the program does is the responsibility of the user.
2. Too little detail casts the programmer in the role of systems analyst—a role he neither wants, nor for which he is trained.

Figure 34 is a program flowchart. Each file is described, each data flow delineated. Careful analysis of this flowchart shows that it accounts for all input, manipulation and output from the combination of programs described.

One common-sense qualification should be added to this description of program flowcharts. The objective is to anticipate problems, not create them. The flowchart

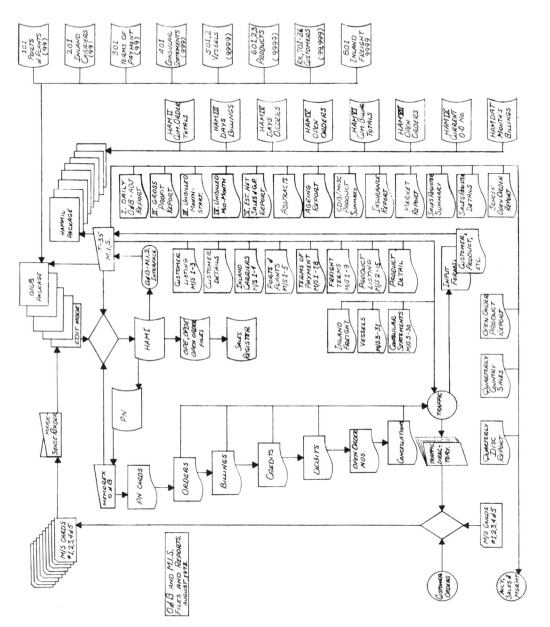

FIGURE 34   PROGRAM FLOWCHART

194

should detail the user's requirements, not those of the programmer. Note in Figure 34 that certain temporary files are indicated, not detailed, i.e. UNPAID, PDINV, etc. These are files used and processed by the programmer and their structure is the prerogative of the programmer.

Thus, as might be expected, a cooperative and understanding interaction must exist between user, systems analyst and programmer. From this interaction should come the most productive final blueprint of the package—the final program flowchart.

Detailed flowcharts are sometimes used by programmers. These break the program down into its component logic, loops, decision points and calculations. They may detail each command given in the program. Such flowcharts should not generally concern the user.

PROCEDURAL FLOWCHARTS

This aspect of a time-sharing operation may be either in the form of a flowchart or a written description. Both techniques are used interchangeably. They are selected for convenience and familiarity.

When describing program operation in this book, we have chosen to use the

COMPUTER   COMMENT   OPERATOR

format. A flowchart can also be used for this purpose. Figure 35 outlines such a flowchart. The program makes several requests of the user, and then outputs a report.

This flowchart design is strictly for the user's benefit. Whichever mode is comfortable should be used. The technique details computer output and user response as interconnected action. Like all flowcharts, the choice of shapes is arbitrary. Diamonds are generally reserved as decision points, but any consistent choice of forms is acceptable. Clarity to the user is the only criterion.

DOCUMENTATION FLOWCHARTS

This name is applied to the flow of paperwork into and out of the time-sharing system. Work is organized to develop and process data for computer input. The output is then charted to each ultimate user.

This type of flowcharting differs from the systems flowcharting described earlier. The former concerns itself with computer input only, the latter with complete flow of information throughout the system. It describes the people and paper flow impacted by the time-sharing activity.

It goes without saying that not all types of flowcharting are applicable to each undertaking. However, once the appropriate flowcharts are prepared, it is time to approach the programmer.

If dealing with the systems analyst is like writing a book, dealing with the programmer is like having it translated into Arabic. Programming is an area so foreign to many users, they may despair of ever fathoming its mysteries. If you fall into this

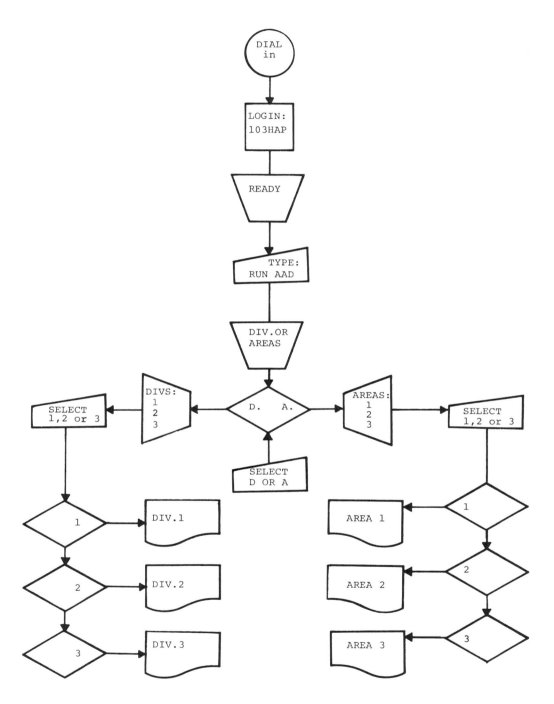

FIGURE 35   PROCEDURAL FLOWCHART

category, go all out in the systems study to delineate every step. Making changes at the programming level will be very difficult.

There are two types of people. Those who can cope with programming and those who can't. Like chess, it either makes sense to you, or it doesn't. No amount of effort will change this. Both types of people can use time sharing. The fact that programming is a mystery does not reduce a user's effectiveness with the computer. Once the program is up and running, programming disappears into the background. You don't have to know how to build a car in order to drive it.

It is important, however, for you to decide where you stand on this subject. It will affect how you deal with the programmer. If programming is a comprehensible subject to you, you can discuss the program in terms of commands, loops and techniques. If a mystery, studiously avoid using the programmer's jargon. Restrict your conversation to what you want done, not how the programmer should work. This advice cannot be emphasized strongly enough. During the programming phase everyone gets caught up in the project. Even the most aloof user picks up some computer terms and programming knowledge.

The best-designed system will require some interaction between programmer and user. If you have decided programming is not for you, answer the question within your own frame of reference. Thus, there are two ways to deal with the programmer:

1. Participate in his programming project.
2. Maintain your own user frame of reference.

A simplistic example might be as follows:

Programmer's Question: "I've collected all these billings in a file. How do you want them output?"

Programming Oriented User's Answer: "I want you to read the file for variables A, E and X, sum on the variable "recv," and output as "North Dist.," "South Dist." and "West Dist."

Nonprogramming User's Answer: "I want the three area totals."

Let's repeat what was said a few paragraphs back. The nonprogramming oriented user explains what's required, not how to do it.

Most programmers would recommend this advice for all users. In the long run, it is the best advice. However, those who find they have a programming proficiency shouldn't be prevented from exercising it.

Although a mixed blessing, a basic familiarity with the programmer's tools can assist on the communications level. In the fifties, programming was handled at a very elementary level. Computers operated on the binary system. That is, a system of numbers having two as its base. In contrast, our decimal system has ten as its base.

The binary system enables the computer to manipulate all numbers on the basis of "on" and "off." These conditions are represented as zero and one in the computer.

Using the binary system, the numbers zero through nine are represented as follows:

BASE 10:	0	1	2	3	4	5	6	7	8	9
BASE 2:	0	1	10	11	100	101	110	111	1000	1001

Commands such as "add," "subtract," "equals" and "compare" can also be reduced to similar nomenclature.

Computer programming began this way. Programs had to be written or "plugged into" the computer as binary commands. Programs had to be written in terms the computer could understand, or "machine language." Obviously, this means of communication with the computer was slow and tedious. To relieve the programmer of thinking in machine language, techniques were devised for the computer to undertake this task.

The first efforts involved purely numeric sequences. The programmer wrote his program as a series of decimal numbers, i.e. 189762518. Based on their position in the line and the numbers themselves, the computer might interpret this as add 762 and 518. Action in the computer would be in binary form. The action within the computer to interpret the programmer's decimal notation to binary was called "compiling."

At Dartmouth College in 1964, a new computer language was devised called "BASIC." This was designed to be as close to English as possible. The objective was to strip programming of its mystique and make it available to all. It succeeded pretty well. Today most college graduates have been exposed to programming, and many use it routinely.

Today programming consists of writing instructions to the computer in this "semi-English" and having the computer translate (compile) this into machine language.

The more sophisticated languages are quite legible. Two of the more commonly used in time sharing are BASIC and FORTRAN. Mathematical nomenclature is used whenever possible. Thus, + means add, - means subtract, and, to accommodate keyboard configurations, / means divide and * means multiply.

Simply:

3 + 2,   three plus two
3 - 2,   three minus two
3 / 2,   three divided by two
3 * 2,   three multiplied by two

The only symbol radically different from its mathematical application is the equals sign. It is used in program writing not to indicate both sides *are* equal, but to instruct the computer to *make* both sides equal. Thus, SUM = 3 + 2 means that from this point in the program on, the variable name "SUM" will be valued as 5.

You'll never learn programming from this book. However, just so the first program text waved under your nose won't be a complete surprise, consider the following.

All you need to know is that a "variable" is a group of letters arbitrarily chosen to represent any number assigned to it. It is similar to the X and Y of algebra Thus, X + 5 might be written ABCAB + 5. Single variable names such as X may be used, of course.

There are two reasons why single-letter variables such as X are not commonly used, however.

1. Usually there are more than twenty-six variables in a program, thus you soon run out of the alphabet.
2. It is customary to use acronyms as variables so they will be identifiable when reading the text, i.e. the variable for "payroll total" might be "paytl."

Selecting examples from both the BASIC and FORTRAN languages, consider these commands:

COMMAND	TRANSLATION
10 LET B = 526	Let the variable name "B" represent the number 526.
20 SVL = BXL - 26	Let the variable name SVL equal the result of the subtraction of 26 from the variable BXL.
30 PCT = (BXL-SVL)/BXL	Solve the expression (BXL-SVL) and divide by BXL. Thus PCT is set equal to the result.

Coding constantly tends toward simplification and readability. The objective is to make encoding simpler, and let the computer do the translation (compiling).

There are numerous program languages. They progress from the binary computer language through "BAL," a basic assemble language to COBOL, a strongly business oriented language.

Languages sometimes are selected because they suit the program to be written. A "powerful" language means a language that will manipulate the various elements required by the program quickly and expeditiously. A sophisticated language is one in which complex mathematical calculations are instituted with a single command.

The user will pick up a smattering of this jargon in time. It may help him communicate with the programmer. As a user, however, emphasis should be put on performance not execution.

TESTING AND DEBUGGING

The most trying phase of any program construction is testing and debugging. You can see the light at the end of the tunnel, but the damn program simply won't run! The user must monitor the accuracy and format of the output, but must avoid getting involved in the mechanics of the operation.

This is the stage that separates the men from the boys, the managers from the technicians. Here the systems work pays off. Here the fudged input, sloppy calculation or poor format sticks out like a sore thumb.

Programmers should not be expected to compensate for the user's initial oversights after the job is done. Inevitably some bugs will creep in, but good systems/user interaction should keep these to a minimum. You, the user, will be held accountable, in no uncertain terms, if you have provided inaccurate information.

The user is now in the middle. The program must output usable information, yet revision becomes a painful process. Only two pieces of advice can be offered:

1. Get it right the first time.
2. Or, grin and bear it.

There is nothing more that can be offered if your design is faulty. There is some advice that can be offered regarding testing and debugging, however. There are a number of pitfalls the user should avoid. Unpleasant as it may be, they can only be enumerated as a series of negative statements.

1. Don't lose sight of your ultimate objectives.
2. Don't compromise because it will take "too long to reprogram."
3. Don't run the program over and over finding error after error; avoid the debugging activity.
4. Insist on a working program before accepting responsibility for it.
5. Don't compromise on output or format.
6. Don't accept clumsy or manually tedious input.
7. Never assume the systems analyst or programmer knows either your job or your requirements.
8. Above all, remember: The program you are building is the house you have to live in.

Unfortunately, the above advice will be greeted most enthusiastically by those who have already lived through the debugging experience. I can only urge that it be taken to heart by those who haven't.

13

PRACTICAL TIME-SHARING DOCUMENTATION TECHNIQUES

Clear, concise documentation is the user's single most important control of the time-sharing environment. By documentation the user puts computer activities into the language he can understand.

Documentation provides the user with a description of how the program operates. It should take the user through those commands that call the program up for implementation; provide the list of commands to activate the program; explain just what input is required, and delineate each step the user must take to run the program.

In the final analysis, because documentation is so vital to the user, he must view it as his responsibility. Even though he will be provided with some sort of documentation, it is better to revise it to his own familiar procedures.

Documentation can proceed at several levels. The first is the programming phase. Here the programmer describes the reasons for his logic. He makes notes on the scope, flow and thrust of his programming. This type of documentation may really be considered as programmer-to-programmer communication. Its purpose is to aid another programmer if, at a later date, he should be required to revise a program he did not originate.

Fortunately, the user doesn't need, nor can he use such documentation. It is noted here merely to alert the user to the fact that such techniques exist. It is noted first since it represents documentation at the basic level of program origination.

CASE IN POINT: A properly designed time-sharing program is easy and efficient to operate. However, one must live in the computer environment to feel comfortable.

To a newcomer, even the simplest commands and responses appear confusing at first blush. Sound documentation protects against confusion.

At a New York department store, certain fast-moving elements of inventory were put on time sharing. This was done at the request of a buyer who then confounded his peers with his timely and current grasp of his operations.

Then the inevitable happened. The buyer was transferred to a suburban store as manager. His replacement was unfamiliar with computer interaction. The new buyer's first attempt at querying the system brought forth a flood of computerese.

"No such file."

"What?"

"File not saved."

"Option 1 or option 2?"

It brought back the former buyer from suburbia and cost both new store manager and new buyer a week of training to acquaint the latter with the system.

Documentation could have saved thousands of dollars, and both men's time and effort.

The user will come in contact, and must use, a variety of documentation techniques. There are almost as many as there are time-sharing companies. Since time sharing is relatively new, no standardized technique has been developed.

Documentation assumes a variety of forms. The most common of these are the following:

1. Top-of-the-program-text documentation.
2. Interactive documentation.
3. Type-defined documentation.
4. Expository documentation.
5. Color-differentiated documentation.
6. Underlining documentation.
7. Stand-alone documentation.
8. Three-column documentation.

Each technique has its advantages and drawbacks. Each method may appear obvious and simple to one user, incomprehensible to another. The best advice is to find with which method you are most comfortable. Once one method works for you, convert all incoming documentation to this format and maintain your own documentation library. This is not as cumbersome as it might appear. Any program is preceded by a learning phase in so far as the user is concerned. Converting the documentation to your style will highlight any omissions in the original documentation. Furthermore, it will give you a dry run of the interaction you will experience on-line.

Usually this type of redocumentation will continue as you run the program. The end result will be a combination familiarization and documentation activity. When completed you will be able to run the program and have documentation to guide others through the program.

Comprehensive and detailed documentation has another value. Personnel does not remain static. Each user adds his own "wrinkles" to program operation. Programs may be changed or modified after original implementation. If the operator leaves or "is run over by a truck" only sound documentation stands between you and total confusion. One-shot scientific programs or library programs can be puzzled out. Your own proprietary programs must be supported by your own documentation.

The insidious part of this situation is the danger of being lulled into a false sense of security. Once incorporated into the daily flow, the system runs smoothly. Months can go by with no reference to the documentation. The computer and operator perform flawlessly. Suddenly, the operator is replaced. Everything is in turmoil. You are back to ground zero. Unless you have solid documentation to fall back on, training and running can become a nightmare.

Documentation is your security blanket; never neglect it. Build the original documentation solidly and completely. Review and update it whenever necessary.

Times to update it occur fairly often for a variety of reasons. Be alert to these times, which may include:

1. Internal programming changes.
2. Enlargement of your own system.
3. Time-sharing company procedural modifications.
4. Addition of new programs.

TOP-OF-THE-PROGRAM-TEXT DOCUMENTATION

For the user, this is the weakest method of documentation. It is known for its brevity and incomprehensibility.

Most time-sharing languages provide this type of capability. They allow for a code designation that instructs the computer to ignore the following text. This text is simply exposition to the user. It tells him what files he needs and what is the purpose of the program.

Such documentation looks like this:

```
C       /√2/->/√B2/->/√FM2/
C       LOAD /√B2/ AS MAIN
C       /√SA/
C       /√SB/
C       /√TLIB/
C       'SPLIB'
C       'LIB'
C       MARK SENSE READ, STORE, SORT
        INTEGER START,DATE,ERTN
        COMMON START,DATE(4),MAIN(2000),FDATA(4,20)
        DIMENSION INPUT(120),FPDATA(4),ICARDS(800),M1001(800),IFORM(5),
           NOX(5)
        DIMENSION IADJUS(20),ICA(5),FRTRT(20)
        EQUIVALENCE (INPUT(1),MAIN(1)),(FPDATA(1),MAIN(122))
       1,(ICARDS(1),MAIN(131)),(NINETY,MAIN(932)),(M1001(1),MAIN(1001))
        EQUIVALENCE (IADJUS(1),MAIN(935)),(ISPADJ,MAIN(999))

C     ICA123=FLAG TO WARN ME ORDER A BILLING BEING RUN AT SAME TIME
        EQUIVALENCE (MAIN(938),ICA123)
C       ASSIGN FORMATS TO IFORM

        ASSIGN 1520 TO IFORM(1)
        ASSIGN 1530 TO IFORM(2)
        ASSIGN 1540 TO IFORM(3)
        ASSIGN 1545 TO IFORM(4)
        ASSIGN 1550 TO IFORM(5)

C       NOW NUMBER OF WORDS

        DATA NWX/17,12,14,11,14/

        GO TO(1,590,2200),START
1       DATA IBLK/3H /
        DO 2 I=1901,1917
```

```
2        MAIN(I)=3H***
         NUP=O
     READ SORTED INPUT
         CALL OPENB(9,1,6H/ERRO/)
         CALL OPENB(4,0,6H/√ORD/)
590      DATA ICARDS,IOB,ICA,NINETY,IEFLO,ISPADJ/O/
         DATA IADJUS/-1/
         IADJUS(9)=99999
         IADJUS(13)=99999
         IADJUS(14)=99999
```

Wherever the letter "C" initiates a line, the computer does not act on what follows. "C" designates "comment" and is only for the programmer's, systems analyst's or user's information.

Specifically, the first comments indicate what other programs will be used in conjunction with this one.

The second line indicates that the source file B2 must be used for input.

The next five lines ennumerate the subsidiary programs used when this program is run.

The eighth line explains the purpose of this program. That is, to activate a specific input device (a mark-sense optical card reader). The program will then store this information and sort it numerically. All this you will note is contained in the brief comment "mark sense read, store, sort."

The next seven lines, not preceded by a "C," are computer commands.

Line 17 is a comment purely for the programmer's edification. It is simply a reminder to himself of a particular program characteristic.

Obviously, this type of documentation is not too informative to the user. It mainly serves the programmer. It can be made as elaborate as necessary, but it is clumsy when incorporated in the program text and is therefore not often used.

Remember that each program has two versions. First is the text of the program. This is in "readable" form. The second is the binary form, that is, the computer language version used by the computer. The normal procedure is to write the program, compile it (which produces the binary version) and save the text off-line. This means it is no longer available at the terminal. Thus, each time the program is run it is necessary to refer to the program text. Usually this is filed separately.

In summary, operating instructions typed as an integral part of the program should be avoided by the user. Specifically, its drawbacks are:

1. Instructions are inserted by the programmer and are too computerized for user legibility.
2. They are usually difficult to access in the timely and intermittent time-sharing environment.

INTERACTIVE DOCUMENTATION

This technique is frequently used with time-sharing library programs. The program belongs to the time-sharing company and is called for use when needed by the user.

Such text typed out at the computer might look like this. The computer types:

The purpose of this program is to fit six curves to data supplied.

The data must be input prior to each run by typing in the following format.

500 data N, N1, N2, N3, N4, N5

510 data N6, N7, N8, N9, N10

520 data N11, N12

Don't use a comma at the end of the line. When data is in type "GO."

Once these instructions have been carried out, the computer processes the data and types:

REGANA.

PLEASE SPECIFY THE NUMBER OF VALUES [N] GIVEN AS DATA FOR THE TWO INPUT VARIABLES, AND THE OUTPUT CODE [D]. [D=1 IF OUTPUT IS TO BE IN ORDER OF INCREASING VALUES OF THE INDEPENDENT VARIABLE, ELSE D=0]. N,D =

The user then inserts

1,1.5,2,2.5,3, etc.

The program then runs and outputs its results:

LEAST-SQUARES CURVEFIT

CURVE TYPE	INDEX	A	B
1. Y=A+[B*X]	5.96246 E-2	4.93421	-.236842
2. Y=A*EXP[B*X]	6.79621 E-3	3.34458	-4.22812 E-3
3. Y=A*[X+B]	4.28484 E-2	3.83113	-.102162
4. Y=A+[B/X]	.135872	2.32305	6.09218
5. Y=1/[A+B*X]	NEGATIVE	.494583	-2.62454 E-2
6. Y=X/[A*X+B]	NEGATIVE	.328644	.148198

FOR WHICH CURVE ARE DETAILS DESIRED [GIVE NUMBER]?   [user types 4]

4. Y=A+[B/X] IS A HYPERBOLIC FUNCTION. THE RESULTS OF A LEAST-SQUARES FIT OF ITS LINEAR TRANSFORM ARE AS FOLLOWS:

X-ACTUAL	Y-ACTUAL	Y-CALC	PCT DIFFER
3	1	4.35378	-77
4	1.5	3.8461	-60.9
5	2	3.54149	-43.5
6	2.5	3.33842	-25.1
7	3	3.19336	-6
8	3.5	3.08457	13.4
7	4	3.19336	25.2
6	4.5	3.33842	34.7

X-ACTUAL	Y-ACTUAL	Y-CALC	PCT DIFFER
5	5	3.54149	41.1
4	5.5	3.8461	43.
3	6	4.35378	37.8
2	6.5	5.36914	21.

This documentation has several advantages. It is self-contained. It is available whenever you wish to run the program. It supplies you with an immediate answer.

It also has several disadvantages. The explanations are brief and cryptic. You don't know what data is needed until the program is run. After you are familiar with the operation, you still get the explanation every time you activate the program. Finally, unless the user is very familiar with his subject, the technical aspects of the explanation may discourage him from exploring new applications or new programs.

Another application of this technique is to add subsidiary text to the program. This information may be called for after the program is activated. It explains how the program should be run. The procedure is to call the program, and then type a separate command that outputs the documentation. This may be in any of the conventional formats.

Such built-in documentation might look like this:

PLEASE LOG IN   HAP 103
RUN   LINREG
TYPE GO, INSTRUCTIONS OR RUN   GO, INSTRUCTIONS

INSTRUCTIONS

THIS IS A LINEAR REGRESSION PROGRAM FOR DATA IN TWO VARIABLES, X AND Y. FROM INPUT POINTS, DESCRIBED BY THEIR X AND Y COORDINATES, AN EQUATION IS PRODUCED THAT BEST FITS THESE POINTS, IN A LEAST SQUARES SENSE

THE RESTRICTIONS ON THE DATA POINTS FOR THE DIFFERENT CURVES ARE:

CURVE TYPE	RESTRICTIONS
1	NONE
2	Y > 0
3	Y > 0 AND X > 0
4	X # 0
5	Y # 0
6	X # 0 AND Y # 0

THE PROGRAM WILL ALSO PRINT OUT YOUR DATA PLUS NEW CALCULATED VALUES OF Y ACCORDING TO THE FORMULAS GIVEN UNDER :CAPABILITIES
THE PROGRAM WILL ASK YOU FOR ONE OF THE FOLLOWING PRINT OPTIONS AT RUN TIME
1) Y-ACTUAL AND Y CALCULATED TABLE
2) ANALYSIS OF VARIANCE TABLE

3) BOTH OF THE ABOVE

4) NONE OF THE ABOVE

THE PROGRAM AUTOMATICALLY GIVES THE CONFIDENCE LIMITS TABLE REGARDLESS OF WHICH OF THE ABOVE OPTIONS YOU CHOOSE. THE CONFIDENCE LIMITS ARE COMPUTED BASED ON THE %-TILE OF STUDENT T-DIST'N YOU GIVE

THE F-STATISTIC IS ALSO GIVEN WITH THE ANALYSIS OF VARIANCE TABLE

THE X,Y POINTS MAY BE ENTERED FROM A FILE OR FROM THE TERMINAL. ENTER THE POINTS IN THE FOLLOWING FORMAT:

ENTER THE POINTS IN THE FORMAT:

Y(1),Y(2),Y(3),Y(4), . . . Y(N)

X(1),X(2),X(3),X(4), . . . X(N)

FOLLOW EACH VALUE BY A COMMA, A SPACE, OR A CARRIAGE RETURN

THE PROGRAM WILL ASK YOU TO SPECIFY THE INPUT SOURCE. FOR FILE INPUT, TYPE THE NAME OF THE DATA FILE; FOR TERMINAL INPUT, TYPE THE WORD 'TEL'.

TYPE-DEFINED DOCUMENTATION

This method attempts to simulate terminal activity. The user commands are shown in lower case. The computer responses are written in capitals. Most time-sharing terminals output in capitals only. This adds a little confusion to this method, but it still can be effective.

Such instructions might appear like this:

```
PLEASE LOG IN:        hap 103
READY
run personnel
INPUT NAME
john adams
INPUT ADDRESS, GRADE, YEAR START
23 oak st, beverly mass, 8, 1968
INPUT DEPARTMENT, SEX, SOCIAL SECURITY NO.
d, m, 020099244
INPUT SALARY, SKILLS, TITLE
18000, g, k, m, resmgr
DO YOU WISH ADDITION TO THE FILE?    yes
FILE ADDED
NEXT?   listing
WHAT QUALIFICATIONS?   salary
WHAT RANGE?   8000, 12000
WHAT PLANTS?   beverly, lynn
```

This method distinguishes between user and computer output. When read in a manual it is fairly easy to follow. It is convenient to type or typeset and therefore has been used in a number of time-sharing manuals.

If you are doing your own documentation, this is probably the easiest to transcribe. Unfortunately, this convenience is offset when you try to use this at a terminal. First, you can't capitalize numbers, therefore confusion can develop as to which numbers are user commands and which are computer responses. Second, most terminals operate only in capitals. Result: The text at the terminal will be all caps whether computer or user originated. This makes comparison between instructions and computer output difficult.

Interaction at the terminal would look like this:

```
READY
RUN PERSONNEL
INPUT NAME
JOHN ADAMS
INPUT ADDRESS, GRADE, YEAR START
23 OAK ST, BEVERLY, MASS, 8, 1968
INPUT DEPARTMENT, SEX SOCIAL SECURITY NO.
D, M, 020099244
etc.
```

In short, this is a convenient transcription method, but difficult to follow at the terminal.

EXPOSITORY DOCUMENTATION

Simple exposition describes the operation of the program. The user reads the text, determines what is needed, and runs the program as described. This type of explanation frequently is used for report-generating programs. These require that the user organize his output before the program can be run. For this reason, more explanations are required. Since expositions such as this are frequently long and complex, only a portion of one is noted below:

A typical place where a T-data type would be useful is in a person's name.

3. Arithmetic may now be done on date fields. For example, if the field DATE1=7-SEP-71 and DATE2=1-AUG-70 then

   a. DATE1-DATE2=402

   b. DATE1-10=28-AUG-71

   c. DATE2+365=1-AUG-71

If we are printing, the values to the right of the equal sign are what is printed.

The following functions are also defined for date fields: (assume $DATE=1-SEP-71)

FUNCTION NAME	ACTION	EXAMPLE	VALUE
$YEAR	returns year of date argument	$YEAR(DATE1)	1971
$MONTH	returns month	$MONTH(DATE1)	9
$DAY	returns day of month	$DAY(DATE1)	7
$AGE	returns number of years between today's date and date argument	$AGE(DATE2)	1
$AGEMON	returns number of months between today's date and date argument	$AGEMON(DATE2)	13
$AGEDAY	returns number of days between today's date and date argument	$AGEDAY(DATE2)	396
$WKDAY	returns day of week of a date (Sunday= 1, Saturday=7)	$WKDAY(DATE2)	3

4. Coded field definitions may have an additional form to reserve space for future additions to the coded list. In the near future, new codes may be added without redefining the entire file. To reserve space at file definition time, we use:

    CN "val" OR "val1"

where n specifies the total number of definitions to reserve space for.

To the novice this method is complicated. In the early stages of time sharing such report-generating programs would not be attempted. Once a certain sophistication is achieved, however, RPGs can be invaluable. They provide great data processing flexibility without the need for programming knowledge. Thus, a knowledgeable user will take the time and effort to master the text in order to reap the rewards an RPG facility can provide.

It must be apparent by now that interaction with the computer cannot be achieved at the snap of the fingers. True, individual, one-shot programs can be run easily. However, as skill and familiarity increase, greater opportunities and applications suggest themselves.

Advanced and complex time-sharing programs are difficult to describe. In many cases straightforward exposition is the only way to document the interaction.

COLOR-DIFFERENTIATED DOCUMENTATION

This technique and the one that follows (underlining computer responses) are essentially the same. They are also the most widely used.

The input/output at the terminal is reproduced just as it occurs. The user's commands are printed in black. The computer responses appear in red. This technique provides a clear differentiation to the user. It is simple and concise. It is so obvious that no lengthy prior instruction or explanation is needed. All the user has to do is open the manual, activate the computer, and follow the text. This technique is exactly similar to the method of underlining the user responses. It is merely that underlining replaces colors.

Although effective, this method has several mechanical drawbacks that reduce its overall usage. First, two-color printing is more expensive and time-consuming. Second, it is used by time-sharing companies, but would be clumsy to use for day-to-day office documentation. Finally, it reduces the flexibility of the time-sharing company. They cannot add new programs or improve old ones without going through a lengthy printing operation.

UNDERLINING DOCUMENTATION

This is the most widely used technique today. Documentation can be done on any typewriter, it is simple, clear and concise. Revision can be made quickly, printed, duplicated or offset and promptly distributed.

Several examples of this technique follow. Note that the programs are ingeniously formatted so that the user has a minimum of input. The words and numbers underlined in this example are all that the user is required to input.

INPUT VARIABLE,LOW VALUE,HIGH VALUE,STEP? 1,15,20,1

NEXT INPUT? 0

PRINT WHICH RESULTS? 3,4

ASSUMPTIONS		RESULTS	
1	UNIT PRICE $	SALES $	PRETAX PROFIT $
	15	998872.	516403.
	16	596046.	214250.
	17	366985.	58789.2
	18	232306.	-21076.4
	19	150734.	-61149.3
	20	100000	-80000

INPUT VARIABLE,LOW VALUE,HIGH VALUE,STEP? 0

NEXT OPTION? STOP

NEXT OPTION? MIN

MINIMIZE WHICH RESULT? 1

INPUTS TO BE ADJUSTED.

VARIABLE,LOW,HIGH? 1,4,5
NEXT INPUT? 0

1 Y	1 X
2.17945	4.5
1.56125	4.75
1.11102	4.875
0.788095	4.9375
0.558143	4.96875
0.394976	4.98437
0.279399	4.99219
0.197604	4.99609
0.139741	4.99805
9.88164E-2	4.99902

STEP SIZE 1
CONTINUE (YES OR NO)? YES

6.98754E-2	4.99951
0.04941	4.99976
3.49383E-2	4.99988
2.47052E-2	4.99994
1.74693E-2	4.99997
1.23526E-2	4.99998
8.73464E-3	4.99999
6.17632E-3	5.
4.36732E-3	5.
3.08816E-3	5.

STEP SIZE 1
CONTINUE (YES OR NO)? YES

2.18366E-3	5.
1.54408E-3	5.
1.09183E-3	5.
7.7204E-4	5.
0	5

FLAT SPOT
FLAT SPOT
FLAT SPOT
FLAT SPOT
FLAT SPOT
FLAT SPOT
STEP SIZE 0.03125
CONTINUE (YES OR NO)? NO

RESTART, CONTINUE OR QUIT? QUIT

NEXT OPTION? STOP

If the above underlined text were printed in red, it would be just as effective. Thus, colors or underlining serve essentially the same purpose.

Using underlining, several techniques can be combined. In the following example considerable explanation precedes the input questions. This technique recognizes that the time-sharing user may call the program infrequently. The question attempts to describe the necessary input to jog the user's memory.

Note the completeness of each question in the following example:

```
NEXT OPTION? DEBUG

LOGIC FILE NAME,DATA FILE NAME? LOGICFIL,DATABAS1
EXPECTED 6 DETERMINISTIC VALUES, FOUND 5
ENTER CORRECT NUMBER OF INPUT VARIABLES? 5
'13' IN LINE 6000 :MID VALUE DOES NOT LIE BETWEEN LOW AND HIGH.
ENTER PROB DATA TO REPLACE 2.3,12,14,13
PROB VARIABLE.TYPE,LOW,MID,HIGH? 2.3,12,13,14
'3.2' IN LINE 6010 :IS THIS THE FIRST ITEM OF THE NEXT PROB DATA GROUP? 1
'100000' IN LINE 6010 :NOT A NUMBER, BAD HIGH VALUE
ENTER PROB DATA TO REPLACE 3.2,80000,92000,100000
PROB VARIABLE. TYPE,LOW,MID,HIGH? 3.2,80000,92000,100000
'4.1'IN LINE 6020 :IS THIS THE FIRST ITEM OF THE NEXT PROB DATA GROUP? 1
5 RESULT VARIABLE NAMES WERE EXPECTED, 4 WERE FOUND.
REENTER CORRECT NUMBER OF RESULT VARIABLES? 4

DATA IS READABLE—WE HAVE STORED:
     5 INPUT NAMES AND DETERMINISTIC VALUES
     4 RESULT NAMES
     4 PROBABILISTIC DISTRIBUTIONS
```

The last two examples represent the most commonly used documentation technique for user interaction with the time-sharing environment. This method is simple, easily understood, and readily duplicated. It is widely used and most manuals and texts employ it with only minor modifications.

STAND-ALONE DOCUMENTATION

This technique is not often used by time-sharing companies. Its greatest value is for the user. It is most effective with problem-solving type programs. The separate input sheet should be considered whenever a volume of formatted data is to be input from the terminal.

Time sharing handles data in three different ways.

1. It looks for a volume of data in a data bank, processes, and outputs the results.
2. It asks questions (as above), performs calculations with the answers, and outputs the results.
3. It requests data (anywhere from one to 100 pieces of input), processes it and outputs the results.

This last category is sometimes difficult for the user to handle. Some preparatory work is necessary to have data available when requested.

For example, you wish to project sales ten years forward, based on sales for the last ten years. You can't simply turn on the terminal and call the program. The first question you get will be "Type last ten years' data?" Obviously, you first must assemble the input data. Since this is necessary, it is better to design a separate input sheet. This will not only format the data, but have all necessary instructions for running the program.

The more self-contained the input sheet is, the better. Properly designed it should be all that is required to run a particular program.

Depending on the time-sharing manual is clumsy. First you locate the program. Then read through the instruction. Next go to the source material and extract the data. Return to the manual to determine formatting requirements. Note the data in the format needed. Then, referring to the manual, log in. Follow the run procedure to the data input request. Finally, type from your formatted data the numbers required for processing.

All this activity can be combined on one piece of paper. If greater data input is required, input by tape or cards should be considered.

The following is an example of a sales projection input sheet.

SALES PROJECTION

Dial 123-4567
LOG IN: HAP 103

Computer Prints	*You Reply*
USER NUMBER?	L1005
LANGUAGE	BASIC
PROGRAM NAME	PROJEX
READY FOR DATA:	

Insert the historical data below: *

	X-data	Y-data	X-data	Y-data
100				
101				
102				
103				
104				
105				
106				
107				
108				

	X-data	Y-data	X-data	Y-data
109				
110				
111				
and				
up				

*(Do not put a comma after the *LAST* digit in the series).
X = THE PERIODS, SUCH AS YEARS.
Y = THE DATA TO BE PROJECTED.

Insert number of X-periods to be projected forward:

800							
802							
804							
806							
808							

(Do not put a comma after the *LAST* digit in the series).

RUN

(data prints out)

END

Keep in mind these sheets are used for frequently run programs. The instructions should be brief, but clear.

Thus, to run a sales projection the procedure is simple:

1. Select the proper input sheet.
2. Fill in the data.
3. Turn on the computer and type in the data as requested (already in the proper format).

THREE-COLUMN DOCUMENTATION

This is the format used throughout this book. It was devised because the preceding methods were not satisfactory. Their greatest weakness is that they fail to take into account the viable and dynamic nature of time sharing.

The first time a user runs a program it is confusing, difficult and tedious. The twentieth time he runs it with ease and skill. A time-sharing user functions differently from an in-house EDP operator. His work is frequently unscheduled. He may run one program twenty times in one day. He may run another once every six weeks.

The time-sharing user may develop a stable of forty programs, some may be run monthly, others daily. This intermittent activity causes a problem in documentation. The user doesn't want to plow through pages of documentation twenty times a day. On the other hand, if he is running a program after a six-month lapse, he needs documentation to refresh his memory.

The three-column format provides this flexibility. In this book we have put comments in the center column, an alternative would be as follows:

After all the employee information has been entered the system will begin asking a series of questions the answers to which are needed for payroll processing. The operator should already have these answers prepared.

COMPUTER	OPERATOR	COMMENTS
8.		
COMPANY NAME IS:	BRAYO	Company name up to 36 characters
9.		
DEDUCTION IDENTIFIERS		
(MAXIMUM 5 LETTERS)	ALMOT	Five (5) letter identifier for DD1
DEDUCTION 1:	$	If DD1 is a dollar amount ($)
$ or %:	%	If DD1 is a percent of gross pay (%)
ACCOUNT NO. TO CREDIT:	187942	Six (6) digit General Ledger Account Number.

This series of questions and answers will be repeated for deductions 2-5.

COMPUTER	OPERATOR	COMMENTS
10.		
MAXIMUM AMOUNT		A *No* response to this question will tell the system to
DEDUCTION 5?	NO	ask for the remainder of the Payroll information
		A *Yes* response will cause
	YES	the system to ask:
MAXIMUM AMOUNT		The operator responds
IN DOLLARS:	500.00	with the maximum dollar figure to be deducted for DD5 in each pay.

COMPUTER	OPERATOR	COMMENTS
11.		
BEGINNING CHECK		Enter beginning check
NUMBER:	129	number
STATE TAX IN		Give tax percentage (the
PERCENT (%):	.05	system will accept 3, 3., or 3.0).
ACCOUNT NO. TO CREDIT:	126221	Give six (6) digit General Ledger Account number.
CITY TAX IN PERCENT (%):	.02	Give tax rate
ACCOUNT NO. TO CREDIT:	52641	Give six (6) digit General Ledger Account Number
ACCOUNT NO. TO DEBIT FOR GROSS WAGES:	365046	Give six (6) digit General Ledger Number.

The standard method puts the comments in the center column. Once logged in you proceed as follows:

COMPUTER	COMMENT	OPERATOR
	The program /GDAT/ is now ready to output orders or billings (depending on the file transferred to /HAMLST/) between any two dates provided.	
	The options given are as follows:	Go /GDAT/
DO YOU WISH AREA OUTPUT? NO = 1, YES = 2	"Yes" will result in further questions to determine *what* area output.	2
	"No" will jump to the question "Do you wish to query orders or billings?"	
DO YOU WISH HARD COPY? NO =1, YES =2		1
	"Yes" will have the computer print out its results as the program runs.	

COMPUTER	COMMENT	OPERATOR
	"No" will allow the computer to write the data to a file, but print nothing.	
WHAT FILES? WESTERN HEMISPHERE 1, OTHER 2,		1
	1 will output CANADA and SOUTH AMERICA. 2 will output EUROPE and the FAR EAST.	
DO YOU WISH TO QUERY BILLINGS (B), OR ORDERS (O)?		B
	This question checks the operating file to determine if /MONBIL/ or /HAMV/ or /HAMVII/ are being processed.	
	If the wrong file is in /HAMLST/ the computer will ask you to check the file.	
DO YOU WISH INFORMATION ON SHIPPING DATES (S), OR PAYMENT DATE (P)?		S
	The computer will select the date requested and output all billings between the two dates given in answer to the next question, as shown:	
LIST ALL SHIPMENTS MADE BETWEEN		25FEB70,28FEB70
	The program now runs by selecting the date or dates requested and outputting it to the terminal or to a file depending on what has been requested above.	

During the familiarization process, all the explanatory text under "Comment" would be carefully read. If the program is run monthly, it serves as a refresher course each time it is activated. The "Comment" column then serves three purposes.

1. For initial familiarization.
2. As a refresher.
3. For others unfamiliar with the program.

When the program is run frequently, the "Comment" column can be ignored. This then reduces activity to a minimum. Such output would then look like this:

COMPUTER	COMMENT	OPERATOR
—		GO /GDAT/
DO YOU WISH AREA OUTPUT. NO =1, YES=2,		2
DO YOU WISH HARD COPY? NO =1, YES=2,		1
WHAT FILES? WESTERN HEMISPHERE 1, OTHER 2,		2
DO YOU WISH TO QUERY BILLINGS (B), OR ORDERS (O)?		B
LIST ALL SHIPMENTS MADE BETWEEN		25FEB70,28FEB70
TOTAL AMOUNT BETWEEN 25FEB70 AND 28FEB70		12140
+		
—		COPY /CANAD/ TO TEL

File is output.

ORDER NO	CUSTOMER NAME	PRODUCT NAME	D TERMS OF SALE	AMOUNT	DATE
A700164	PROTORCAN	SESQUI	O N30	1435.	27FEB70
—		Second file is output.			
—				COPY /SOAMA/ TO TEL	

ORDER NO	CUSTOMER NAME	PRODUCT NAME	D TERMS OF SALE	AMOUNT	DATE
C700136 ETC.	MULTICHEM	STPP	I DDBL30	7565.	28FEB70

The advantage of this system is obvious. During the first few runs, every word is read and considered. The comments clarify the computer requests and guide the user. Once familiarity with the program is achieved, however, these explanations are superfluous. They can be ignored.

It has one drawback. It is unfamiliar, and for some takes a bit of getting used to. The novice bridge player tries to develop a strategy by counting winners. It takes a little getting used to to count his losers, the technique the experts use.

Documentation is critical for the time-sharing user. To protect himself, therefore, in the computer environment he must rely on meticulous documentation at the use level.

Time sharing's greatest asset to the user is that he need not be intimately familiar with hardware or software. This leaves program documentation as his only means of communication with the computer environment. For this reason, the user must establish solid documentation techniques.

14

EVALUATING COST-EFFECTIVE
TIME-SHARING SERVICE

SELECTING A TIME-SHARING COMPANY

Chapter 1 outlined a "quick and dirty" way to get time sharing "on-stream." Eight characteristics were listed to enable the novice to get time sharing up and running. "Quick and dirty" is computer jargon meaning to get the job done fast without worrying about economics or the niceties of program efficiency.

For the novice this approach is the best. There is no better way to approach time sharing than to be on-line.

The eight criteria established in chapter 1 also govern the sophisticated user's time-sharing company selection. Their priority is different, however.

To review, the eight criteria are:

1. Operational procedures.
2. Language used.
3. Operations assistance.
4. Editing capability.
5. Up time.
6. Library.
7. Response time.
8. Cost.

The experienced user weighs the above quite differently from the novice. Up time, languages and library content can be reviewed, checked and evaluated in a single discussion. To the experienced user a single session at the terminal will tell him all he needs to know about operational procedures, editing capability and response time. As was mentioned in chapter 1, such familiarization sessions are offered free by any time-sharing company.

The knowledgeable user evaluates time-sharing services on two major characteristics:

1. ECONOMICS
2. OPERATIONS ASSISTANCE

ECONOMICS

Costs are the name of the game. If you can do the same job in-house, don't go outside. If twenty monkeys on twenty typewriters can, in fact, output the results, hire twenty monkeys.

The uniqueness of time sharing's interactive environment sometimes blinds the user to this fact. The day will come, however, when output and cost comprise the final yardstick against which the user's performance is judged. Isn't that always the case? Why should it be different with time sharing?

It is not different, but it can be complex. Costs incurred on time sharing are the sum total of many things, some the user can control, some program design can control, and some programming can control. The more knowledgeable the user, the better he can maintain cost surveillance of his time-sharing charges. If money can be saved, the details and methods are well worth detailing.

Before we investigate how costs may be controlled, however, let's first inspect how they are generated. Time-sharing companies bill their clients in various ways. The most common of these are:

1. Computer Processing Units (CPU)
2. Storage
3. On-line time
4. Formula charge

COMPUTER PROCESSING UNITS (CPU)

CPU is computer time, the number of seconds the computer has devoted to your job. The time-sharing computer may have ten, twenty or fifty customers on line at the same time. It proceeds by taking in one customer, doing some work, putting it aside and going to the next. This procedure is followed over and over for each customer. All are thus serviced intermittently many times per second.

CPU is the time your job has been actually on the computer. It is related to the complexity of the program—the number of calculations called for, the number of sort routines requested, or the number of data banks that must be opened, read and closed.

STORAGE

Data banks and programs must be stored from day to day. These are stored in the computer on discs, tapes, or drums. They are made available when you command the program to run, by being brought into computer core.

This storage is calculated on a daily, weekly or monthly basis. It is calculated as so many dollars per thousand words. A "word" is defined as so many computer "bits." Thus, a one hundred line program might be twenty-five hundred words. At a rate of one dollar per thousand words, this might cost $2.50 per day in storage.

ON-LINE TIME

This charge is incurred from the moment you log in until you log out. It is based on the time the terminal is connected to the computer. Charges vary from time-sharing company to time-sharing company. They further vary based on output speed.

Output speed is the number of characters per second printed by the terminal. For example, a terminal may print ten characters per second (cps) or sixty cps depending on its setting, model or type. Thus, a ten-page report may take an hour to print out at ten cps or ten minutes at sixty cps. Prices don't reflect this ratio exactly. Ten cps on-line charges might be ten dollars per hour while sixty cps might be fifteen.

Two factors govern output speeds. The speeds available from the time-sharing system, and the type of terminal you have. Possible speeds range from 10 cps to 2,400 cps. The range from 10 cps to 120 cps is customary on typewriter-type terminals. Ranges above this are available with CRT (cathode ray tube) terminals. Output speeds and devices up to and over 200 lines per minute are available, of course. It is unlikely, however, that a time-sharing user would have these in-house.

If a hundred-page report is to be output, such hardware is necessary. Most time-sharing companies have high-speed printers available. It is simple and inexpensive to have your voluminous reports output on their premises.

FORMULA CHARGE

Some time-sharing companies develop a formula combining CPU time, file opening and closing, data base searches, input/output charges and other elements. Each time a program is run, these times are processed through a formula. The computer then outputs a number that represents the operational costs. This type of formula naturally varies from time-sharing company to time-sharing company.

Thus, a time-sharing user is billed on the sum of three charges.

1. CPU or formula charge
2. Storage
3. On-line time

Simple comparison of the quoted time-sharing rates will not pinpoint the least expensive time-sharing service, although competition forces most rates into the same ball park.

Fortunately, time-sharing contracts are usually on a monthly basis. This enables the user to run for a month and examine the service provided. This is the best way. Compare service and cost after a month or two months. The risk is small and the result is actual prices, not guesstimates.

OPERATIONAL ECONOMICS

During the initial stages of time sharing, lots of flexibility is available to the user. He should use this period to evaluate as many time-sharing services as possible. Keep in mind that later on, once complex interacting programs have been devised, changeover can be difficult.

Costs from time-sharing service to time-sharing service do vary. However, your particular requirements are more likely to dictate choice than cost alone. Comparing time-sharing rates and evaluating services are essential ingredients in the selection of time-sharing services. However, there is a much more positive way to approach the economics of time sharing.

The most controllable costs are those generated by the user. The great temptation with time sharing is to turn it on, do your thing and log out. It is so convenient and easy, the user frequently falls into the habit of doing his thinking at the terminal. This can cost money.

Time sharings' ease of operation frequently encourages sloppy economic habits. No matter how many might be warned against, human ingenuity will find others. With this caution in mind, we enumerate some of the most flagrant cost consumers.

SLOPPY ON-TIME

Approach the terminal with your work well planned. If data is to be input, have it properly formatted and organized. If a series of commands are to be given, it is better to write them out beforehand.

Don't turn the terminal on, then get up to find a reference, a bit of data or some additional instruction. Concentrate on the input and output job. Avoid distractions such as conversations, phone calls, or another job while the computer is running.

While you are logged in, the cliche "time is money" is a reality.

CASE IN POINT: Consider the following example of sloppy on-time.

Turn on the console, log in, and initiate the program. It requests option 1 or 2. You are unsure of which one to choose. You think option one, you strike 1.

"Number of pounds?" the computer queries. The phone rings. You chat with a colleague. You then return to the console.

You wanted a dollar, not a poundage run. You escape.

A friend drops in. You explain what you are doing. He is impressed. You return to the computer.

This type of activity can be described for as long as patience and imagination will allow.

When you log out twenty minutes later, the computer notes you have spent twenty-seven dollars.

With the organized approach, you log in with the data in front of you. You note you are to strike option 2. You input the data requested. You log out. The job took five minutes and cost $2.35.

INEFFICIENT DATA INPUT

Although a terminal may look like a typewriter, no one types thirty, forty or fifty characters a minute while on one. The hunt-and-peck method predominates. For this reason input via the terminal should be limited to those times when an interactive mode prevails.

Data input over 100 characters can be input faster and more efficiently via paper tape or keypunched tab cards than hunting and pecking. Furthermore, typographical errors are clumsy to correct even in an interactive mode. There are many alternative methods.

First, large data bases can be keypunched. Either in-house, outside on a contract basis or through your time-sharing service data can be keypunched and fed to the computer.

Second, many terminals can make paper tapes. Terminals have two modes "on-line" and "local." When on "local," the terminal responds like an electric typewriter. It types, you can "cut" paper tape, but you are not connected to a time-sharing service. There is no charge.

This capability allows you to make a paper tape of a large data bank in your own good time and speed. When complete, you log in to time sharing and run the tape into the computer. This may be run in at 10 cps or 60 cps, whatever the terminal allows. This technique allows you to cut the tape over a period of hours, yet run it in with a minimum of on-line time.

Another method is to type the data into a data bank and edit it before activating a program to run it. This technique reduces the chance that the program will attempt to process bad data. Computer programs are tightly formatted. If the program finds a letter where a number should be, it will stop until someone fixes it. Output such as "Bad data in input" would signal such a situation. If a lot of processing had occurred before that point, you would be charged for the work.

The most frustrating situation occurs when several typos come to light in the same input. The program starts and runs through sixty percent of the data bank processing as it goes.

```
Bad data in input
STOP
CPU 72
```

You locate the error, correct it (at the cost of more CPU and on-line time) and rerun. The program proceeds until it is 75% complete.

```
Bad data in input
STOP
CPU 110
```

You locate and correct the error, and rerun. The program proceeds to the 90% mark.

```
Bad data in input
STOP
CPU 130
```

Locate and correct. Note that if there is bad data in the data base, the program can only proceed to that point. Bad data further along will only appear after you have fixed the previous bad data.

The program now runs to completion.

STOP
CPU 150

The program costs 120 CPU. The bad data has forced you to use a total of 462 CPU.

> CASE IN POINT: Time and CPU wasted in this fashion is expensive. Coverting these figures to dollars, both in CPU and time consumed, works out to a considerable loss. The well-run operation took ten minutes and 120 CPU—cost $14.00. The bad data increased running time to sixty minutes and 462 CPU—cost $56.00.

There are three ways this can be avoided. First, put the data in carefully. With small, independent time-sharing programs this is sometimes the only way.

Second, have the computer check the data before processing. This merely means that all the data is read in and errors noted before the main program starts processing the data. This technique requires just as much corrective effort on the part of the user. It expends less CPUs, however, since the main processing does not start until all the data passes the check.

Finally, with complex programs, a separate program might be written to do nothing but check the data and format it precisely. It, too, will output errors that must be corrected. However, once it reformats the data bank, the major program will run without interruption.

I have passed over error correction rather superficially with the casual comment "locate and correct." Don't be misled. Locating errors in a data bank is one of the most frustrating things you can experience.

For example, you are anxious to run the program. A schedule must be met. The computer has rejected your data bank twice before. You get the message

Bad data in input
STOP

You type out the line that's bad.

573.91,TOMSTLC,761924,0,I,MT,597,806,NY,SFT30

What's wrong with the line? You type the preceding line, which you know is correct (because the computer has passed it).

879.53,LOVSITC,761925,0,I,ST,511,706,FR,LMS60

All formats, fields, and data appear to be correct. Don't bother to find the "bad data." What you can't see, but what the computer knows, is that element four, namely ,0, should be the letter "O," but is in fact a numerical zero. To the computer, this is two totally different things, to the human eye the same.

There are several solutions to this situation:

1. Use a type face with a slash through all numerical zeros ($\emptyset$).

2. Have the computer indicate precisely the bad data, like this:

573.91,TOMSTLC,761924,0,I,MT,597,806,NY,SFT30
                                      ^

3. Print out an error message:

Bad data in field 4

All are reasonable solutions. All are routinely used. Unfortunately, errors must be anticipated before the computer can be programmed to pinpoint them.

In complex programs it is impossible to anticipate all possible errors. The anticipated errors you correct, the unanticipated you sweat.

STORAGE

Storage can be costly, especially when data no longer needed is retained. Constant housekeeping is required to neaten up the files, that is, the programs and data banks.

Unnecessary storage charges are incurred in several ways.

1. While compiling programs
2. While debugging programs
3. While running programs

1. Compiling Programs

Program compiling is a highly interactive process. The initial version is input, compiled and error messages noted. The text is then corrected, and the program recompiled. If further corrections are required, they are made and the program compiled again.

Sometimes the corrections don't work, and further work is required on the text. After an hour of this, it is difficult to tell what the original version of the text looked like. To safeguard himself, the operator frequently saves the text by assigning it another name. Thus he has two versions of the same text. One called *Samson,* which he compiles, one named *Delila,* which he saves. If anything goes wrong with *Samson,* he can always start again with *Delila.* This is perfectly acceptable procedure. Unfortunately, once the euphoria of a successful "compile" envelops the operator, he is likely to shout "Eureka!" and log out. You are left paying storage charges on several alternative texts.

These alternative texts should not be retained for two reasons. First, they run up storage charges. Second, after a week it may be difficult to recall which is the final version.

CASE IN POINT: In the example described above, the file SAMSON contained 32,000 characters at $1.00 per thousand. That's thirty-two dollars per day. The duplicate of the file cost the same amount. In this case, it was created by a programmer helping a medium-sized exporter neaten up his system.

The duplicate file DELILA remained in the system until an end-of-the-month housecleaning uncovered it. This simple oversight cost the user $220.00 unnecessary dollars.

In other cases, complete program packages have been left in the system and thousands of necessary dollars have been lost.

It is not uncommon to find that an intermediate version has been corrected and compiled for some minor modification rather than the final version. When this occurs, further changes again must be made, changes that were already made in the later version. At these times you can't escape the feeling that you are taking two steps backward for every one step forward.

Thorough house cleaning after each compiling session should be a must.

2. Debugging and Writing Programs

The same situation prevails with debugging and writing programs. Alternative texts or revisions are renamed and put aside for later reference.

During the writing or debugging stage it is customary to generate several optional versions. These optional versions run up storage costs. They should be monitored as strictly as possible.

The best solution to this problem is to assign one individual to the housekeeping chore. His job should be to output a listing of the computer programs and data bases periodically and question the value of each.

3. Running Programs

Many programs, when run, write new data banks. These may be stored and used as the data base for a second program. Once these data bases have served their purpose, they should be deleted. Frequently, a computer file will be found full of obsolete data banks. These cost money.

When documenting a program, deletion of unnecessary data banks at the conclusion of the run should be included as part of routine operations.

For example:

COMPUTER	COMMENT	OPERATOR
	Dial 123-4567	
LOG IN		HAP 103
READY		
		RUN AREAS
WHICH AREA?		1,3,7
AREA DATA 1,3,7 WRITTEN		
STOP		
READY		TYPE TO TEL 1
	All details for Area 1 are now typed out	

COMPUTER	COMMENT	OPERATOR
		TYPE TO TEL 3
	The second data bank for Area 3 is typed out.	
		TYPE TO TEL 7
	Area 7 is output.	

Now, clutching the output for Areas 1, 3 and 7 in his hot little hand, the user could log out and go about his business. However, he would be leaving three data bases (Areas 1, 3 and 7) stored in the computer. Depending on their size, he could be charged anywhere from two dollars to one hundred dollars a day for this oversight. The documentation should instruct the user to delete this unnecessary data.

COMPUTER	COMMENT	OPERATOR
	Before logging out delete data banks 1, 3 and 7.	
READY		DELETE 1,3,7
		LOG OUT

DOCUMENTATION

It is a great temptation to log in and "wing it." Don't depend on your memory of the last session and keep punching keys until you get what you want. A great amount of money is lost this way. Sometimes the program is run three times before the right output is produced. Documented procedures should always be available, not only to assist the novice user, but also to guide the regular user through the most economical procedures.

Storage costs are controllable. The user should make every effort to limit storage to the essentials.

PROGRAM OPERATION

Avoiding excessive storage is only one aspect of uneconomical program operation. As mentioned above, documentation provides a means of controlling costs. By properly documenting operational procedures the danger of reruns is reduced. You do it right the first time.

Another method of controlling costs is to assemble all the input beforehand. When you turn on the computer you should be ready to go. To control this (as described earlier) an input data sheet can be used. All the information is collected, assembled on the input sheet and ready for processing.

Thus, program operation should be organized and standardized. It is not the time to do your thinking and running around after the program is started. Do it first.

Time at the terminal is money. Spend your time there quickly and efficiently. Realize that your time at the terminal requires your total concentration. Don't try to do other things or allow yourself to be distracted. An incorrect command can send you all the way back to square one.

While at the terminal, I have noted one interesting human inconsistency. When you are at a terminal, you, in effect, are on the telephone. The entity at the other end is a computer not a person, but interaction is the same. Where does the human inconsistency come in? From those people who interrupt you. No one would every try to talk to you while you are having a phone conversation. However, while on a terminal, someone will inevitably say, "While you're not doing anything, could you answer a question for me?" For your own peace of mind, and for the cost savings involved, try to avoid interruptions during computer activity.

Economical program operation can be assured by:

1. Proper documentation
2. Efficient data input organization
3. Avoidance of interruptions while on-line.

LIBRARY PROGRAMS

The most expensive operations on time sharing are programming and debugging. If library programs are available, use them.

Library programs can help the user in a number of ways. They may be incorporated into a package of programs, used as subroutines, or, in the case of a sort program, used to organize data for simpler data base handling.

Don't write a new program if one is already available. Know your library programs and design program packages to take full advantage of them.

Following is a simple example. Open orders were output by their date of scheduled shipment. Since they had been received over a period of months, they form a scrambled list of data. Their only common information is the month in which they were to be shipped. Such a list might look as follows:

SHIPMENTS SCHEDULED BETWEEN FEB. 1 AND FEB. 31

ORDER NO	CUSTOMER	PRODUCT NAME	QUANTITY	AMOUNT	DATE
W732755I	ICIAUS	STRONTIUM CARB	51,MT	24926.	11FEB74
W733036I	CROWNSOAF	SAPP	220,CWT	3641.	10FEB74
W733181I	USCHINA	STPP	2200,CWT	30250.	1FEB74
W7332060	ORKIMYA	KP 140	55,CWT	3351.	10FEB74
W7332050	KASLOWSKI	KP 140	55,CWT	3351.	10FEB74
W733242I	RBRYCENZ	TSP ANHY	44,CWT	675.	1 FEB74
W7332700	ATAKA	DAPON 35	960,CWT	68640.	1FEB74
W733306I	PROTINDUS	SAPP	220,CWT		10FEB74
W733306I	PROTINDUS	DSP	220,CWT	8120.	10FEB74
W733307I	PROTINDUS	MKP	110,CWT		14FEB74

W7333071	PROTINDUS	DKP	110,CWT	5600.	14FEB74
W7333391	BAKERS	SAPP	440,CWT	8782.	15FEB74
W7333630	AMAIRSING	RS1840	350,CWT	11025.	4FEB74
W7334181	COLGATEAUS	TKPP	748,CWT	15110.	4FEB74
W7335351	COLGATEMAL	STPP	4000,CWT	52000.	1FEB74
W7335581	RBRYCENZ	PHOS ACID	756,CWT		1FEB74
W7335581	RBRYCENZ	PHOS ACID	756,CWT	12461.	1FEB74
W7336151	BROWNINGCH	PHOS ACID	3300,CWT	54450.	1FEB74
W7336211	FEASTTEXT	H202 50	49,MT	18891.	1FEB74
W7336241	HUATRAD	H202 50	49,MT	17992.	15FEB74
W7336381	SWIFTAUS	TKPP	395,CWT	7580.	1FEB74
W7403491	MANFUNG	H202 50	49,MT	23027.	10FEB74
W7403511	MANFUNG	AMMPERSULPHATE	150,CWT	3375.	10FEB74
W7403741	SERQUIM	SHMP	132,CWT	2034.	15FEB74
W7403811	CHEMSERVS	DSP	132,CWT		22FEB74
W7403811	CHEMSERVS	SHMP	132,CWT		22FEB74
W7403811	CHEMSERVS	TSPP	132,CWT		22FEB74
W7403811	CHEMSERVS	TKPP	132,CWT	10903.	22FEB74
W7404451	MITSUPISHI	STRONTIUM CARB	110,ST	31350.	2FEB74
W7404461	MITSUPISHI	STRONTIUM CARB	110,ST	31350.	18FEB74
W7404500	CALTEXAFR	KTX AA	53,CWT	2332.	28FEB74
W7404521	PRESERVENE	SESQUI	100,ST	5825.	8FEB74
W7401611	HOLPRO	CLAUBER'S ANHY	31,MT	2496.	5FEB74

This is an abbreviated example. These lists frequently run several pages long. It is the sales department's responsibility to "birddog" these orders.

Unfortunately, the sales department thinks in terms of product sales. They control the order flow by checking different plants for different products. This scrambled list is difficult to use. It is out of context with the salesman's thinking.

To remedy this, it was decided to output the list by product. Here the true value and flexibility of time sharing become apparent. No reprogramming or reorganization of the system was required to implement this decision. The next output was merely processed by one of the time-sharing library programs. The result looked like this:

SHIPMENTS SCHEDULED BETWEEN FEB. 1 AND FEB. 31

ORDER NO	CUSTOMER	PRODUCT NAME	QUANTITY	AMOUNT	DATE
W7405330	WILSINDIA	ACETO ORTHO	32,CWT	2112.	10FEB74
W7403511	MANFUNG	AMMPERSULPHATE	150,CWT	3375.	10FEB74
W7404561	LATDOWAUS	AMMPERSULPHATE	100,CWT	2250.	11FEB74
W7406411	ICIAUS	CDB CLEARON	354,CWT	23385.	1FEB74
W7409851	RERYCENZ	CDB CLEARON	48,CWT	4553.	28FEB74
W7332700	ATAKA	DAPON 35	960,CWT	68640.	1FEB74

W733307I	PROTINDUS	DKP	110,CWT	5600.	14FEB74
W733306I	PROTINDUS	DSP	220,CWT	8120.	10FEB74
W740381I	CHEMSERVS	DSP	132,CWT		22FEB74
W740432I	CALTEXNY	DSP	31,CWT	759.	4FEB74
W740708I	INTSELTAI	FERROPHOS	50,LT	4750.	20FEB74
W740161I	HOLPRO	GLAUBER S ANHY	31,MT	2490.	5FEB74
W733621I	FEASTTEXT	H2O2 50	49,MT	18891.	1FEB74
W733624I	HUATRAD	H2O2 50	49,MT	17992.	15FEB74
W740349I	MANFUNG	H2O2 50	49,MT	23027.	10FEB74
W7332060	ORKIMYA	KP 140	55,CWT	3351.	10FEB74
W7332050	KASLOWSKI	KP 140	55,CWT	3351.	10FEB74
W7406440	RFRYCENZ	KP 140	46,CWT	2840.	6FEB74
W7406450	RERYCEAUS	KP 140	46,CWT	2840.	6FEB74
W7406460	ATAKA	KP 140	46,CWT	2840.	6FEB74
W740759I	PROTINDUS	KPERSULPHATE	111,CWT	3052.	15FEB74
W7404500	CALTEXAFR	KTX AA	53,CWT	2332.	28FEB74
W7406210	ASAHICHEM	MAC	399,CWT	25137.	1FEB74
W7406220	ASAHICHEM	MAC	197,CWT	10857.	1FEB74
W733307I	PROTINDUS	MKP	110,CWT		14FEB74
W733558I	RPRYCENZ	PHOS ACID	756,CWT	12461.	1FEB74
W733615I	BROWNINGCH	PHOS ACID	3300,CWT	54450.	1FEB74
W733558I	RFRYCENZ	PHOS ACID	756,CWT		1FEB74
W7333630	AMAIRSING	RS1840	350,CWT	11025.	4FEB74
W733306I	PROTINDUS	SAPP	220,CWT		10FEB74
W733036I	CROWNSOAF	SAPP	220,CWT	3641.	10FEB74
W733339I	BAKERS	SAPP	440,CWT	8782.	15FEB74
W740452I	PRESERVENE	SESQUI	100,ST	5625.	8FEB74
W740440I	NEWPORTCHE	SHMP	110,CWT	1064.	4FEB74
W740374I	SERQUIM	SHMP	132,CWT	2034.	15FEB74
W740381I	CHEMSERVS	SHMP	132,CWT		22FEB74
W740647I	EASTSEAKO	SHMP	330,CWT	4653.	4FEB74
W740814I	CONTLMININ	SHMP	166,CWT	3503.	25FEB74
W740815I	CONTLMININ	SHMP	125,CWT	2677.	25FEB74
W733535I	COLGATEMAL	STPP	4000,CWT	52000.	1FEB74

The list is now sorted by product, yet contains the same estimated shipment date information as the original. Without skipping a beat, the output was accommodated to the user's requirements. Thus, one run through the data bank outputs all the information needed in the report. The library sort program sets it up.

There are many other built-in programs the user can take advantage of. Dates, time, projections, library programs, all should be used to make proprietary programs more efficient.

Computer technology is moving so fast, the user should always be sure he isn't reinventing the wheel.

REPORT-GENERATING PROGRAMS (RGP)

RGPs bypass program writing and allow the user to design, format and output his own reports. They are well worth investigation as a quick, relatively inexpensive way to output information. They are designed to satisfy user requirements in different fields.

There are financial RGPs, sales RGPs and a variety of others. Each has its specific value and uses, but each user must make an individual determination as to whether an RGP will fit his needs.

THE TIME-SHARING LOG

If the user doesn't watch his pennies, no one will. A record should be kept of each log in and the charges incurred.

Sometimes the user is charged unjustifiably. The time-sharing service cannot know this unless the user brings it to their attention.

You log in. Prepare a data base for processing by editing and adding data. The program is started, initiates output and continues to process and output data for half an hour.

The system crashes. The appropriate message appears at the terminal (right in the middle of your beautifully formatted output):

COMPUTER MALFUNCTION. PLEASE WAIT FIVE MINUTES AND LOG IN AGAIN.

You dutifully wait, log in and find that you are back to square one, editing and adding data before you can run.

In some cases the work done before such a crash would not have been charged to your account. In other instances it would be. In every case you should check with the time-sharing company and note the circumstances in your log.

Another type of malfunction is the telephone disconnect. This may or may not be the time-sharing company's fault. However, if your log indicates too many of these disconnects, lines should be checked.

Telephone disconnects that force you to rerun your program are just as expensive as computer malfunctions. Unfortunately, they are much more difficult to receive credit for.

Another type of unjustified charge occurs when you activate a program, it runs for forty minutes, and then outputs:

NO DATA BASE AVAILABLE.

This could be your fault. However, the time-sharing company sets up your files each day. Some days they miss. Errors caused by faulty setup are to the time-sharing company's account.

Consider this situation. At day's end all your work, programs, data bases, etc. are written to a disc storage device. The next day they are reloaded in the computer for you to access and run. Furthermore, the disc data is saved from day to day. If you delete a program accidentally on Thursday, it is not irretrievably lost. It can be recovered from Wednesday's "dump" and made available to you.

This can work against you. If, upon reloading, the time-sharing company experiences a malfunction, they might lose some of your work for the preceding day. They might reload from the day before. All your program names could be in place, but they would be from the day before, not yesterday. All your updates of yesterday would be lost.

Under such circumstances, you have every right to expect credit for that day's work. This will only partially recompense you since you will have to redo all the work.

A few lines of a time-sharing log might look like this:

DATE	LOG IN TIME	JOB DESCRIPTION	CPU	COST
5/14	9:15	DATES	12:15	$25.65
5/14	10:25	SORT OF M.I.S.	4:22	7.85
5/14	3:25	PROGRAM DEBUG	18:26	60.25
5/15	10:30	COMPILE TRETS	1:20	3.50
5/16	10:10	BORGI–CRASH	—	—
5/16	11:30	BORGI	12:55	32.50

CASE IN POINT: Consider the following computer horror story from the early days of time sharing. A complete order-entry system was established on time sharing. Daily entry of orders and constant extraction of reports was established.

This small time-sharing company operated with one computer. (Today, as many as twenty interlinked and backup computers are commonplace.) Total computer charges for this company's services ran about four thousand dollars per month. These charges broke down to about twenty-eight hundred for CPU time and twelve hundred in storage.

The computer crashed and was off the air for four days! Fifteen minutes before the system went back to manual, the computer came back on.

At the month's end the bill came in. Still the usual $4,000 charge. To some extent, this was acceptable. Despite the inconvenience, overtime and confusion, the same amount of output had been produced. However, what about the storage charges? Daily storage for the four down days was included, a time when files and the whole system were unavailable to the customer.

This is a moot point. A few hours, even a day, of off-the-air can be ignored. Four days of mythical storage charges, however, added to the inconvenience of being "off" is a bit much. Two hundred and fifty dollars in credits was negotiated.

This extreme example is unusual. Usually, credits accumulate at the rate of ten dollars here and twenty dollars there.

More reliability is constantly being built into time sharing. In the near future, credits will probably almost disappear with increasing reliability of the systems.

You should simply be aware that you are entitled to this type of consideration, should the occasion warrant it.

Your time-sharing service has all costs and charges computerized. So does your friendly neighborhood bank. Unfortunately, like everything else in this world, if you want something done right, you'd better do it yourself.

The time-sharing log monitors your computer operation, and can save you dollars every month.

SUMMARY

Evaluation of both services and costs are the user's responsibility. Without exaggeration, time-sharing charges can vary by 100% between sloppy and efficient procedures.

Maintaining a time-sharing log is essential. Not only will it pinpoint costly procedures, but it will monitor time-sharing service costs.

15

PROFITABLE USER INTERACTION WITH TIME-SHARING EQUIPMENT

Initially, there may be competition between in-house EDP, when it exists, and time sharing. The two capabilities should, however, complement one another.

The time-sharing user is a new breed of cat. Make no mistake about it, for some time he will be an amateur in a field of professionals. His objectives are, and should be, different from those of the EDP establishment.

It is a major responsibility to implement, maintain and operate a computer facility valued in the millions of dollars. The EDP community has accepted, carried out and built such structures. Time sharing's highly interactive mode is inimical to the in-house EDP environment. The time-sharing user should not infringe on this area.

Time-sharing users fall into five categories:

1. The manager-user.
2. The intermittent user.
3. The time-sharing manager.
4. The time-sharing supervisor.
5. The EDP technician user.

THE MANAGER-USER

The manager-user represents time sharing at its best use. He is a man managing a business, division or department who can interact directly with the computer. This individual employs the computer to provide him with timely, specifically targeted information. He functions effectively within the interactive mode.

The computer serves as a tool to achieve his objectives. It maintains, processes, assembles and manipulates data and outputs information that enables the individual to manage, monitor and control his area of responsibility.

This should be the user of today; it will be the user of tomorrow. All the hardware and software exist to make this possible. Today's managers are sometimes too busy with the art of management to employ the science of management.

THE INTERMITTENT USER

Most managers of divisions, departments or projects fall into this category. They utilize time sharing on a one-time basis. Time sharing is used when a regression analysis is required. Time sharing is employed when a profitability analysis is needed.

Today the intermittent user dominates time sharing. It relieves personnel of tedious, time-consuming calculations. It allows application of complex management science formulae to everyday business operations. The intermittent user has been time sharing's entry into the business community. He is and will be essential to its continued growth.

It is rare, however, when the intermittent user can function on his own. He requires support both economically and procedurally. Economically because his intermittent use does not justify the overhead generated by maintaining a console, data set and program storage. Procedurally because, between runs, the intermittent user can forget the processing commands (how to run the program). This is why careful documentation and update must be maintained.

In large companies costs can be allocated over five, ten or fifty users to justify overhead for a terminal. Procedurally, however, they must maintain their own records, or the next type of user must be justifiable, i.e. a time-sharing manager.

THE TIME-SHARING MANAGER

As the textbooks like to point out, computers may replace people in the short term, but they will create new jobs in the long term. The time-sharing manager is the perfect example of this. His function is to organize, build and maintain the facilities to offer time sharing to his company. Naturally, this position can only be justified when time-sharing services are offered throughout a fairly large corporation.

At this early stage of time-sharing growth, such managers have developed from two sources. First from the management sciences groups, and second from line individuals who develop capabilities on time sharing that are applicable to a wide spectrum of the company. Unfortunately, the most obvious source of such talent has not been tapped. The EDP establishment has only rarely spun off individuals interested in time sharing.

The new position of time-sharing manager is a fascinating one. It requires not only computer expertise, but also demands a special insight into the requirements of line and staff personnel. It can expose the time-sharing manager to accounting, sales, production and research problems. Above all else, it is diversified.

A time-sharing manager has three major functions. First, to make time-sharing facilities available to those who can use it. Second, to maintain records, programs and facilities. Third, to explore, develop and apply time-sharing capabilities to his corporation's advantage.

This third function is of the utmost importance. Interaction with the computer is still a unique characteristic. To introduce time-sharing advantages, the manager must also function as an in-house salesman. His first job is to ferret out time-sharing applications. His second, to sell these uses to the line and staff people involved. In this effort, recognition and support from the highest echelons of the company are essential. Without such support, his efforts will fail as they encounter the "don't bother me, I'm too busy" syndrome.

Time sharing is new enough so that if it is not aggressively promoted, it will wither on the vine. Thus, the time-sharing manager's major responsibility is the introduction of and use of time sharing in all appropriate aspects of company activity.

THE TIME-SHARING SUPERVISOR

The workhorse of the time-sharing operation is the time-sharing supervisor. His function is to maintain and sustain a smooth and efficient environment.

No matter how desirable user-computer interaction may be, there will always be some users who cannot manipulate their own programs. Someone must do it for them.

In well-structured time-sharing packages, there is much updating and housekeeping to be done. As the system grows, its smooth operation demands frequent attention. The supervisor supplies this input.

Specifically, the time-sharing supervisor maintains the log, updates and maintains data files, cross checks time-sharing charges, and generally keeps the programs available and running. The skill with which these duties are carried out frequently determine the success of the whole time-sharing effort. The time-sharing supervisor is the utility man on the time-sharing team.

WHAT THE USER NEEDS TO KNOW

Unlike EDP personnel, what the time-sharing user needs to know involves little hardware expertise. The time-sharing user's emphasis is on getting his job done. The computer thus becomes the means to this end, not the end itself.

Design is the time-sharing user's end. The accurate and meticulous design of systems for computer manipulation is the time-sharing user's objective. Recognition of this objective is essential to successful time-sharing use. This point cannot be emphasized strongly enough.

Until computers became available most business, educational, and even scientific problems were handled as generalities. To apply computers to these activities specifics are required. Unless the system can be described in absolute detail, it cannot be computerized.

This fact has been both the greatest advantage and greatest drawback to time sharing. Advantage because in-depth study of the prospective computer application is required before implementation. Disadvantage because many people, managers, educators or scientists, are reluctant to detail the broad generalizations they have been successfully using in their day-to-day operations

Thus the time-sharing user's emphasis is where it should be—on his own needs, his own operation and his own applications. Hardware and software become secondary to his requirements. Design and operation are everything, computers and computerese incidental to his objectives.

Time sharing offers a variety of ways to implement this objective. The user can employ library programs, write his own, build packages of programs or use report-generating programs. All these techniques are available to help him get his job done. With time sharing, all are user oriented.

TIME-SHARING FRAME OF REFERENCE

The most effective attitude the user can adopt is to be objective oriented. Consider the computer a "little black box." Build systems and procedures to achieve your goals. Don't ask how the computer can do it; concentrate on demanding what needs to be done.

Except for the most massive of computer processing jobs, almost any business, educational or scientific job is easily within the scope of time-sharing hardware. Computer power is truly available today to anyone who wants to apply it, yet its potential will only be realized as more time-sharing users learn to make greater demands on these services.

THE COMPUTER

The hardware available naturally limits the capabilities allowable to the user. As mentioned above, however, capabilities are so great today, almost no limitations are apparent. Furthermore, time sharing is further expanding its capacity at a remarkable rate. The extraordinary advances in hardware technology have saved many a user, systems analyst and programmer.

A good example of this is a New York concern that built an order and billing system on time sharing. The original system was built to accommodate eight hundred customers and output about fifty invoices daily. Furthermore, it incorporated an accounting, sales and credit reporting system. No appreciable increase in volume was anticipated. This level of activity had prevailed for the past five years.

The system included a data bank of 250 products and numerous daily, weekly and monthly reports. A comprehensive market report was also output each month.

Once the system was up and running, things started to happen. Over a period of six months, an acquisition increased customers by fifty percent and products by one hundred percent. The success of the M.I.S. reports generated requests for additional output. Government requirements dictated new programs. Internal growth added substantially to the invoice output.

During this same period of time, new time-sharing features came on stream. The system was upgraded from 10 characters per second to 30 cps. Invoice production dropped from six minutes per document to two minutes. A random access feature was added resulting in much faster manipulation of the files. Rather than searching eight hundred customers one by one, the computer went directly to any of the twelve hundred customers for data. Finally data bank storage was increased enormously.

At the end of six months both company growth and time sharing reached a new equilibrium. The same system and updated programs were operating at a level about 100% above the original design specifications. Sheer dumb luck? Not completely, rather, indicative of the rapid growth and sophistication of time-sharing services in the last few years.

This rapid growth makes it impossible to provide a directory of hardware. Any listing of equipment is obsolete within a short period of time.

The present most widely used time-sharing computers are the SDX-40, PDP-10 and the IBM 360 and 370. This is goobledygook to the novice user, and basically unimportant to him. What is important is the various criteria established in the preceding chapters. The output of the computer, regardless of its type, is what is important to the user.

OUTPUT AND INPUT HARDWARE

The time-sharing user is most intimately concerned with input and output devices. From terminals to couplers to card and tape readers, these are the user's prime concern.

> CASE IN POINT: Selection of the right tool to do the right job is important in every trade. The terminal or console is the time-sharing tool of the trade.
>
> A large Boston plastics company established a time-sharing system of considerable scope and complexity. A timely series of reports, charts and graphs were output for all levels of management.
>
> In a burst of enthusiasm, they had a cathode ray tube installed in the office. This was ostensibly to monitor the systems activities. Actually, it was suspected that it was used to impress colleagues.
>
> Unfortunately, the system was primarily report-generating oriented. It constantly cumulated and output current totals. Thus, most programs, if run, changed both the stored data and the next scheduled run. Thus, most of these programs could not be action run.
>
> After the first few weeks, the unit languished. After several thousands of dollars in rental fees, it was removed.

TERMINALS

The proliferation of terminals in the last few years has been astounding. Greater sophistication at lower cost has been the watchword. Specifically, several basic types are in common use. The most widely used are the following.

1. The T-33 and T-35

These terminals are the workhorses of time sharing. They most closely resemble typewriters and are familiar to most as the "Teletype."

The T-33 and T-35 have been changed little in the past years. Their reliability and simplicity of operation make them the terminals of choice for simple, straightforward time-sharing use. At present they are limited to 10 cps and usually use carriage widths of 72 characters.

Until greater sophistication of use is required, however, they provide the time-sharing user with excellent service.

2. Electronic Terminals

The newer generation of terminals employs electronics to a much greater degree than the T-33 and T-35. This characteristic provides greater flexibility, but also greater sensitivity in day-to-day use, requiring more servicing and upkeep.

Such machines as the Terminet 300, Memorex 1240 and Univac DCT 500 typify this type of terminal. Greater speed is their primary advantage. Speeds from 10 cps to 120 cps are common. Carriage widths of 120 characters are common.

Selection of these machines is based entirely on the user's requirements. Large reports might dictate one machine, output of orders and billings another. Each terminal has its strong and weak points. Know your major end uses. Select a terminal best suited to your requirements.

3. CRT (Cathode Ray Tube) Terminals

This type of terminal is used in a highly interactive environment. Programming, querying files, and editing data bases is accomplished efficiently. These terminals can operate at speeds of 2,400 characters per second. They function like a TV tube with a keyboard.

Normally, CRTs are used where hard copy is not required. For considerable extra cost, attachments are available to generate hard copy.

Again, the terminal is selected to meet the user's requirements. If editing capability, speed and data retrieval are of prime concern, CRT units should be considered. If hard copy is required frequently, other terminals would be more economical.

Data Sets

These devices are used to connect the terminal to the telephone. The old reliable T-33 and T-35 don't require data sets, they are "hard wired," but electronic terminals use them.

These are of little concern to the user. The terminal manufacturers can usually recommend a suitable device. Acquisition of the terminal should be coordinated with an appropriate data set.

INPUT-OUTPUT DEVICES

Aside from typing at the terminal, other means are available. These include:

a. Paper tape
b. Punch cards
c. Magnetic tape
d. Optical readers

All these means allow input or output of large volumes of information. The most common and convenient for time sharing is paper or magnetic tape.

The T-33 and T-35 have built-in paper tape devices. These punch on paper tape whatever is input or output at the terminal. Paper tape allows several economies. A large file may be typed "off-line" at no charge, then run in at 10 cps. Thus faster input and less computer on-time. Files may be typed out of the computer and saved on paper tape without incurring storage charges. Paper tape is the simplest and most convenient input and output method available to the time-sharing user.

Punch cards are widely used in conventional EDP operations. They require keypunch and card-reading capability. These are not generally available to time sharing users. Special jobs, voluminous one-shot inputs and other mass processing situations might require keypunch consideration. Day-to-day time-sharing activities, however, do not lend themselves to tab card application.

Magnetic tape is another means of saving data and programs off-line. This capability usually requires additional equipment. The size of the time-sharing effort would indicate whether such auxiliary devices are justifiable. Such a decision will not immediately face the novice user. Magnetic tape can be acquired most readily as an adjunct to CRT equipment. When this type of device is considered, magnetic tape devices can be explored as possible adjuncts.

Optical card readers are the latest input devices. This equipment reads tab cards marked in pencil rather than punched. These devices provide the sophisticated time-sharing user with a way around keypunching. The user marks a mark-sense card in pencil. The mark-sense reader reads these marks in the same way a card reader reads a keypunched card. Pencil marks replace punched holes.

An example of this is an order and billing system developed by a New York exporter. Compare the following:

Conventional System	*Mark-sense System*
1. An order expediter receives the customer order.	1. Same.
2. Prepares the details and fills in a "trigger form" writing in details of the order.	2. The order expediter marks the mark-sense card.
3. The trigger form is keypunched.	3. —
4. The tab cards are fed into the card reader.	4. The pencil-marked cards are read by the mark-sense reader.
5. The data is output via computer.	5. Data is output via the computer.

With this technique one full step is eliminated from the input process. This step is extremely important. It not only reduces personnel (keypunch operators), but eliminates two sources of errors. First, when filling out the form, second when keypunching the data.

This review of hardware has been purposely general. Advances in hardware are extremely rapid. Significant changes can and have occurred over six-month periods. Time-sharing service companies are the best source of up-to-the-minute hardware recommendations. It is to your advantage to utilize equipment known to be compatible with their service.

SUMMARY

Time sharing puts computer power in the user's hands. With this new capability comes the opportunity to utilize the computer over a much broader range than heretofore.

Only the user, that is, the business manager, educator, or scientist, can fully develop this new potential.

Glossary of Terms

BASIC—A computer program-writing language.

Batch—A single, homogeneous assemblage of data.

Batch Processing—Computer operation on one assemblage of data at a time.

Binary File—The source file, once it has been "compiled," to computer binary notation.

Compiling—Transforming a program from programmer language (BASIC, FORTRAN) into computer language (binary).

Computer Language—A special binary notation used only by the computer.

Connect Time—Time a user is "logged in" to the computer.

Console—A typewriterlike device, sometimes using a cathode ray tube, to input and output data to the computer.

Constant—A program code word that remains the same throughout the program.

CPS—Characters per second.

CR—Carriage return.

Crash—A computer malfunction.

CRT Unit—Cathode Ray Tube terminal.

Cutting a Tape—Making a paper tape at the terminal.

Data Base/Data Bank—Operational data stored by the computer.

Data Set—Telephone/computer interface device.

Debug—Correct errors in a computer program before it can run.

Dedicated Unit—Any device restricted to a single use.

Editing—Revising and correcting computer files and programs.

EDP—Electronic Data Processing.

Elementary Languages—Easy-to-learn programming languages.

Field—Area in the data base or program text containing one character.

File Name—The name assigned a data base or data bank.

Files—Computer-stored programs and data; also called a data bank or data base.

Format—The structure of data or the makeup of a page of output.

Formulae—Any mathematical expression used in the program text.

FORTRAN—A computer programming language.

GIGO—Garbage In, Garbage Out.

Hardware—The computer and its peripheral devices.

Headers—Captions on output data.

ID—Computer user identification number.

Languages—Written instructions to the computer.

Library—A series of ready-to-run programs available to a time-sharing company's customers.

Log In—A procedure to obtain recognition from the computer and to initiate computer activities.

Looping—Running a computer program, reviewing the results, changing the input and rerunning.

Machine Language—A binary language used only by the computer.

MAD Bank—Multiple Access Data Bank.

Massaging—Processing data banks over and over.

Mode—Method of operation.

Nanosecond—One billionth of a second.

Operational Procedures—Human/computer interaction.

On-line—Communicating with the computer via a terminal.

Package—An interconnected assemblage of computer programs.

Parasitic—Situation where one entity lives on another to its detriment.

PI—Profitability Index

Powerful Language—A language able to perform a wide variety of tasks.

Processing—The act of a computer manipulating data.

Programs—Sets of instructions for the computer.

Proprietary Programs—Programs owned exclusively by the user.

Quick and Dirty—A hasty programming job with details left out or ignored.

Response Time—How quickly the computer responds to commands.

RPG—Report Generating Program.

Scientific Languages—Computer instruction, science-oriented.

Sequential—Consecutive, one after the other.

Software—Computer instructions, programs.

Source File—The alphanumeric version of a computer program.

Storage—The ability of the computer to retain data.

Symbiotic—Situation where one entity helps the other; opposite of parasitic.

Tab Cards—Also known as IBM cards; keypunched cards used to input data to the computer.

Template—A device used in flowcharting to trace the symbols.

Terminal—A typewriter-type console or CRT unit.

Up Time—The time a computer is available and running.

Variable—A program code word that changes as it is set equal to new or adjusted data.

Index

A

Acquisition output, 61-65
ALGOL, 20
Alphanumeric configuration, 156
Assistance, time-sharing company, 176
Availability, data, 180-181

B

BAL, 199
BASIC, 19, 20, 173, 198, 199, 243
Batch, 243
Batch processing, 17, 243
Batch-processing languages, 19
Beyond Freedom and Dignity, 105
Billing, 25
Billing report, 104
Binary file, 243
Binary information, 156
Binary system, 197-198
"Bits," 221
Budget projections, 138-140
Business, 74-75
Business information system, 86
Business managers, 29

C

Calculation of profitability index, 44-45
Capacity, 19
Cathode ray tube terminal, 115, 240, 243
Central processing unit charge, 26
Charges:
    central processing unit, 26
    minimum monthly, 25-26
    on-line, 26
    storage, 26-27
Chart, 77
Clarity, 19
Classes, regular, 177
COBOL, 20, 199
Color-differentiated documentation, 209-210
Commands, 18
Company selection:
    central processing unit charge, 26
    computer languages, 19-20
    editing capability, 21-22

Company selection *(cont.)*
    evaluation, 220-234 (*see also* Evaluation)
    library, 23-25
    minimum monthly charge, 25-26
    on-line charges, 26
    operational procedures, 18-19
    operations assistance, 21
    response time, 25
    storage charges, 26-27
    up time, 22-23
Comparisons, performance, 18-28 (*see also* Company, selection)
Compiling, 226-227, 243
Computer, 238-239
Computer language, 243
Computer Processing Units, 221
Computer programs free, 66-80 (*see also* Free computer programs)
Computer terminal, 31
"Computer utility," 81
Connect time, 243
Console, 48, 243
Constant, 243
Contract:
    long-term, 18
    outside, 171, 172
    with single individual, 21
Corrections, 30
Cost analysis, 187-188
Cost-justifiable programs, 82
Costs, 25-27 (*see also* Charges)
CPS, 243
CR, 243
Crashes, 22-23, 243
Credit card data base, 156
Credit cards, 156
CRT unit, 243
Cutting a tape, 243

D

Daily report, 105
Data:
    availability, 180-181
    collection, study, recording, 188
    input, 182-185
    reliability, 181-182
    timeliness, 185-186